The Sundance Writer

A Rhetoric, Reader, Research Guide, and Handbook

FIFTH EDITION

The Sundance Writer

A Rhetoric, Reader, Research Guide, and Handbook

FIFTH EDITION

Mark Connelly
Milwaukee Area Technical College

WADSWORTH
CENGAGE Learning™

Australia • Brazil • Japan • Korea • Mexico • Singapore • Spain • United Kingdom • United States

WADSWORTH
CENGAGE Learning

The Sundance Writer: A Rhetoric, Reader, Research Guide, and Handbook, Fifth Edition
Mark Connelly

Senior Publisher: Lyn Uhl

Publisher: Monica Eckman

Acquisitions Editor: Margaret Leslie

Senior Development Editor: Judith Fifer

Assistant Editor: Amy Haines

Editorial Assistant: Danielle Warchol

Associate Media Editor: Janine Tangney

Managing Media Editor: Cara Douglass-Graff

Executive Marketing Manager: Stacey Purviance

Marketing Coordinator: Brittany Blais

Marketing Communications Manager: Courtney Morris

Content Project Manager: Aimee Bear

Senior Art Director: Jill Ort

Senior Rights Specialist: Dean Dauphinais

Cover Designer: Sarah Bishins

Cover Image: gettyimages.com

For product information and technology assistance, contact us at
Cengage Learning Customer & Sales Support, 1-800-354-9706

For permission to use material from this text or product, submit all requests online at **www.cengage.com/permissions**. Further permissions questions can be e-mailed to **permissionrequest@cengage.com.**

Library of Congress Control Number: 2011936486

ISBN-13: 978-1-111-83908-6

ISBN-10: 1-111-83908-5

Wadsworth
20 Channel Center Street
Boston, MA 02210
USA

Cengage Learning is a leading provider of customized learning solutions with office locations around the globe, including Singapore, the United Kingdom, Australia, Mexico, Brazil and Japan. Locate your local office at **international.cengage.com/region**

Cengage Learning products are represented in Canada by Nelson Education, Ltd.

For your course and learning solutions, visit **www.cengage.com.**

Purchase any of our products at your local college store or at our preferred online store **www.cengagebrain.com.**

Instructors: Please visit **login.cengage.com** and log in to access instructor-specific resources.

Printed in the United States of America
1 2 3 4 5 6 7 15 14 13 12 11

For Larry Riley

TEACHER • MENTOR • FRIEND

CONTENTS

EXPANDED CONTENTS

Part Two   **THE READER**

Part Three THE RESEARCH PAPER

Part Four **WRITING IN COLLEGE**

Part Six   GRAMMAR AND HANDBOOK

PREFACE

Valued for its real-world emphasis and focus on critical thinking, *The Sundance Writer* is the complete textbook for composition courses. Going beyond the standard presentation of readings, grammar, and the writing process, *The Sundance Writer* presents strategies for professional writing, conducting research, analyzing and using images, and interpreting literature. *The Sundance Writer*'s balance of theory and strategy, blend of readability and intellectual rigor, critical thinking focus, and practical emphasis on writing for the "real world" make it a flexible teaching and learning tool.

New to This Edition

The fifth edition was thoroughly reviewed by composition instructors from across the country, who called it "unparalleled to comparable texts" and praised its "impressive" readings and assignments. The new *Sundance Writer* builds on the proven success of previous editions, maintaining its readable style and easy-to-navigate format while offering innovative new features for the ever-evolving needs of today's classroom.

Updated MLA and APA Styles

The documentation in this text has been thoroughly updated to reflect current MLA and APA styles. The updates are based on the seventh edition of the *MLA Handbook for Writers of Research Papers* and the sixth edition of the *Publication Manual of the American Psychological Association*.

New Readings

The fifth edition features fourteen new readings, including classic pieces, such as Martin Gansberg's "Thirty-Eight Who Saw Murder and Didn't Call the Police," as well as new essays, such as Sharon Begley's "What's in a Word?" and Christopher Jencks's "Reinventing the American Dream."

New Critical Issues Online Readings with Research Assignments

Organized by mode, the reader portion of *The Sundance Writer* includes a thematic anthology of ninety-nine electronic readings that students can access through the Cengage CourseMate for this text. The new edition offers expanded commentary and critical thinking questions. E-readings can be used as controlled resources units for writing research papers, allowing instructors to monitor documentation and plagiarism on nine critical issues:

1. Immigration
2. The Health Care Crisis
3. Debtor Nation
4. The War on Terrorism
5. The Environment
6. The Job Market
7. The Criminal Justice System
8. Privacy in the Electronic Age
9. Public Schools

E-Sources

Throughout *The Sundance Writer*, students are referred to reliable online resources that will assist them in every step of the writing process.

Key Features

The Sundance Writer is divided into six sections: The Rhetoric, The Reader, The Research Paper, Writing in College, Writing in the Information Age, and Grammar and Handbook.

The Rhetoric

The Sundance Writer focuses on critical stages in the writing process, providing students with techniques to improve their writing and overcome common problems. *The Sundance Writer* encourages students to see English as a highly practical course giving them skills they need in future classes and in any field or occupation they pursue—the ability to reason logically, organize ideas, and communicate effectively.

Writing does not occur in a vacuum but in a context that consists of the writer's objective, the reader, the discourse community, and the nature of the document. After introducing strategies for establishing context and enhancing critical thinking, *The Sundance Writer* guides students in developing and supporting a thesis. Students also are given practical directions for revising and editing.

The Reader

Organized by rhetorical mode, this section presents fifty entries, including classic essays by George Orwell, Martin Luther King Jr., and Bruce Catton, as well as recent works by John Taylor Gatto, Sharon Begley, and Anna Quindlen. Women, African

Americans, Asians, and Hispanics are all well represented. The subjects cover a range of issues: public schools, American Muslims, getting a job, privacy, and the homeless.

The wide variety of topics on science, law, culture, business, and social issues make *The Sundance Writer* suitable for thematic courses. In addition, this textbook has several features that make it a useful teaching tool for college instructors:

A range of readings Each chapter opens with brief, easy-to-read entries that clearly demonstrate the rhetorical mode, followed by longer, more challenging essays. Instructors have the flexibility to assign readings best suited to their student populations.

Brief entries suitable for in-class reading Many of the essays are short enough to be read in class and used as writing prompts, thus reducing the need for handouts.

An emphasis on critical thinking *The Sundance Writer* stresses critical thinking by including essays such as Samuel Scudder's "Take This Fish and Look at It," which dramatizes the importance of detailed observation.

SPECIAL FEATURES

Writing beyond the classroom *The Sundance Writer* places a unique emphasis on the practical value of writing skills. Each chapter ends with a sample of "real-world" writing that illustrates how professionals use the modes in different fields.

Blending the modes Each chapter highlights an essay that demonstrates how writers use different modes to relate a narrative, make a comparison, or outline a definition.

Opposing viewpoints Paired essays present different opinions on four critical issues: legalizing drugs, ethnic identity, bankruptcy, and nuclear energy.

Student papers in annotated and final draft for each mode Samples of student writing offer models of common assignments and demonstrate the revision process.

Collaborative writing Each reading concludes with directions for group writing.

Responding to images Classic and contemporary photographs prompt student writing, class discussion, and collaborative analysis.

The Research Paper

The Sundance Writer offers students a complete discussion of writing research papers, initially addressing common student misconceptions. Defining *what a research paper is not* is very effective in preventing students from embarking on misguided, time-consuming endeavors. Updated to focus on using Internet sources, *The Sundance Writer* gives guidelines to help students locate, evaluate, and document electronic material.

SPECIAL FEATURES
- Strategies for selecting and evaluating sources
- Strategies for overcoming problems with research
- Strategies for evaluating Internet sources
- Strategies for conducting interviews and surveys
- Strategies for locating and documenting visual images
- Separate MLA and APA research papers

Writing in College

The Sundance Writer includes chapters on writing essay examinations and writing about literature.

SPECIAL FEATURES
- Sample essay examination questions and responses
- An introduction to major literary terms
- A complete short story, two poems, and a dramatic scene
- Sample literary essays

Writing in the Information Age

The Sundance Writer includes chapters on analyzing and using photographs, graphs, tables, and charts in both academic and business writing. In addition, *The Sundance Writer* provides strategies for writing effective e-mail, résumés, letters, and business reports. Strategies are also presented to communicate in a range of special writing contexts:

- collaborative writing
- online writing groups
- writing as the representative of others
- writing to mass audiences
- writing to multiple readers
- giving multimedia and oral presentations
- writing portfolios

Grammar and Handbook

The Sundance Writer presents an overview of grammar, explaining the parts of speech and basic sentence structure in a separate review chapter. The handbook is designed for easy use and focuses on the most common problems in grammar and mechanics.

SPECIAL FEATURES

■ Strategies for detecting and revising sentence fragments, run-ons, dangling modifiers, faulty parallelism, unnecessary commas, and other errors

■ Lists of commonly confused and misspelled words

English CourseMate

Cengage Learning's **English CourseMate** brings concepts to life with interactive learning, study, and exam preparation tools that support the printed textbook. **CourseMate** includes

■ An interactive eBook

■ Interactive teaching and learning tools, such as

  ■ Quizzes, flashcards and videos

  ■ An online study guide devoted to the writing process, modes of exposition, research and the research paper, special kinds of writing, and grammar/sentence skills

  ■ Engagement Tracker, a first-of-its kind tool that monitors student engagement in the course.

Learn more at **www.cengage.com/coursemate.**

Enhanced InSite for *The Sundance Writer, Fifth Edition*

Insightful, effective writing begins with **Enhanced InSite™**. From a single, easy-to-navigate site, you can manage the flow of papers online, check for originality, access electronic grade-marking tools, and conduct peer reviews. Students can also access an interactive eBook, private tutoring options, anti-plagiarism tutorials, and downloadable grammar podcasts. Learn more at **cengage.com/insite.**

Interactive eBook

Students can do all of their reading online or use the eBook as a handy reference while they're completing their other coursework. The eBook includes the full text of the print version with user-friendly navigation, search and highlight tools, and more.

Online Instructor's Manual

Available for download on the instructor companion site, accessed at **login.cengage .com,** this manual offers resources such as teaching tips, syllabus planning, and lesson organization that help instructors prepare for class more quickly and effectively.

Acknowledgments

This book and previous editions have benefited tremendously from the critiques and recommendations of the following instructors:

Booker Anthony, *Fayetteville State University*

Janet Bland, *Marietta College*

Patricia Bostian, *Central Piedmont Community College*

Suzane Bricker, *DeVry University*

Linda Caine, *Prairie State College*

Shery Chisamore, *SUNY Ulster*

Nandan Choksi, *American InterContinental University*

Kathryn Cid, *Gibbs College*

Lynn Coleman, *DeVry University*

Karen Compton, *Emmanuel College*

David Cooper, *Northwestern Business College*

Everett Corum, *American Public University System*

Jennifer Dahlen, *Northland Community and Technical College*

Jonathan Dewberry, *New Jersey City University*

William Donovan, *Idaho State University*

Robert Dunne, *Central Connecticut State University*

Daniel Fitzstephens, *University of Colorado*

Luisa Forrest, *El Centro College*

Leanne Frost, *Montana State University–Billings*

Sharon George, *College of Charleston*

Paul Goodin, *Northern Kentucky University*

Rima Gulshan, *Northern Virginia Community College*

John Hardecke, *East Central College*

Shannah Hogue, *Cedarville University*

Marjanna Hulet, *Idaho State University*

Parmita Kapadia, *Northern Kentucky University*

Roba Kribs, *Ancilla College*

Jane Lasarenko, *Slippery Rock University of Pennsylvania*

Chad Littleton, *University of Tennessee–Chattanooga*

Keming Liu, *Medgar Evers College*

Brad Marcum, *Pikeville College*

Laura McCullough, *Vance-Granville Community College*

Jim McKeown, *McLennan Community College*

Karen Miller, *University of Minnesota–Crookston*

Amy Minervini-Dodson, *Arizona Western College*

Dorothy Minor, *Tulsa Community College, NEC*

Adrielle Mitchell, *Nazareth College*

Torria Norman, *Black Hawk College*

Ben Railton, *Fitchburg State College*

Marsha Rutter, *Southwestern College*

Shawn Schumacher, *DeVry University*

Jennifer Swartz, *Lake Erie College*

Susan Swetnam, *Idaho State University*

Mary Trent, *Oral Roberts University*

Ben Varner, *University of Northern Colorado*

Paul Vasquez, *El Paso Community College*

Kymberli Ward, *Southwestern Oklahoma State University*

Vernetta Williams, *Southwest Florida College*

All books are a collaborative effort. My special thanks goes to PJ Boardman, editor-in-chief; Lyn Uhl, senior publisher; Monica Eckman, publisher; Margaret Leslie, acquisitions editor; Judith Fifer, senior development editor; Amy Haines, assistant editor; Janine Tangney, associate media editor; Danielle Warchol, editorial assistant; Jason Sakos, marketing director; Stacey Purviance, executive marketing manager; Brittany Blais, marketing coordinator; Jill Ort, senior art director; Aimee Bear, content project manager; Samantha Ross, production manager; and Dean Dauphinais, senior rights specialist.

Why Write?

A writer is someone who writes, that's all.

—Gore Vidal

Few students intend to become writers. You probably think of writers as people who write for a living—reporters, playwrights, and novelists. But all professionals—all educated men and women, in fact—write to achieve their goals. Police officers and nurses document their daily activities in reports and charts, knowing that whatever they write may be introduced in court as evidence months or years in the future. Salespeople send streams of e-mail to announce new products, introduce themselves to new accounts, respond to buyers' questions, and inform management of their progress. A young couple opening a bed-and-breakfast will find themselves writing to secure financing, develop brochures, create a website, answer guests' e-mail, and train employees. Men and women entering any profession soon realize that they depend on writing to share ideas, express opinions, and influence people.

Thinking about your future career, you probably envision yourself in action—a doctor treating patients, an architect walking through a construction site, a choreographer directing a rehearsal. But whether your goal is Wall Street or the Peace Corps, writing will be critical to your success.

WRITERS AT WORK

I don't know any writer who thinks that writing is fun. It's hard work, and the way I do it is just as if I'm doing any other job. I get up in the morning and I have breakfast and read the newspapers and shave and shower and get dressed. But [then] I go down in my cellar, where I have my study, and work. I try to get to my machine by eight or nine o'clock in the morning. Sometimes I'll run out of steam in the afternoon, but sometimes I'll go until midnight. But you have to treat it as a job; you have to be disciplined. You don't sit around waiting for inspiration. If you do, you're never going to get anything done because it's much more fun taking the dog out for a walk along the canal than sitting down there and writing. But the thing that keeps you going, I think, is that you have these peaks in which you really do begin to feel that you're getting the story told and this chapter looks pretty good. Very often it looks good, and you put it aside; you look at it two weeks later and it looks terrible. So you go back and work on it again.

Stanley Karnow, journalist
SOURCE: *Booknotes*

As a college student you will be judged by the papers, essay examinations, research papers, and lab reports you produce. After graduation you will have to write a convincing letter and résumé to secure job interviews. Throughout your career you will encounter challenges and problems that demand a written response.

Learning to write well sharpens your critical thinking skills, improving your ability to communicate. The strategies you learn in a writing course can also enhance your performance in oral arguments, presentations, job interviews, and meetings. By learning to think more clearly, analyze your audience, and organize your ideas, you will be a more effective communicator in any situation.

THE GOALS OF THIS BOOK

The Sundance Writer **has been created to**

✔ increase your awareness of the importance of writing

✔ help you appreciate the way context shapes writing

✔ improve your critical thinking skills

✔ provide practical tips in overcoming common writing problems

✔ increase your ability to analyze and use visual images

✔ introduce you to writing research papers, business documents, and literary criticism

Above all, *The Sundance Writer* was created to help you develop the skills needed to succeed in composition, other courses, and your future career. Because no single text can fully address every aspect of writing, *The Sundance Writer* provides links to online support.

Using *The Sundance Writer*

The Sundance Writer is divided into six parts: the Rhetoric, the Reader, the Research Paper, Writing in College, Writing in the Information Age, and Grammar and Handbook.

I. The Rhetoric

Rhetoric is the art of communicating effectively. The twelve chapters in Part 1 of *The Sundance Writer* explain stages in the writing process, providing practical strategies to help you develop ideas, overcome writer's block, and avoid common problems.

In addition to guiding you in writing a thesis, supporting your ideas, and improving sentence and paragraph structure, *The Sundance Writer* emphasizes the importance of context and critical thinking. **E-Writing** activities help you explore writing resources on the Internet.

II. The Reader

The Sundance Writer includes more than fifty examples of professional and student writing, each illustrating one of nine modes of writing: description, narration, example, definition, comparison/contrast, process, division/classification, cause and effect, and argument and persuasion. These chapters feature works by George Orwell, Malcolm X, Julianne Malveaux, Anna Quindlen, and Martin Luther King, Jr. The subjects cover a range of issues: cell phones, reading, the job search, homelessness, terrorism, and student loans.

Chapters open with a discussion of the mode, pointing out strategies you can use to improve your writing and avoid errors. Sample writings illustrate how writers in different fields or professions use a particular mode to develop their ideas.

Readings are followed by questions focusing on key aspects of good writing.

- ▪ *Understanding Context* Analyze the writer's thesis, purpose, and interpretation of events or ideas.
- ▪ *Evaluating Strategy* Review the writer's methods, use of support, and appeals to readers.
- ▪ *Appreciating Language* Study the writer's choice of words, tone, and style.

Each entry includes writing suggestions, allowing you to use essays as starting points for your own assignments.

Special Features

Blending the Modes. Each chapter highlights an essay demonstrating how writers use different modes to relate a narrative, establish a comparison, or outline a definition.

Writing Beyond the Classroom. All chapters conclude with a brief example of how writers use the modes in real-world writing such as ads, web pages, and business documents.

Responding to Images. Each chapter includes an image to analyze and discuss or write about.

Opposing Viewpoints. Paired essays present differing opinions on four critical issues: legalizing drugs, ethnic identity, bankruptcy, and nuclear power.

Student Papers. Each chapter includes an instructor-annotated and revised version of a student essay that serves as a model for the kind of paper you may be expected to write.

Critical Issues. Each chapter offers a summary of articles available online through your English CourseMate. This site, which can be accessed at **www.cengagebrain.com**, provides additional readings on nine key issues: immigration, health care, the national debt, the war on terrorism, the environment, the job market, criminal justice, privacy in the electronic age, and public schools.

English CourseMate, accessed at **www.cengagebrain.com**, also provides support for each mode and supplies additional assignments, exercises, checklists, and sample papers. Throughout *The Sundance Writer,* CourseMate icons and descriptions guide you to this online support.

Enhanced InSite for Composition™, available through **www.cengagebrain.com**, provides tools for composition such as anti-plagiarism tutorials, grammar podcasts, exercises, private tutoring options, peer review, online paper management, and more.

III. The Research Paper

The Sundance Writer provides a full discussion of the research paper, including strategies to overcome common misconceptions and problems that often frustrate students. Useful research guides include

- two complete research papers in MLA and APA formats
- strategies for using Internet sources

IV. Writing in College

Writing the Essay Examination

Throughout your college career you may encounter essay examinations. *The Sundance Writer* includes sample questions and strategies for preparing for examinations and writing better responses.

Writing about Literature

Many courses require students to write about works of literature. This chapter defines common literary terms and includes strategies for reading and analyzing fiction, poetry, and drama.

V. Writing in the Information Age

Increasingly, we communicate in images as well as words. The Internet, camera phones, and desktop publishing allow people to attach photographs, charts, and graphs to e-mail, letters, and reports. Bloggers include images and videos on their web pages. Digital photography has made it possible for an image to be broadcast around the world instantly. The opening chapters in this part of the book explain how to analyze, interpret, and use images to enhance your critical thinking and writing.

Writing outside of college takes place in a special context. To be effective in your future career you need to appreciate the needs of writing in the workplace. *The Sundance Writer* provides strategies for writing e-mail, résumés, cover letters, and reports.

The final chapter of Part 5 provides advice on the following special writing situations you may encounter in college and your future career:

- writing in groups, in person, and online
- writing as the representative of others
- writing to a mass audience
- writing to multiple readers
- giving oral and multimedia presentations
- preparing portfolios

VI. Grammar and Handbook

The word *grammar* brings to mind complex rules and mysterious terms, such as *gerunds, nonrestrictive elements, faulty parallelism,* and *dangling modifiers.* But grammar is simply a pattern, a way of putting words into sentences that communicate clearly. The grammar chapter provides a simple explanation of sentence structure and the parts of speech.

The handbook focuses on repairing common writing problems and answers questions students frequently ask: When do I capitalize words? Should it be "it's" or "its"? What's a run-on? Where do commas go?

In addition to grammar explanations and writing strategies, *The Sundance Writer* contains glossaries of grammar terms and commonly confused words, as well as lists of writing topics and frequently misspelled words.

Strategies for Succeeding in Composition

1. **Study your course materials and syllabus carefully.** Become acquainted with the indexes, glossaries, and tables of contents in your textbooks to quickly locate information. Make sure you understand your instructor's policies on incompletes, late papers, and grading. *Record assignment due dates on a calendar.*

(Continued)

2. **Review *all* the assignments in the syllabus.** Reading all the assignments at the beginning of the course lets you think ahead and plan future papers.

3. **Read descriptions of assignments carefully.** Be sure you fully understand what your instructors expect before you begin writing. Review these instructions *after* completing the first draft to make sure you are headed in the right direction. Talk to instructors about topics you are considering and show them rough drafts to make sure your paper will meet the goals of the assignment.

4. **Write when you are focused.** Writing requires concentration. Write at the beginning of a study session when your energy level is high.

5. **Utilize down time.** Review drafts while riding the bus or waiting for a class to begin.

6. **Talk to other students about writing.** Bounce ideas off classmates. Ask for comments about your topic, your thesis, your approach, and the evidence you present.

7. **Read papers aloud before handing them in.** The easiest and fastest way to improve your grades is to read your papers aloud. It is easier to *hear* many errors than *see* them.

8. **Keep copies of all your papers.**

9. **Study returned papers to improve your grades.** If you do poorly on a paper, your first instinct may be to discard it or bury it under some books. But this paper holds the key to getting better grades in the future. Read your instructor's comments and list the mechanical errors you made. If you have a tendency to write run-ons or overlook needed commas, target these items when you edit future assignments. Refer to the handbook section of this book for further assistance.

10. **Read with a "writer's eye."** Whether reading for class or personal enjoyment, notice how other writers select details, choose words, and organize ideas. When you discover a passage you find interesting, study how it is constructed.

11. **Write as often as you can.** Like driving a car, writing improves with practice. The more you write, the more natural it will feel to express yourself on paper. Besides the common advice to keep a journal, there are many other strategies that can help you squeeze practice writing into your busy schedule.
    - *Take notes in other classes.* Even if you understand the material in lecture courses, take notes. You can easily get in hours of practice writing by listening to a professor's remarks and restating them in your own words.

- *Text, e-mail, and instant message friends.* The liveliest chats on the Internet force you to express yourself in writing.
- *Freewrite whenever you can.* Riding a bus or waiting for the dryer to switch off, scribble your thoughts in a notebook.
- *Keep a daily journal.* Write at least a paragraph a day in a diary. Comment on political events, what you have seen on television, the latest gossip, or the way your job is affecting your ability to study.
- *Blog.* Join the millions of people who post their thoughts, experiences, opinions, and feelings online. Ask readers to respond to you. Notice how people react to your ideas and your choice of words.
- *Post comments on what you read online.* Become part of a discourse community by responding to opinions or news items. Read the comments of others and determine which writers make sensible arguments and which ones simply vent their emotions, convincing no one.

Avoid Plagiarism

In writing college papers, you often include ideas, facts, and information from outside sources. Whenever you copy material or restate the ideas of others in your own words, you must indicate the source. Presenting the words or ideas of others as your own is called *plagiarism,* which is a serious academic offense. Students who submit plagiarized papers are frequently failed or expelled.

Strategies for Avoiding Plagiarism

1. **When you copy a source word for word, indicate it as a direct quote with quotation marks:**

   Original source:

   The airbag is not the most important automotive safety device. It is a sober driver.

   William Harris, address before National Safety Council

   Quotation used in student paper:

   Speaking before the National Safety Council, William Harris said, "The airbag is not the most important safety device. It is a sober driver."

   (Continued)

2. **When you state the ideas of others in your own words, you still must acknowledge their source:**

   Paraphrase used in student paper:

   According to William Harris a sober driver is a better safety device than an airbag.

3. **When working on drafts, color-code quotations and paraphrases to distinguish them from your own words.** In writing a paper over several days, you may forget where you used outside sources. Whenever you cut and paste material into a paper, color-code it or place it in bold as a reminder that it needs to be treated as a quotation or a paraphrase in final editing.

4. **Always record the source of outside material.** When you cut and paste or paraphrase material, always copy the information needed to cite the source: the author, title, website or publication, dates, and page numbers.

   Refer to pages 547–553 for information on using and citing outside sources.

The Writing Process

An Overview

You learn how to write by writing.

—Stanley Weintraub

What Is Writing?

Writing is a process as well as a product. Writing requires creativity, concentration, and determination. Even professional writers struggle with the same problems you face in college—setting the right tone, explaining complicated ideas, sharing experiences that are difficult to put into words, deciding which details to add and which to delete, and, often toughest of all, just getting started.

Hollywood depicts writers as people who work in bursts of inspiration. Tough reporters rush to their typewriters and pound out flawless stories that they tear off and hand to copyboys without changing a line. Poets gaze dreamily at the portrait of a lost love and in a flash of creativity dash out a masterpiece, the soundtrack soaring in the background.

In reality, most writers don't have time to wait until inspiration strikes, and they rarely get it right the first time. Writing, like building a table or creating a computer program, takes effort. Although it helps to think about a topic, it rarely pays to wait, hoping for a sudden insight to automatically guide you. *The best way to begin writing is to write.*

Developing a Composing Style

Writing is highly personal. Many writers prefer to work at certain times of day, in specific rooms, or in a favorite coffee shop, and use pencils, an antique fountain pen, or a laptop. Some writers work in two- or three-hour blocks; others work in fits and starts, continually interrupting themselves to study for a quiz or run an errand.

If you have not been accustomed to writing, it may take you a while to discover when, where, and how you will be most productive. If you find writing difficult, consider changing the time, place, and conditions in which you work. Even if you achieve high grades, you may be able to improve your productivity and save time by examining the way you write.

WRITERS AT WORK

In the old days, when I used to write on a typewriter, I would start my drafts on that yellow paper. I just opened my mind and just kept going. I would never know exactly what I was going to say until my fingers were on the keyboard and I'd just type. And a lot of it would be junk, so I'd retype it, and then I'd put in more, and it would get better. These were called "zero minus drafts," and they were on the yellow paper. And then I would cut them up, and cut and paste, and I'd have these cut-and-paste yellow pie sheets. Then finally it would begin to look like it should, and then I'd start typing on white paper, and then I'd have white paper with yellow parts on it. By the time it got to all white paper, that was the first draft. Now I write on a computer, but I just do endless drafts.

Nell Irvin Painter, historian
SOURCE: *Booknotes*

Writing does not always occur in fixed stages. It is often a *recursive* process—writers repeat steps, often carrying out two or three simultaneously. Writing on a computer makes it easy to scroll up and down, jotting down ideas for the conclusion, then moving back to change a word or two to polish the introduction. Though they may not follow them in any particular order, most good writers follow six stages:

Prewrite   Explore topics and develop ideas.

Plan   Establish context and outline points.

Write   Get your ideas on paper.

Cool   Put your writing aside.

Revise   Review your draft and rewrite.

Edit   Check the final document.

At first glance, a six-step process may appear time-consuming, but mastering these strategies can improve the speed and quality of your writing. Follow these steps, altering them if needed, to create your own composing style.

1. **PREWRITE—Explore topics and develop ideas.** Good writing does not just express what you "feel" about a subject or repeat what you have read online or heard on talk radio—it explores issues, challenges commonly held beliefs, engages readers, and moves beyond first impressions and immediate responses. Effective prewriting begins with critical thinking strategies:

   ■ **observing details**

   ■ **asking questions**

- **checking facts**
- **distinguishing between fact and opinion**
- **looking for patterns or relationships between ideas**
- **searching for further evidence**

The goal of prewriting is to discover a subject, identify supporting details, and determine what you want to say.

2. **PLAN—Establish context and outline ideas.** Once you have established your subject, develop your thesis—your main idea—and supporting details in a context formed by four factors:

- **your goal as a writer**
- **the needs of your reader,**
- **the standards of the discourse community (a particular discipline, profession, community, culture, or situation)**
- **the conventions of the document**

If you are responding to a school assignment, for example, make sure your plan addresses the instructor's requirements. Develop an outline listing the items you need to achieve your goal and the best way to arrange them in a logical pattern:

- **the introduction—attracts attention, announces the subject, and prepares readers for what follows**
- **the body—organizes main ideas in a logical pattern**
- **the conclusion—presents a final fact, observation, quotation, or question to make a lasting impression**

An outline does not have to be a formal plan using Roman numerals and capital letters; it can be a simple list or a diagram that allows you to visualize the essay on a single sheet of paper. Outlining helps to organize ideas, spot missing information, and prevent writing in circles or going off topic.

Long projects should also include a budget or timeline. If you are working on a research paper that will take weeks to complete, consult a calendar to break the process into steps. Don't spend six weeks conducting research and expect to write and revise a twenty-page paper over a weekend. Make sure you devote enough time for *each* stage in the writing process.

3. **WRITE—Get your ideas on paper.** After reviewing your plan, write as much as possible without stopping, using the following guidelines:

- **Record *all* your thoughts.** It is easier to delete ideas later rather than try to remember something you forgot to include.
- **Do not break your concentration to look up a fact or check spelling.** Instead, make notes as you go. Underline words you think are misused or misspelled. Leave gaps for missing details. Write quick reminders in parentheses or the margins.

■ **Place question marks next to passages that may be inaccurate, unclear, or ungrammatical.**

■ **If writing on a computer, use color or bold font for passages needing further attention.**

Above all, keep writing!

4. **COOL—Put your writing aside.** This is the easiest but one of the most important steps in the writing process. It is difficult to evaluate your work immediately after writing because much of what you wish to say is still fresh in your mind. Set your draft aside. Work on other assignments, run an errand, watch television, or read a book to clear your mind. Afterward, you can return to your writing with more objectivity. Just ten minutes of "cooling" can help you gain a new perspective on your work, remember missing details, and eliminate errors you may have overlooked.

5. **REVISE—Review your draft and rewrite.** Before searching your paper for misspelled words or fragments, evaluate it holistically using these steps:

■ **Review your assignment and your plan.** Does your draft meet the needs of your audience? Does it follow the format expected of this document?

■ **Does the paper have a clear thesis or goal?**

■ **Did you include enough details to support your thesis?** If you have developed new ideas, are they relevant? What facts, ideas, or quotes do you need to add? Are there any passages that should be deleted?

■ **Is the paper logically organized?** Are there clear transitions between paragraphs? Can readers follow your train of thought?

6. **EDIT—Check the final document.** When you have completed your last revision, examine it for awkward sentences, grammatical errors, and misspelled words.

■ **Review your diction.** Have you used the right words?

■ **Revise sentences.** Are there wordy or repetitive phrases that could be shortened or deleted?

■ **Examine the format.** Does your writing meet the needs of the document? Should it be single- or double-spaced? Do you include required course information or list sources?

Reading a paper aloud can help you spot errors and awkward passages.

Finally, keep in mind that each writing assignment is unique. For example, a narrative requires attention to chronology, a comparison paper demands clear organization, and a persuasion essay depends on the skillful use of logic. You may find some papers more challenging than others. Because it is often difficult to determine how hard a particular assignment may be, start writing as soon as possible. Just ten minutes of prewriting will quickly reveal how much time and effort you need to devote to a paper.

CREATING A COMPOSING STYLE

✔ **Review your past writing.** Consider how you have written in the past. Which papers received the highest and lowest grades in high school? Why? What can you recall about writing them? What mistakes have you made? What comments have teachers made about your work?

✔ **Experiment with composing.** Write at different times and places, using pen and paper or a computer. See what conditions enhance your writing.

✔ **Study returned papers for clues.** Read your instructors' comments carefully. If your papers lack a clear thesis, devote more attention to prewriting and planning. If instructors fill your papers with red ink, circling misspelled words and underlining fragments, you should spend more time editing.

Writing on a Computer

Almost every business and profession today requires computer literacy. If you find yourself overwhelmed by technology, as many professional writers do, consider taking a computer course. Many colleges offer one-credit courses or free seminars. If nothing else, ask a friend or classmate to show you how he or she uses a computer to write.

Strategies for Writing on a Computer

1. **Appreciate the advantages and limitations of using a computer.** Computers can speed up the writing process and allow you to add ideas, correct spelling, and delete sentences without having to retype an entire page. Computers, however, will not automatically make you a better writer. They cannot refine a thesis, improve your logic, or enhance critical thinking. *Don't confuse the neatness of the finished product with good writing.* An attractively designed document must still achieve all the goals of good writing.

2. **Learn the features of your program.** If you are unfamiliar with writing on a computer, make sure you learn how to move blocks of text, change formats, check spelling, and, most importantly, master the print and save functions. *Find out if your program has an undo function. This can save the day if you accidentally delete or "lose" some of your text.* This function simply undoes your last action, restoring deleted text or eliminating what you just added.

3. **Write in single-spacing.** Most instructors require that papers be double-spaced, but you may find it easier to compose your various drafts in single-spacing so that you can see more of your essay on the screen. You can easily change to double-spacing when you are ready to print or e-mail the final version.

(Continued)

4. **Date and color-code your drafts.** To make sure you do not accidentally turn in an earlier, unedited draft of a paper, always put today's date in the header to identify the most recent version. In writing and editing a longer paper, highlight passages and change colors. You might highlight passages needing grammatical editing in red and those needing fact checking or additional details in blue. Marking up drafts like this can make final editing easier. When you complete editing a section, change the text color to black. When the entire document is free of red or blue paragraphs, you know you have fully edited the paper.

5. **Save your work.** If your program has an automatic save function, use it. Save your work to a flash drive or Internet-based space (such as DropBox). If you are writing on a college or library computer and do not have a flash drive, e-mail your work to yourself, or print a hard copy. Don't let a power shortage or a keystroke error make you lose your work!

6. **Print drafts of your work as you write.** Computer screens usually allow you to view less than a page of text at a time. Although it is easy to scroll up and down through the text, it can be difficult to revise on screen. You may find it easier to work with a hard copy of your paper. Consider double- or even triple-spacing before you print, so you will have room for handwritten notations.

7. **Make use of special features.** Most word-processing applications allow you to count the number of words, check spelling, and use a built-in thesaurus. Some programs will aid you with grammar and usage rules.

8. **Use spelling and grammar checkers but recognize their limitations.** A spell-checker will go through your document and flag words it does not recognize, quickly locating many mistakes you might overlook on your own. Spell-checkers do not locate missing words or recognize errors in usage, such as confusing *there* and *their* or *adopt* and *adapt*. Grammar checkers sometimes offer awkward suggestions and flag correct expressions as errors. **Reading your text aloud is still the best method of editing.**

Writer's Block

Almost everyone experiences writer's block—the inability to write. With a paper due in a few days, you may find yourself incapable of coming up with a single line, even unable to sit at a desk. You can feel frustrated, nervous, bored, tired, or anxious. The more time passes, and the more you think about the upcoming assignment, the more frustrated you can become. There is no magic cure for writer's block, but there are some tactics you can try.

Strategies for Overcoming Writer's Block

1. **Recognize that writer's block exists.** When you have the time to write, *write*. If you have two weeks to complete an assignment, don't assume that you will be able to write well for fourteen days. Get as much writing as possible done when you can. If you delay work, you may find yourself unable to write as the deadline nears.

2. **Review your assignment.** Sometimes the reason you feel that you have nothing to say is that you have not fully understood the assignment. Read it carefully and turn the instructions into a series of questions to spark critical thinking.

3. **If you are having trouble selecting a subject, review the assignment for keywords and search the Web.** If you don't have access to the Web, look up these words in a dictionary or encyclopedia. Even wholly unrelated references can spark your imagination and help you develop ideas.

4. **Write anything.** The longer you delay writing, the harder it will be to start. If you have trouble focusing on your assignment, get into the mood for writing by sending an e-mail to a friend. Use an online chat room to get into the rhythm of expressing yourself in writing.

5. **Discuss your assignment or goal with others.** Talking with a friend can often boost your confidence and reduce your anxiety about an assignment. A spirited discussion can generate free associations about your topic, helping you to view your subject from new angles.

6. **Force yourself to write for five minutes.** Sit down and write about your topic for five minutes nonstop. Let one idea run into another. If you have trouble writing about your topic, write about anything that comes to mind. Even writing nonsense can break the physical resistance you may have to sitting down and working with a pen or keyboard. Try to steer your experimental writing to the assigned task. If your draft is going nowhere, save your work and stop after five minutes. Take a walk or run some errands; then return to your writing. Sometimes seeing a word or phrase out of context will lead to significant associations.

7. **Lower your standards.** Don't be afraid to write poorly. Write as well as you can, making notes in the margin as you go along to remind yourself of areas that need revision. Remember that writing is recursive, so even badly written statements can form the foundation of a good paper.

8. **Don't feel obligated to start at the beginning.** If you find yourself unable to develop a convincing opening line or a satisfactory introduction, begin writing the body or conclusion of the paper. Get your ideas flowing.

9. **Switch subjects.** If you are bogged down on your English paper, start work on the history paper due next month. Writing well on a different subject may help you gain the confidence you need to return to a difficult assignment.

(Continued)

10. **Record your thoughts.** If you find writing frustrating, consider talking into a recorder or listing ideas on index cards. You may find working with different materials an effective method of getting started.

11. **Try writing in a different location.** If you can't work at home because of distractions, go to the library or a quiet room. If the library feels stifling and intimidating, move to a less formal environment. You may discover yourself doing your best work while drinking coffee in a noisy student union.

12. **If you still have problems with your assignment, talk to your instructor.** Try to identify what is giving you the most trouble. Is it the act of writing itself, finding a topic, organizing your thoughts, or developing a thesis?

WRITING ACTIVITIES

THE SIX STAGES OF THE WRITING PROCESS

1. Choose a topic from the list on pages 751–752 and use the six-step method described in this chapter to draft a short essay. As you write, note which stages of the process pose the greatest challenges. Alter your composing style in any way that improves your writing.

2. Select an upcoming assignment and write a rough draft. Use this experience to identify areas that require the most attention. Save your notes and draft for future use.

3. E-mail a friend about a recent experience. Before sending it, set the letter aside, letting it "cool." After two or three days, examine your draft for missing details, awkward or confusing phrases, misspelled words, or repetitious statements. Notice how revision and editing can improve your writing.

e-writing

Exploring Writing Resources Online

1. The Web offers an ever-growing variety of resources for student writers: dictionaries, encyclopedias, grammar drills, databases of periodicals, library catalogs, editing exercises, and research guides.

2. Review your library's electronic databases, links, and search engines. Locate online dictionaries and encyclopedias you can use as references while writing assignments.

3. Using a search engine, such as Yahoo! or Google, enter keywords, such as *pre-writing, proofreading, narration, capitalization, thesis statement, comma exercises, editing strategies,* and other terms that appear throughout the book, the index, or your course syllabus. In addition to formal databases, many instructors and writing centers have constructed online tutorials that can help you improve your writing, overcome troubling grammar problems, and research specific assignments.

4. Ask your instructors for useful websites. Use your browser's bookmark function to keep track of these and other sources you find useful.

For Further Reading

Elbow, Peter. *Writing without Teachers.*

Flesch, Rudolf, and A. H. Lass. *The Classic Guide to Better Writing.*

Strunk, William, and E. B. White. *The Elements of Style.*

Zinsser, William. *On Writing Well: The Classic Guide to Writing Nonfiction.*

E-Sources

Writing in College: A Short Guide to College Writing
   http://writing-program.uchicago.edu/resources/collegewriting

Online Writing Lab at Purdue University
   http://owl.english.purdue.edu/handouts/general

The Nuts and Bolts of College Writing
   http://nutsandbolts.washcoll.edu/

 Access the English CourseMate for this text at **www.cengagebrain.com** for further information on the writing process.

The Writing Context

You don't write because you want to say something;
you write because you've got something to say.

—F. Scott Fitzgerald

What Is Good Writing?

No doubt you have read things that break the "rules" of good writing. Advertisements include slang. Novels contain fragments. Scientific journals run multisyllabic terms into paragraph-long sentences. Government reports are filled with indecipherable acronyms.

Writing can be judged only in context. Writing does not occur in a vacuum but in a context shaped by four factors:

- The writer's purpose and role
- The knowledge base, attitudes, needs, expectations, and biases of the reader
- The discipline or profession, community, culture, or situation in which the writing takes place
- The conventions of the document or publication

Another way of thinking of context is to think of a *genre*—a kind or type of writing. The genre a writer is working within takes into account all four factors. Genre explains why a story about an airplane crash in the *Chicago Tribune* differs from a National Transportation Safety Board (NTSB) report or the airline's condolence letter to the victims' families. Stated simply and printed in narrow columns for easy skimming, a newspaper account briefly describes current events for general readers. An NTSB investigation will produce multivolume reports, including extensive test results and testimony of survivors and witnesses. Directed to aviation safety experts, the report is presented in technical language largely incomprehensible to the average reader. In contrast, the airline's letter to victims' families addresses people experiencing confusion, grief, loss, and anger. Carefully drafted by crisis communications experts and reviewed by attorneys, it attempts to inform without admitting liability or appearing falsely sympathetic.

Writing that is successful in one context may not be acceptable in another. The lecture notes you write to prepare for an upcoming examination may be totally useless to other students. If you keep a diary, you may be reluctant to alter the context by allowing your roommate to read it. The essay about sexual harassment that impresses your instructor and classmates in English might be

WRITERS AT WORK

I sit at my computer and write, and then when I have a couple of sentences, I read them over aloud to see how they sound—not what they look like, but how they sound. Could a reader get the meaning of this? Could he follow the words and sound of it? . . . I talk to myself as

I write in the hope of getting something of the spoken language into the written page because I think that's the way people read.

David Herbert Donald, Lincoln scholar
SOURCE: *Booknotes*

rejected by the editor of the college paper as "too wordy" for the editorial page. A psychology professor may find your essay's comments about male and female sexual behavior simplistic and unsupported by research. An attorney could dismiss your thesis, arguing the policies you urge the university to accept would be unconstitutional.

To be an effective writer, it is important to realize that there is no standard form of "good writing" that is suitable in all circumstances.

QUESTIONS

1. Can you recall situations in which you had difficulty expressing yourself because you were unsure how your reader would react? Did you have problems finding the right word or just getting your ideas on paper?

2. Have you found that professors have different attitudes about what constitutes good writing? How is writing a paper in English literature different from writing one in psychology or economics?

3. Have you noticed that magazines and websites have strikingly different writing styles? What do articles in the *Nation, Car and Driver, Cosmopolitan, Time, People,* and *Rolling Stone* reveal about their readers? How does The Huffington Post differ from TMZ?

The Writer

The Writer's Purpose

Everything you write has a goal. The note you scribble on a Post-it® and stick on your computer screen reminds you of an upcoming test. Research papers demonstrate your skills and knowledge in college courses. The résumé you submit to employers is designed to secure an interview.

Good writing has a clear goal—to inform, to entertain, or to persuade. Students and professionals in all fields face similar writing tasks. The way they present their ideas, the language they use, and even the physical appearance of the finished document are determined in part by their purpose. Although each writing assignment forms a unique context, most writing tasks can be divided into ten basic modes or types:

Description *creates a picture or impression of a person, place, object, or condition.* Description is an element in all writing and usually serves as support of the writer's main goal. Descriptions can be wholly factual and objective, as in an accident report, encyclopedia article, or parts catalog. In other instances, descriptions are highly subjective, offering readers a writer's personal impressions of a person or subject.

Narration *relates a series of events, usually in chronological order.* Biographies, histories, and novels use narration. Business and government reports often include sections called *narratives* that provide a historical overview of a problem, organization, or situation. Narration can be fictional or factual, and it can be related in first or third person.

Example *presents a specific person, place, object, event, or situation as representative or symbolic of a larger subject.* A writer may isolate a particular event and describe it in detail so readers can have a fuller appreciation of a larger or more abstract topic. The fate of a single business can illustrate an economic or technological trend.

Definition *explains a term, condition, topic, or issue.* In many instances definitions are precise and standard, such as a state's definition of second-degree murder. Other definitions, such as the statement of what makes a good teacher or parent, may be based on a writer's personal observation, values, experience, and opinion.

Comparison and Contrast *examines the similarities and differences between two or more subjects.* Textbooks often employ comparison or contrast to discuss different scientific methods, theories, or subjects. Comparisons may be made to distinguish items or to recommend one theory as superior to others. Comparison can also be used to present a "before and after" view of a single subject or contrast a myth with reality.

Process *explains how something occurs or demonstrates how to accomplish a specific task.* Writers can explain how nuclear power plants generate power, how the Internet works, or how the liver functions by breaking the process down into a series of events or stages. Writers also use process to provide directions. Recipes, operator's manuals, and first-aid books provide step-by-step instructions to accomplish specific tasks.

Division *names subgroups in a broad class.* Writers can make complex topics understandable or workable by dividing them into smaller units. Insurance can be divided into life, health, homeowner's, and auto policies. Writers can develop their own divisions, often creating names or labels for each category.

Classification *places subjects in different classes or levels according to a standard measurement.* Homicides are classified as first, second, or third degree according to circumstances and premeditation. Burns are classified first, second, and third degree based on their severity. As with division, writers often establish subjective classifications, creating a personal system to rate people, products, or ideas.

Cause and Effect *examines the reasons for an occurrence or explains the results of an event.* A writer can detail the *causes* of a decrease in crime, a rise in the stock market, or the extinction of a species. Similarly, he or she could describe the *effects* a decrease in crime will have on property values, how rising stock values will impact pension funds, or what effect the loss of a species will have on the environment.

Argument and Persuasion *influences opinion and motivates actions.* Writers persuade readers using logical appeals based on evidence and reasoning, ethical appeals based on values or beliefs, and emotional appeals that arouse feelings to support their views. Columnists and commentators try to influence readers to accept their views on issues ranging from abortion to casino gambling. Fund-raising letters motivate readers to donate to charities or political campaigns.

QUESTIONS

1. Consider how you have used these modes in the past. How often have you used them to achieve your goals in communicating with people? Can you think of essay questions that directed you to demonstrate your knowledge by writing comparison or cause and effect? Have you used comparison, division, or cause and effect to organize e-mails or business letters?

2. How often do you use modes such as comparison or classification in organizing your ideas and solving problems? Before you buy a product, do you compare it to others? Do you classify the courses you would like to take next semester by their difficulty or desirability? Do you seek solutions to problems by applying cause-and-effect reasoning?

A Note about Modes

Modes refer to a writer's basic goal. Few writing tasks, however, call for use of a single mode. In most instances, writers blend modes to achieve their goals. A biographer's main purpose is to tell a story, to *narrate* the events of a person's life. Within this narrative, the author may use *cause and effect* to explain the forces that molded a person's childhood, draw *comparisons* to illustrate how that person differed from his or her peers, and *persuade* readers to accept the subject as an *example* or role model.

When you write, select the mode or modes that best suit your purpose. Don't feel obligated to fit your paper into any single pattern.

The Writer's Role

The way writers create documents is shaped by their role. An independent blogger may spew out whatever comes into his or her head to amuse, influence, annoy, or infuriate nameless readers in cyberspace. A corporate attorney drafting a response to an angry customer demanding a refund is guided by company policy, the standards of the legal profession, and the peers and superiors he or she is representing.

In college your role is like that of a freelance writer. Your essays, reports, and research papers are expected to reflect only your own efforts. In general, your work is judged independently. The grades you receive in psychology have no effect on the way your English papers will be examined. In addition, college instructors are supposed to be objective. In a composition class, your papers are likely to be graded by *how* you state your views, not *what* they are. Your opinions on controversial topics are not likely to be raised in future courses or at job interviews.

Beyond the classroom, your role may be more complicated. First, you will be seeking more than an endorsement of your writing ability. Instead of working toward an A, you will be asking readers to invest money, buy a product, give you a job, accept your idea, or change their opinions on an important issue. In addition, you may have an ongoing relationship with your reader. If you give a client bad news in November, you cannot expect that he or she will read your December letter with much enthusiasm. It is important to consider how one message will affect the way future messages will be evaluated.

In many instances your profession dictates a role that greatly influences the kind of writing you will be expected to produce. Police officers and nurses, for example, are required to provide objective and impersonal records of their observations and actions. Fashion designers, decorators, and advertising copywriters, who are judged by their creativity and originality, are more likely to offer personal insights and write in the first person.

QUESTIONS

1. Consider the jobs you have had in the past and organizations you have worked for. What writing style would be considered appropriate for employees in these fields? Was objective reporting more important than personal opinion? Can you think of instances where an employee could jeopardize his or her job by making inappropriate statements to customers or clients? What image did the organization try to project in its memos, ads, websites?

2. What kind of writing would be effective in your future career? How does writing in engineering or medical malpractice law differ from writing in sales, hotel management, or charities? Does your future profession demand strict adherence to government or corporate regulations or allow for personal expression?

The Reader

Writing is more than an act of self-expression; it is an act of communication. To be effective, your message must be understood. The content, form, style, and tone of your writing are shaped by the needs, expectations, and attitudes of your readers. A medical researcher announcing a new treatment for AIDS would write an article for *Immunology* very differently from one for *Newsweek* or *Redbook*. Each magazine represents a different audience, knowledge base, and set of concerns. Doctors and scientists would be interested in the writer's research methods and demand detailed proof of his or her claims. Most readers of nonmedical publications would need definitions of scientific terms and explanations of data they would be unable to interpret on their own. Readers of *Newsweek* would be interested in a range of issues such as cost, government policy, and insurance coverage. Subscribers to a women's magazine might wonder if the treatment works equally well for both sexes or is suitable for pregnant women.

As a writer you have to determine how much knowledge your readers have about your subject. Are you writing to a general audience or specialized readers from the same discipline, profession, or area of interest? Do technical terms require definition? Are there common misunderstandings that should be explained? In addition to your reader's level of knowledge about your subject, you should consider your readers' goals, needs, and expectations. Is your audience reading for general interest or seeking information needed to make decisions or plan future actions?

It is also important to take into account how your readers will respond to your ideas. Who are your readers? Are they likely to be friendly, uninterested, or hostile to you, your ideas, or the organization you might represent? What are their interests and concerns? Environmentalists and real estate developers have conflicting philosophies of land use. Liberals and conservatives have opposing concepts of the role of government. When presenting ideas to audiences with undefined or differing attitudes, you will have to work hard to overcome their natural resistance, biases, and suspicions.

Individual Readers

The papers you write in college are usually read by a single instructor evaluating your work within the context of a specific course. Teachers and professors form a special audience because they generally provide clear instructions outlining requirements for each assignment. They are obligated to read your writing and are usually objective in their evaluations.

Beyond the classroom, however, you may have to persuade people to read your work. No one is required to read your résumé or proposal. Your readers will be expected to do more than evaluate how effective your writing is. You will be asking readers to give you a job, buy your product, or accept your opinions. You may ask readers to invest substantial resources on your behalf, conceivably placing their careers in your hands. When you write to individuals, you will have to carefully analyze their needs, concerns, and objections.

The more you learn about the individual you are writing to, the better equipped you will be to shape an effective message. If possible, speak with or e-mail this person to gain greater insight about his or her background, needs, interests, and concerns. Before submitting a long report, you may be able to test your ideas by sending a letter or preliminary draft for consideration and discussion before committing yourself to a final document.

Extended Audiences

In college your papers are graded and returned. Beyond the classroom, there are often two audiences: immediate readers who receive your documents and a second, extended audience. In most professional situations, letters and reports are retained for future reference. The angry e-mail you send to an irate customer may be passed on by the consumer to your supervisor, the Better Business Bureau, or an attorney. At a trial, it may be entered into evidence and read to a jury. The safety inspection report you write in March may be routinely skimmed and filed. But if a serious accident occurs in April, this report will be retrieved and closely examined by insurance investigators, state inspectors, and attorneys for the injured. Whenever you write beyond the classroom, realize that many people other than your immediate readers may see your documents. Avoid making remarks that may be misunderstood out of context.

The Perceptual World

To appreciate the way readers will respond to your ideas, it is useful to understand what communications experts call the *perceptual world*—the context in which people respond to new information and experiences. As individuals or as members of groups, readers base their responses on a variety of factors that have varying significance. Advertising and marketing executives analyze the perceptual world of consumers to design new products and commercials. Trial attorneys assess the perceptual world of juries to determine their most persuasive argument. Biographers and psychologists often construct the perceptual world of an individual to explain past actions or predict future behavior. Political candidates take polls, conduct interviews, and operate focus groups to establish the perceptual worlds of voters.

The perceptual world is often depicted as a circle to indicate that its elements are not ranked in any particular order and often operate simultaneously.

Social roles, such as being a parent, civic leader, or homeowner, influence how people interpret new ideas. A thirty-year-old with two small children has concerns that differ from those of someone of the same age with no dependents.

Reference groups include people or institutions readers respect and defer to in making judgments. A physician unsure about prescribing a new drug may base his or her decision on recommendations by the American Medical Association.

Past experiences influence how people react to new information and situations. Readers who have lost money in the stock market will be more skeptical of an investment offer than those who have enjoyed substantial profits. People who have a history of conflict with law enforcement may view police officers differently from those who rely on their services to protect their property.

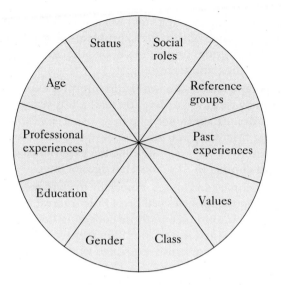

The Perceptual World

Values, whether religious, political, or cultural, shape how readers react to ideas. Although often unspoken, these values may be deeply held. People's attitudes about money, sexual behavior, drug use, politics, technology, and child rearing frequently stem from a core set of beliefs.

Class influences attitudes. Wealthier people may be more optimistic about the economic system that has worked for them, whereas poor people may feel pessimistic, seeing few examples of success among their peers.

Gender has proved to affect people's judgments. Polls about a president's popularity, for example, often show a gender gap between men and women. Although gender may have no impact on how people evaluate their pension plans or the introduction of computers in the workplace, it can influence how readers respond to issues such as child care, divorce laws, and sexual harassment.

Education, both formal and informal, shapes the intellectual background against which new ideas are examined and tested. Readers with greater academic training are in a stronger position to measure ideas, evaluate evidence, and analyze the validity of a writer's conclusions. Education in specific disciplines will influence how readers consider the evidence writers present. Scientists and mathematicians, for example, are more likely than the general public to question advertising claims that use statistics.

Professional experiences, along with training and career responsibilities, form people's attitudes about a number of issues. An economics professor with tenure may more easily embrace a new tax policy than does a struggling business owner worrying about meeting next week's payroll would. Occupations expose readers to a range of situations, problems, and people, leading them to develop distinct attitudes and values about the government, success, crime, relationships, money, and technology.

Age affects how people look at the world and interpret experiences. An eighteen-year-old naturally views life differently than a fifty-year-old does. In addition, people's attitudes are influenced by their experiences. People who came of age during the brief Gulf War of 1991 have different views about using military power than does the generation whose experience of war was shaped by the protracted conflict in Afghanistan a decade later.

Status influences people's responses, especially to change. A proposed modification in Social Security policies will be of little interest to high school students but of immediate importance to those collecting benefits. An entry-level employee with little invested in a corporation may feel less threatened by rumors of a merger than does a senior executive whose hard-won position may be eliminated.

Other aspects of the perceptual world can include physical stature, ethnic background, and geography. In determining your readers' perceptual world, it is important to realize that in some instances people will respond to your ideas based on their entire life experiences. In other circumstances, they may respond in solely a professional role or because your ideas trigger a specific reaction. In assessing perceptual worlds, avoid basing your assumptions on stereotypes. Not all older people are conservative, and not all minorities support affirmative action. Many elements of a reader's perceptual world are unconscious and cannot be easily ascertained. But by learning as much as you can about your readers, you can better determine which strategies will influence them to accept your ideas.

QUESTIONS

1. How would you describe your own perceptual world? Which factors most influence the way you respond to new ideas?

2. How would you describe the perceptual world of your parents, coworkers, and friends? Are there sharp individual differences? Are there shared values and experiences that might lead them to respond as a group in some circumstances? How would they respond to a letter urging them to donate money to a homeless shelter, support a handgun ban, or vote for a candidate? Which issues would be difficult to present to them? Why?

3. Have you ever tried to understand someone you hoped to influence? In practicing a presentation, preparing for a job interview, or seeking the right words to discuss a difficult issue with family or friends, do you consider how your audience will react? Is understanding people's perceptual worlds something we engage in every day?

4. Examine the photographs on pages 624, 626, 629, and 630. How do your attitudes, experiences, social roles, and values affect the way you perceive these images? Can you predict how other people might respond to them?

Evaluating Readers

In many situations you will be unable to learn much about your readers. A want ad may offer only a box number to respond to. Foundations and government agencies sometimes have strict policies that limit information given to applicants. In most cases, however, you can learn something about your reader or readers that can guide your writing.

General Readers

1. Envision your readers. Who are you writing to? What kind of person are you addressing? How do you want people to respond to your ideas?

2. Consider your purpose. What are you asking your readers to accept or do? What objections might they have to your thesis? How can you answer their questions or address their concerns? Play the devil's advocate and list all the possible objections people may have to your ideas, evidence, and word choice. How can you overcome these objections?

3. Test your writing. Before sending a mass e-mail, show it to a small group of people who represent your wider audience. Ask if they can detect errors, misleading statements, or inappropriate comments you may have overlooked.

Individual Readers

1. As a college student, ask instructors for further guidelines about upcoming assignments and request comments on an outline or rough draft.

2. For writing beyond the classroom, learn as much as you can about your reader. If you cannot obtain personal information, learn what you can about the organization he or she is associated with. What does your reader's profession suggest about his or her perceptual world?

3. Before submitting a résumé or proposal, call ahead and see whether you can speak to the person who will evaluate your work. Even a brief conversation with a receptionist or an assistant can provide insight about your reader.

Extended Readers

1. Determine who else may see your writing. How will the administration respond to an article you write for the student newspaper or a comment about the college you post on the Internet? Will your managers approve of the tone and style of the e-mails you send customers?

2. Review your writing to see if it reflects the kind of image your organization or professional peers feel is appropriate.

3. Realize that your writing may surface months or years later. Think how what you write today will affect your future options. Can anything you write today blemish your future?

The Discourse Community

The communication between writer and reader takes place in a particular environment, discipline, profession, community, culture, situation, or publication. A doctor responding to a reader's question for an advice column in a women's magazine has different concerns and responsibilities than one answering an e-mail from one of his or her patients. A lawyer discussing the first amendment in a law review article may use hypothetical examples and discuss abstract legal principles. The same lawyer drafting a motion for a judge about a specific case will have to limit his or her writing to evidence relevant to a single situation and a single defendant. Effective writers are sensitive to the role the discourse community has in how their ideas will be received and evaluated. Like the perceptual world of the reader, the discourse community may contain several elements operating simultaneously with varying degrees of influence.

Discipline. Each discipline has a unique history that can dictate how writers collect information, evaluate evidence, measure results, and propose ideas. In the humanities, research usually involves an individual's interpretation of specific works. Such fields as physics, biology, and chemistry demand that a thesis result from experiments using standard methods that can be replicated by independent researchers.

Profession. Each profession has its own context of historical experience, technical training, areas of concern, responsibilities, and political outlooks. Law enforcement officers approach a case of suspected child abuse with the goal of determining if there is enough evidence to file charges. Mental health professionals are more interested in the well-being of the child, regardless of whether the situation meets the legal definition of abuse.

Community. People are influenced by those around them. A community may be a geographic region, organization, or collection of people with shared interests. Residents of midtown Manhattan have different interests, concerns, and challenges than Midwestern farmers. The U.S. Navy, IBM, the National Organization for Women, the Catholic Church, and NASA each form a distinct community with a unique history, values, problems, and philosophies. Communities form when people share a common interest. AIDS patients, Iraq War veterans, and adopted children have special concerns about government regulations and public policy.

Culture. National, regional, religious, and ethnic groups have common histories and values that influence how ideas are expressed and evaluated. Although Americans generally respect individuality, other nationalities may value conformity. What may appear to Westerners as frank and honest writing may be viewed by others as brash and disrespectful.

Situation. A discourse community can be altered by a specific event. The way a manager writes to employees will change during a strike. An international crisis will influence the way the president addresses senators opposed to his policies. A crisis may bring writer and reader together as they face a common threat, or it may heighten differences, creating mutual suspicion and hostility.

QUESTIONS

1. Examine textbooks from different courses. What do they indicate about the values, standards, and practices in each discipline? Do sociologists write differently from psychologists? What do the books' glossaries reveal about how terms are defined?

2. Consider your future career. What values, attitudes, and skills are important? How will they influence the way you would write to peers? What kind of writing would be considered unprofessional or inappropriate?

3. Think of jobs you have had. Did each workplace form a specific community or culture? Did one office, warehouse, or restaurant have a different atmosphere or spirit than others? Would you word an e-mail to employees in one business differently from those in another?

4. How can a dramatic event shape the way messages are written and evaluated? How would you word a statement announcing the death or injury of a fellow classmate, teammate, or employee?

The Document

The nature of the document influences reader expectations. Memos and e-mail may include informal abbreviations and slang that would be unacceptable in a formal report. Readers expect newspaper articles to be brief and simply stated. Because reporters must write quickly, their readers anticipate that factual errors or inaccurate quotes may appear in print. However, the same readers would have higher expectations of a scholarly journal or a book, because the writers have weeks or years to check their sources and verify facts.

Certain documents such as research papers, résumés, wills, legal briefs, military action reports, dissertations, and press releases have unique styles and formats. Writers who fail to follow the standard forms may alienate readers by appearing unprofessional.

Strategies for Writing Specialized Documents

1. **Make sure you understand the form, style, and rigor expected in the document.** Legal documents, grant proposals, and academic dissertations have distinct standards. If no formal directions or guidelines exist, review existing samples, or ask an instructor or manager what is expected.

2. **Determine if the document suits your purpose.** The importance of your message, the amount of information, and the style of writing should match the form. E-mail is suited for routine information and reminders. But announcing salary changes or job reclassifications in an informal document will strike readers as callous and impersonal.

3. **Use more than one document to achieve your goals.** If an accident prompts you to immediately alert employees of new safety regulations, you can state

(Continued)

them in a short e-mail. If, however, you find yourself producing pages of text, consider writing a formal report or set of guidelines. Use e-mail to quickly alert readers of the most important actions they should take and tell them to expect detailed regulations in the near future. Sometimes formal documents restrict your ability to highlight what you consider significant. Attach a cover letter or send a preliminary report that allows greater freedom of expression.

Strategies for Establishing Context

Whenever you write, consider the context.

Your Purpose and Role

1. What is your goal? To provide information, change opinions, or motivate action? Have you clearly determined what you want to express?
2. Are you presenting your own ideas or those of others? If you serve as a representative of a larger group, does your writing reflect the needs, style, attitudes, and philosophies of your peers or superiors? Do you avoid making statements that might jeopardize your position or expose the organization to liability? Will your peers and superiors approve of your ideas and the way you express them?

Your Reader

1. Define your readers. What is their perceptual world?
2. What objections might your readers have to your ideas?
3. Are there potential extended readers? Who else may see this writing? Have you made any statements that could be misunderstood out of context?

The Discourse Community

1. Are you operating in a general or specific discourse community? What is expected in this discipline, community, or profession?
2. Is your writing affected by a specific event or situation that could change in the future? Should you qualify your remarks so they will not be misunderstood if read out of context later?

The Document

1. Does the document have any special requirements? Do you fully understand what is required, what your readers expect?
2. Does the document suit your purpose? For example, are you using e-mail to transmit a message better stated in a personal letter?
3. Should you use more than one document? Would preliminary messages, attachments, or cover letters assist in communicating to your reader?

Strategies for College Writing

The College Writing Context

Each college course can constitute its own unique context. A literature professor may encourage original interpretations of a short story, while a physics instructor demands lab reports follow objective guidelines free of personal observations or opinions. There are, however, some general strategies for writing in college:

Write Objectively

Except for personal essays written for a composition class, college papers generally avoid first-person statements such as "I think" or "I feel."

Demonstrate Critical Thinking

College instructors expect papers to reflect intellectual rigor and accomplish more than simply repeat facts or summarize other sources. A literature professor requires a college paper to go beyond a plot summary of a novel to show original and thoughtful analysis that might examine a character's motivation, the author's use of symbols, or the book's depiction of a social problem. In the sciences, lab reports must reflect accuracy and objective reporting that can be verified by others.

Use Scholarly Sources for Support

In high school you may have relied on newspapers, newsmagazines, and popular websites to find support for research papers. College instructors expect students to obtain evidence from government documents, professional publications, and peer-reviewed academic journals.

Evaluate Sources

In addition to including evidence to support your thesis in college papers, it is important to comment on the quality and reliability of the sources you use.

Do not simply cut and paste quotations or statistics without explaining their significance and reliability.

Write in Standard Edited English

College instructors expect you to master the diction used by professionals in your intended field. Avoid slang and conventional phrases you might use in an e-mail to a friend such as "back in the day" or "way bad." Write in full sentences, avoiding texting shorthand such as "u" or "thru."

College instructors expect papers to be free of spelling and punctuation errors. Proofread your work carefully.

(Continued)

Use Words Precisely

In addition to learning specialized vocabulary used in a college course, make sure you know the difference between words like *continual* and *continuous* or *imply* and *infer*. Avoid awkward phrases that add little meaning to your sentences. Be aware of words that may reflect bias. Do not attempt to impress professors by cluttering your paper with big words that only obscure what you are trying to say. Read professional journals and your textbooks to determine the style of language used in your field.

WRITING ACTIVITIES

Choose one or more of the following situations and develop writing that addresses the needs of the writer, immediate and extended readers, the discourse community, and the document.

1. You serve on a student committee concerned with underage and binge drinking that was formed after a fraternity party erupted in violence and led to dozens of arrests and a serious drunk-driving accident. Write a brief statement to each of the following readers, urging greater responsibility. Consider their perceptual worlds and invent any needed details. Keep the extended audience in mind. How will other students, student organizations, the administration, and local media respond to your messages?
   - the president of the fraternity
   - the liquor distributor who promoted the event
   - incoming freshmen
   - a local disc jockey who had repeatedly urged listeners to "crash the party and get blasted"

2. Write a short letter asking for funds to support a shelter for homeless and battered women. Consider how each reader's perceptual world will influence responses.
   - the director of women's studies at a university
   - small-business owners in a neighborhood that has become a gathering place for homeless people
   - local ministers
   - the chamber of commerce
   - a local organization of women entrepreneurs

e-writing

Exploring Context Online

The Internet offers a quick lesson in the diversity of writing contexts: academic journals, corporate websites, commercial catalogs, political messages, and personal expressions.

1. Using InfoTrac College Edition (available through your English CourseMate at **www.cengagebrain.com**), find relevant articles by entering a search word, such as diabetes, racial profiling, terrorism, income tax, or any topic in the news. You may also search using one of your library's databases. Scan down the list of articles and select a variety to review. How do the style, format, vocabulary, and tone of a medical journal or law review differ from an article in a popular magazine? What does the language reveal about the intended audience? Can you determine the kinds of readers the writers were trying to reach?

2. If you use e-mail, review recent messages you have received. Do e-mails from friends reflect their personality, their way of speaking? Do personal e-mail messages have a different tone than promotional messages you might receive?

3. Analyze the language used in blogs, chat rooms, Facebook, or Twitter. Have these electronic communities produced their own slang or jargon? Do chat rooms of car enthusiasts differ from those dedicated to child care or investments? Do people with special interests bring their particular terminology and culture into cyberspace?

4. Using a search engine, such as Yahoo! or Google, enter the following search terms to locate current sites you might find helpful:

perception	*audience analysis*
persuasion	*perceptual world*
making presentations	*influencing readers*
reader analysis	*communications skills*
writing genres	

E-Sources

Paradigm Online Writing Assistant—The Writing Context
    http://www.powa.org
Online Writing Lab—Identifying an Audience
    http://owl.english.purdue.edu/owl/resource/658/04/
University of North Carolina Writing Center—Audience
    http://www.unc.edu/depts/wcweb/handouts/audience.html

Access the English CourseMate for this text at **www.cengagebrain.com** for further information on context.

Critical Thinking

Seeing with a Writer's Eye

*It is part of the business of the writer . . . to examine
attitudes, to go beneath the surface, to tap the source.*

—James Baldwin

What Is Critical Thinking?

Good writing is not a repeat of what you have read online or seen on television, and it is more than a rush of thoughts and feelings. Too often we tend to respond to ideas and experiences based solely on our existing perceptual worlds. We allow our emotions to color our judgment and guide our decisions. We confuse opinions with facts, accept statistics without question, and allow stereotypes to influence our evaluations. In short, we let our perceptual world short-circuit our thinking, and we rush to judgment:,

Pete Wilson was a great quarterback—he'll make a great coach.

Nancy's driving a BMW—her new restaurant must be a success.

Alabama improved reading scores 12 percent using this program—our schools should use it, too.

Jersey Lube ruined my car—two days after I went there for an oil change my transmission went out.

All these statements make a kind of sense at first glance. But further analysis will lead you to question their validity.

Does a skilled quarterback necessarily know how to coach—how to inspire, manage, and teach other players, especially those on defense?

Does Nancy even own the BMW she was seen driving? Did she get it as a gift, pay for it with existing savings, borrow it from a friend, or lease it at a low rate? Does the car really prove anything about the success or failure of her restaurant?

Alabama may have improved reading scores with a particular program, but does that really prove the program will work in Nevada or Minnesota? Could children in other states have low reading scores caused by reasons other than those in Alabama?

Did Jersey Lube ruin your transmission? The technicians may have only changed the oil and never touched the transmission, which was due to fail in two days. Had you driven through a car wash the day before, could you just as easily blame them?

WRITERS AT WORK

There are difficult moments where you think you're never going to get a handle on it. You end up with a bulging computer with all these little disparate items of information. Some of them you got four years ago and you can't figure out where in the world they fit. They look like they belong to a different jigsaw puzzle, and [as if] you shouldn't be bothering with them at all. Until you get a handle on it, it can be very difficult. I always write a first draft that has everything in it, and it reads about as interesting as a laundry list—"first he did this, and then he did this." I just have a chronological laundry list of everything that happened to him and that he did on a given day. Only after dealing with that, and wrestling with that by just getting it down on the page, which is a chore, do murky shapes begin to appear. Then you just go with those, and you test them and make sure that they work before you finally decide to use them. It's really feeling in the dark for a while, and it can be discouraging. But I always knew he was there somewhere for me, and so I wasn't going to let him go.

Clare Brandt, biographer of Benedict Arnold
SOURCE: *Booknotes*

Errors like these are easy to make. Unless you develop critical thinking skills, you can be impressed by faulty evidence that at first glance seems reliable and convincing.

Critical thinking moves beyond casual observation and immediate reactions. Instead of simply responding with what you *feel* about a subject, critical thinking guides you to *think*—to examine issues fully and objectively, test your own assumptions for bias, seek additional information, consider alternative interpretations, ask questions, and delay judgment.

How to See with a Writer's Eye

Good writers are not passive; they don't simply record immediate responses. They *look closely, ask questions, analyze, make connections,* and *think.* Learning to see with a writer's eye benefits not just those who write for a living but all professionals. In any career you choose, success depends on keen observation and in-depth analysis. A skilled physician detects minor symptoms in a physical or follows up on a patient's complaint to ask questions that lead to a diagnosis others might miss. A successful stockbroker observes overlooked trends and conducts research to detect new investment opportunities. A passerby might assume a busy store must be successful, but a retail analyst would observe what merchandise people are purchasing and how they are paying for it. If all the shoppers are buying discount items and paying with credit cards, the store could be losing money on every sale.

Asking questions can help you become a critical consumer of information and a better writer as you test the validity of assumptions. Consider a passage from a freshman essay:

> America must restrict immigration. Millions of people are coming to this country, taking jobs and running businesses while Americans are out of work. A lot of these people don't even speak English. With a recession deepening, this country should promise jobs to people who have lived here and paid taxes, not to new arrivals who are willing to work cheap.

The thesis—that America must restrict immigration—is clearly stated. But where is the proof? The student mentions "millions" of immigrants—but is there a more precise number? Just how many people are we talking about? What evidence is there that immigrants are "taking jobs" from others? Could they work in jobs that others wouldn't take? Does the country "promise" jobs to anyone? What relationship is there between paying taxes and being qualified for a job? Do immigrants really "work cheap"? A thesis makes an assertion; it states a point of view. But without credible support, it remains only an opinion.

Critical thinking reveals that the student needs to conduct research and refine his or her arguments. Should the paper make a distinction between legal and illegal immigrants? In addition, the writer should consider what opponents will say. Can he or she call for restrictions on immigration without appearing to be racist? What proof can be offered to support the need for restrictions?

Strategies for Increasing Critical Thinking

There is no quick method of enhancing critical thinking, but you can challenge yourself to develop a writer's eye by asking questions to improve your prewriting, drafting, and editing skills.

1. **How much do you really know about this subject?** Do you fully understand the history, depth, and character of the topic? Are you basing your assumptions on objective facts or only on what you have read on blogs or heard on talk shows? Should you learn more by conducting research or interviewing people before making judgments?

2. **Have you looked at your topic closely?** First impressions can be striking but misleading. Examine your subject closely, ask questions, and probe beneath the surface. Look for patterns; measure similarities and differences.

3. **Have you rushed to judgment?** Collect evidence but avoid drawing conclusions until you have analyzed your findings and observations.

4. **Do you separate facts from opinions?** Don't confuse facts, evidence, and data with opinions, claims, and assertions. Opinions are judgments or inferences, not facts. Facts are reliable pieces of information that can be verified by studying other sources:

FACT: This semester a laptop, petty cash, and an iPod were taken from the tutoring lab while Sue Harper was on duty.

OPINION: Sue Harper is a thief.

The factual statement can be proved. Missing items can be documented. The assumption that Sue Harper is responsible remains to be proved.

5. **Are you aware of your assumptions?** Assumptions are ideas we accept or believe to be true. It is nearly impossible to divorce ourselves from what we have been taught, but you can sharpen your critical thinking skills if you acknowledge your assumptions. Avoid relying too heavily on a single assumption—that IQ tests measure intelligence, that poverty causes crime, that television has a bad influence on children.

6. **Have you collected enough evidence?** A few statistics and quotations taken out of context may seem convincing, but they cannot be viewed as adequate proof. Make sure you collect enough evidence from a variety of sources before making judgments.

7. **Do you evaluate evidence carefully?** Do you apply common standards to evaluate the data you collect? Do you question the source of statistics or the validity of an eyewitness? The fact that you can find dozens of books about alien abductions does not prove they occur.

Common Errors in Critical Thinking

When you attempt to understand problems, evaluate evidence, draw conclusions, and propose solutions, it is easy to make mistakes. These lapses in critical thinking include *logical fallacies*. In establishing your reader's perceptual world, developing your ideas, and interpreting information, avoid these common mistakes.

Avoiding Errors in Critical Thinking

In reading the works of others and developing your own arguments, avoid the following errors in reasoning:

- **Absolute statements.** Although it is important to convince readers by making strong assertions, avoid absolute claims that can be dismissed with a single exception. If you write, "All professional athletes are irresponsible," readers only need to think of a single exception to dismiss your argument. A qualified remark, however, is harder to disprove. The claim that "Many professional athletes are irresponsible" acknowledges that exceptions exist.

- *Non sequitur* **(it does not follow).** Avoid making assertions based on irrelevant evidence, such as "Jill Klein won an Oscar for best actress last year—she'll be great on Broadway." Although an actress might succeed on film, she may lack the ability to perform on stage before a live audience. The skills and style suited for film acting do not always translate well to the theater.

■ **Begging the question.** Do not assume what has to be proved. "These needless math classes should be dropped because no one uses algebra and geometry after they graduate." This statement makes an assertion, but it fails to prove that the courses are needless or that "no one" uses mathematics outside of academic settings.

■ **False dilemma.** Do not offer or accept only two alternatives to a problem; for example, "Either employees must take a 20 percent wage cut, or the company will go bankrupt." This statement ignores other possible solutions such as raising prices, lowering production costs, selling unused assets, or increasing sales. If a wage cut is needed, does it have to be 20 percent? Could it be 15 percent or 10 percent? Before choosing what appears to be the better of two bad choices, determine if there are other options.

■ **False analogy.** Comparisons make weak arguments. For example, if you write, "Marijuana should be legalized since Prohibition did not work," you are forgetting that marijuana and alcohol are different substances. Alcohol has been consumed by humans for thousands of years. Marijuana, however, has never had wide social acceptance. The fact that Prohibition failed could be used to justify legalizing anything that is banned, including assault weapons, child pornography, or crack cocaine.

■ **Red herring.** Resist the temptation to dodge the real issue by making emotionally charged or controversial statements, such as "How can you justify spending money on a new football stadium when homeless people are sleeping in the streets and terrorists are threatening to destroy us?" Homelessness and terrorism are genuine concerns but have little to do with the merits of a proposed stadium. The same argument could be used to attack building a park, a zoo, or an art gallery.

■ **Borrowed authority.** Avoid assuming that an expert in one field can be accepted as an authority in another. One example is "Senator Goode claims Italy will win the World Cup." A respected senator may have no more insight into soccer than a cabdriver or a hairdresser does. Celebrity endorsements are common examples of borrowed authority.

■ *Ad hominem* (attacking the person). Attack ideas, not the people who advocate them. "How can you accept the budget proposed by an alderman accused of domestic violence?" The merits of the budget have to be examined, not the person who proposed it.

Other errors in critical thinking can occur when writers conduct research, collect evidence, or make observations. Make sure that in collecting and evaluating evidence, you avoid making the following errors:

■ **Hasty generalizations.** If your dorm room is robbed, a friend's car stolen from the student union parking lot, and a classmate's purse snatched on her way to class, you might assume that the campus is experiencing a crime wave. The evidence is compelling because it is immediate and personal. But it does not prove there is an increase in campus crime. In fact, crime could be dropping, and you and your friends may simply have had the misfortune to fall into the declining pool of victims. Only a comparative review of police and security reports would prove if crime is increasing. *Resist jumping to conclusions.*

■ **"Filtering" data.** If you begin with a preconceived thesis, you may consciously or unconsciously select evidence that supports your view and omit evidence that contradicts it. Good analysis is objective; it does not consist of simply collecting facts to support a previously held conviction. A list of high school dropouts who became celebrities does not disprove the value of a diploma. Avoid selecting anecdotal examples that counter a general trend.

■ **Ignoring alternative interpretations.** Even objective facts can be misleading. If research shows that reports of child abuse have jumped 250 percent in the last ten years, does that mean that child abuse is on the rise? Could those numbers instead reflect stricter reporting methods or an expanded definition of abuse, so that previously unrecorded incidents are now counted?

■ **Mistaking a time relationship for a cause** *(post hoc, ergo propter hoc).* Can the president take credit for a drop in unemployment six months after signing a labor bill? Because events occur in time, it can be easy to assume an action that precedes another is a cause. A drop in unemployment could be caused by a decline in interest rates or an upsurge in exports and may have nothing to do with a labor bill. Do not assume events were caused by preceding events.

■ **Mistaking an effect for a cause.** If you observe that children with poor reading skills watch a lot of television, you might easily assume that television interferes with their reading. In fact, excessive viewing could be a symptom. Because they have trouble reading, they watch television instead.

■ **Assuming past events will predict the future.** The 2008 recession was caused, in part, because mortgage brokers believed that real estate prices would continue to rise 6 percent annually. When home values fell as much as 50 percent, millions of homeowners faced foreclosure and investors lost billions of dollars. Past trends cannot be assumed to continue into the future.

WRITING ACTIVITIES

1. Select a recent editorial and examine it for lapses in critical thinking. Does the writer make statements that rest on untested assumptions, false analogies, or insufficient data? Write a critique, commenting on the writer's use of logic to support his or her views.

2. Select a topic from the list on pages 751–752 and identify the types of errors in critical thinking you might face in addressing this issue.

3. Examine a session or two of cable news or radio talk shows. How many guests engage in arguments that are laced with errors in critical thinking? Can you identify people who use guilt by association, anecdotal evidence, and faulty comparisons? Do interviewers or guests try to persuade viewers by begging the question or creating false dilemmas?

CRITICAL THINKING CHECKLIST

✔ Examine your writing for evidence of critical thinking.

✔ Have you carefully examined your subject or relied solely on casual observation?

✔ Is your main idea clearly and logically stated?

✔ Have you collected enough information to make judgments?

✔ Are your sources reliable and unbiased?

✔ Have you considered alternative interpretations?

✔ Have you avoided errors in critical thinking such as hasty generalizations?

e-writing

Exploring Critical Thinking Online

You can find a range of sources on the Web dedicated to critical thinking, ranging from sites maintained by academic organizations to those created by individual teachers posting information for their students.

1. Using InfoTrac College Edition (available through your English CourseMate at **www.cengagebrain.com**) or one of your library's databases, enter *critical thinking* as a search term and locate articles that may assist you in your writing course and other classes.

2. Locate the online version of a national or local newspaper and review recent editorials. Can you detect any lapses in critical thinking? Do any editorials rely on hasty generalizations, anecdotal evidence, faulty comparisons, filtering data, or false authorities?

3. To learn more about critical thinking, enter *critical thinking* as a search term in a general search engine such as Yahoo! or Google, or enter one or more of the following terms:

coincidence	*anecdotal evidence*
post hoc	*circular reasoning*
red herrings	*guilt by association*
hasty generalizations	*fact and opinion*

For Further Reading

Barnet, Sylvan, and Hugo Bedau. *Critical Thinking: Reading and Writing.*

Dauer, Francis Watanabe. *Critical Thinking: An Introduction to Reasoning.*

Hirschberg, Stuart. *Essential Strategies of Argument.*

Packer, Nancy Huddleston, and John Timpane. *Writing Worth Reading: The Critical Process.*

Paulos, John Allen. *Innumeracy: Mathematical Illiteracy and Its Consequences.*

Rosenwasser, David, and Jill Stephens. *Writing Analytically.*

E-Sources

The Critical Thinking Community
http://www.criticalthinking.org

 Access the English CourseMate for this text at **www.cengagebrain.com** for additional information on critical thinking.

Prewriting Strategies
Getting Started

I think best with a pencil in my hand.

—Anne Morrow Lindbergh

What Is Prewriting?

Writing is more than a means to create a document; it can be a method to discover topics and explore ideas. *Prewriting* is practice or experimental writing—writing that helps you get started and measure what you know, identify new ideas, and indicate areas requiring further research. Prewriting can sharpen your skills of observation and evaluation. Like an artist making quick sketches before beginning a mural, you can test ideas, explore a range of topics, list points, and get a feel for your subject. Prewriting can help you save time by quickly determining which ideas are worth developing and which should be discarded. *Prewriting puts critical thinking into action.*

Prewriting Strategies

Writers use a number of strategies to discover and develop ideas. Prewriting can be highly focused or totally open. You may wish to target a specific assignment or explore ideas that might generate topics for a number of papers.

People think in different ways. Review these methods and experiment with them. Feel free to combine strategies to create your own method. If you are responding to a specific assignment, consider all the elements of the context:

- **the writer**—your goal and the demands of the assignment, especially your thesis or main idea
- **the reader**—the knowledge and attitudes of your audience and the kind of support needed to convince them
- **the discipline**—the culture, history, and methods used to express and support ideas
- **the document**—the purpose, rigor, style, length, and format of the finished product

Make sure you understand what your instructor expects and how your paper will be evaluated. If you are unsure, talk to your instructor or other students. Sometimes even a casual conversation about an upcoming assignment will reveal different perspectives and insights.

WRITERS AT WORK

I write by longhand. I like to see the words coming out of the pen. And once they distribute themselves, one has the stylistic struggle to try to turn that clumsy sentence on the page into something lucid. That can take a long time. I remember once spending seven hours on one sentence—seven hours. And I looked at it the next morning, it was a pretty banal sentence. That's writing. Writing is a reduction to essentials, elimination, and that takes time.

Edmund Morris, historian
SOURCE: *Booknotes*

Freewriting

Freewriting records your thoughts, ideas, impressions, and feelings without interruption and without any concern for spelling, grammar, punctuation, or even logic. Don't confuse freewriting with writing a rough draft of an essay; instead, it is a method of discovering ideas. Freewriting is like talking to yourself. It has no direction: it can skip from one topic to another without rational transitions; it may contain contradictory statements. Freewriting produces "running prose," like a recording of a rambling telephone conversation. The goal is to discover ideas. Here are some tips:

- **Write as fast as you can.**
- **Don't pause to correct spelling or check facts—but make notes as you go.**
- **Don't feel obligated to write in full sentences—list ideas and key words.**
- **Keep writing and record everything that comes to you—remember your goal is to explore ideas, not write a rough draft.**

Having spent the evening searching the Web for material for a paper, a student switched to a word processing program and rapidly recorded her thoughts on the information superhighway:

> The information superhighway links anyone to the world. A college student, sitting in a dorm or libary, can connect to sources in New York, London, or Tokio. Web pages link you to sources you would nevre find on your own or now about. Within fifteen minutes tonight I printed off twenty pages of infomation that would take hours to find in a conventional libary. The interent is the ultimate consumer guide. I could find online catalogs and read product descriptions and prices for things I thought about buying for xmas gifts and presents. I could even check sticker prices on new cars. Xxxxxxxxxxxxxxxx xxxxxxxxx.
>
> But switching from web page to web page, bieng hit with all kinds of data from around the owrld wears off after a while. The internet is exciting but like having cable TV, you get used to having 80 channels instead of four or five.
>
> Years ago Clinton promised to have every shcool in America wired to the interent.

But one wonders. If children have trouble reading, what does the internet provide books don't? The information super highway bombards us with statistics and facts. The real question is can people analyze it? Do we have the wisdom to know what to make of all this material. I see students in the lib. Get excited as they see the stacks of information slipping from the printers. But like students forty years ago who were the first to be able to use a Xerox machine and copy an article instead of haivng to take notes—I wonder what will they do with all this informaiton when they get home?

Wisdom vs. Knowledge. X xxxxxxx x xxxx x Being able to synehisize data. xxxxxxxxxx

CNN tells us about a crisis in Iraq or a stock plunge in Korea in seconds. The TV screen flashes with images and numbers. We hear soundbites from experts. But do we know enough history of the Middle east to now what this crisis means? Do we know enough about international business and trading to know how the Korean markets effect ours? What does information mean if we dont appreciate what it means?

This freewriting is a loose, repetitive, and misspelled collection of ideas, switching from the Internet to cable television without connection. But within the text there are the germs of ideas that could lead to a good essay about the information super-highway and critical thinking.

Advantages

- **Freewriting can help overcome writer's block.** Giving yourself the freedom to write anything—even meaningless symbols—forces you to overcome the idea that every time you write you must come up with significant insights and flawless prose.

- **Freewriting is useful when you simply have no idea what to write about.** It can help you discover a subject by free association.

Disadvantages

- **Because of its unrestricted nature, freewriting can spin off a lot of interesting but inappropriate ideas.** You may find yourself writing off track, getting farther from the writing needed to meet the needs of your readers. You can focus your freewriting by considering the needs of your readers. Study your instructor's guidelines for the paper before starting to write. *Write with your reader in mind.*

- **Freewriting can be tiring.** Feel free to list or cluster ideas to save time. *Don't feel obligated to write in complete sentences.*

WRITING ACTIVITY

FREEWRITING

Select one of the following issues and write about it for at least five minutes without stopping. Don't worry about making sense, keeping on topic, or connecting ideas. Remember, this is not a rough draft, but an exploration of ideas. The topic is simply a catalyst, a jumping-off point. Let your free associations flow. If the topic of your hometown leads you to comment on your neighbors' divorce, go with it. *Keep writing!*

your hometown	campus child care	roommates	reality TV shows
job interviews	blind dates	student loans	unemployment
best friends	diets	mortgages	first day at work
gay rights	binge drinking	the Internet	outsourcing

Brainstorming

Brainstorming is another method of finding ideas to write about. Brainstorming can take different forms, the most simple being making lists. As in freewriting, do not attempt to be selective; just follow these guidelines:

- **Write down every idea you can come up with, whether it makes sense or not.**
- **Don't stop to check facts or spelling—list ideas.**
- **Cluster or group ideas to make connections if you can.**
- **Make notes or write short paragraphs to record important ideas you may forget.**

A psychology student searching for a subject for a term paper might begin listing the following thoughts and topics:

mental illness—schizophrenia
inability to function in society
insanity defense
mental illness/homelessness
mentally ill off medication
public disturbances by mental patients
institutions/group homes
commitment laws, decision to protect patients against their will
human rights versus incarceration without trial
committing the homeless to mental health institutions for their own safety

Through brainstorming the student moves from the general topic of mental illness and legal issues to a subject suitable for a research paper—institutionalizing homeless mentally ill patients. With further prewriting, the student can develop this topic to compare past and present practices, argue for more group homes, study the causes of homelessness, or debate the merits of a local ordinance.

Brainstorming can help you develop writing even when the topic is clearly defined and the context is fixed. Having observed a shoplifter race out of her store with a jacket, the owner of a dress shop who plans to write an incident report to the manager of the shopping mall jots down the following list:

time/date of incident
item(s) stolen—get values wholesale/retail
location of video cameras? (Check)
security guard took 6 minutes to respond
guards never at north end of mall

>   problems at other stores—check video & computer stores
>   need for security
>   lease expires in three months/may not renew

From this list, the store owner identifies the information needed to document the problem and comes up with the threat of leaving the mall to dramatize her position and prompt a response.

Advantages

- **Like freewriting, brainstorming can help you get started when you have no topic in mind.**
- **Brainstorming allows you to jot down rapid-fire ideas,** freeing you from the need to write complete sentences.
- **Brainstorming can quickly identify information needed to support your points.**

Disadvantages

- **Brainstorming sometimes produces nothing more than a shopping list of unrelated ideas.** Use other techniques, such as freewriting, to flesh out superficial ideas.
- **Because it rests on free associations, brainstorming can lead you far astray from an assigned topic.** If you are working on a specific assignment, keep your syllabus or instructor's guidelines in front of you to help focus your train of thought.

WRITING ACTIVITY

BRAINSTORMING

Select one column from the topics below and build on it, adding your own ideas. Jot down your thoughts as quickly as possible. Allow your thoughts to flow freely. Do not worry about changing direction or coming up with an entirely different subject.

men/women	success	campus housing
attitudes about relationships	careers	dorms/off campus
ending relationships	salaries	having your own apt.
how men and women cope with failed relationships	the perfect first job	advantages/disadvantages of living alone

---

Asking Questions

Asking questions is a method of exploring ideas that can focus your thoughts and identify not only a thesis but information you need. For over a century reporters, working under tight deadlines, have been trained to approach a news story by asking the Five Ws: *Who? What? Where? When? Why?* Asking questions can help you avoid writing in circles and can highlight important issues.

You can use the modes (see pages 22–23) to generate questions.

- **description:** What are the key details of your subject?
- **narration:** What happened? Can you explain the background or history of your subject? What events are significant? What do they mean?
- **example:** Does your subject illustrate a larger trend, issue, or problem?
- **definition:** Do key terms or the subject itself need to be precisely defined?
- **comparison:** How does your subject compare to another? Are there similarities or differences?
- **process:** Can you explain how your subject occurs or operates?
- **division/classification:** Can your subject be divided into types or ranked in varying degrees?
- **cause and effect:** Can you explain what caused your subject or describe its influence or results?
- **argument and persuasion:** What will you have to present to convince readers to accept your ideas?

A student in a literature class has chosen to write a research paper about Arthur Miller's play *Death of a Salesman.* Note the number of questions that stem from one of the modes:

Death of a Salesman
How can you describe Willy's values?
Is Willy a victim of society or of his own delusions?
What role does Uncle Ben play? Is he an example of Willy's dream?
Is Willy's suicide caused by despair or a last attempt at success?
What effect does Willy's infidelity have?
Biff steals a suit and a fountain pen. What do these objects symbolize?
Linda knows Willy has lost his salary but does not confront him about it. Why?
Why does Miller compare Willy and Biff to Uncle Charlie and Bernard?
Is the play an attack on the American dream?
Why causes Willy to reject Charlie's job offer?
This play is world famous but the hero is abusive, selfish, and short-tempered. Why is the play so popular?
What is the purpose of the requiem at the end? How would the play be different without it?

Asking questions can help target other forms of prewriting, giving direction to your freewriting and brainstorming. In addition, questions can help spark critical thinking. Exploring the whys and hows of people, places, and events can help you move beyond simply recording first impressions and superficial observations.

Advantages

■ **Asking questions can help transform a topic into a thesis** by directing you to state an opinion or take a position.

■ **Questions, if carefully worded, force you to think and test your preconceived notions and attitudes.**

■ **Questions reveal needed information,** guiding you to conduct research.

Disadvantages

■ **Questions in themselves are not necessarily effective in provoking thought.** Unless you are careful, you may find yourself simply creating pat questions that lead to simple answers. If your answers simply restate what you already know or believe, write tougher questions or try another prewriting method.

■ **Asking too many questions, especially misdirected ones, can lead you on a scattered mission, finding unrelated or trivial information.** Edit your questions when you complete your list. Don't feel obligated to consider every question you jot down.

WRITING ACTIVITY

ASKING QUESTIONS

Select one of the topics below and develop as many questions as you can. If you find yourself blocked, choose another topic or create one of your own. List as many questions as you can and don't worry about repeating yourself. Consider using one or more of the modes to develop questions:

campus crime	credit cards	online shopping	drinking age
prisons	stalking laws	online dating	fashion
cell phone etiquette	health clubs	divorce	media images of women

Look over your questions and circle those that suggest interesting topics for papers.

Clustering

Clustering is a type of prewriting that helps people who are visually oriented. If you have an artistic or technical background, you may find it easier to explore ideas by blocking them out on a sheet of paper or computer screen. Clustering is a form of directed doodling or informal charting. Instead of listing ideas or writing paragraphs, sketch your ideas on paper, as if arranging index cards on a table. People who use clustering often develop unique visual markers—using rectangles, arrows, and circles to diagram their ideas.

Thinking about his sister's decision to adopt a baby from China, a student clustered a series of observations and questions:

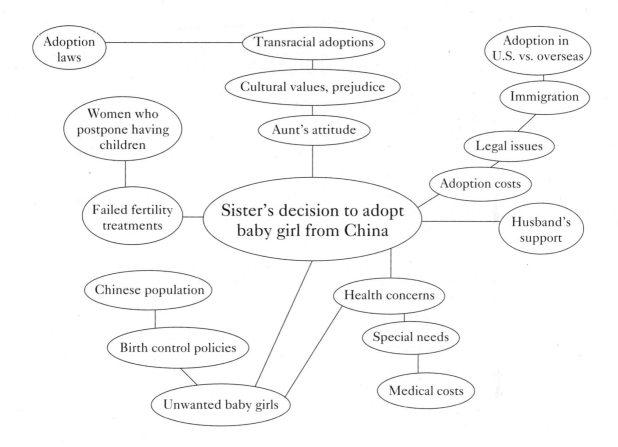

In this case, clustering helps chart the positive and negative elements of transracial adoptions.

Advantages

- **Clustering is suited to people who think spatially and find it easier to draw rather than write.**
- **Clustering is a good method to explore topics for comparison and classification papers.**
- **Clustering can save time.** Freewriting, brainstorming, and asking questions all list ideas in the order in which they occur to the writer rather than in relationship to each other. These ideas have to be examined and reorganized. Clustering allows you to create several lists or groupings, ranking ideas in importance and immediately showing links between related ideas.
- **Clustering can help place ideas in context.** You can group ideas in columns to contrast advantages and disadvantages or create a spectrum, showing the range of ideas.

Disadvantages

■ **You can become so absorbed in the artistic elements of clustering that you spend more time toying with geometrical designs than with the ideas they are supposed to organize.** Keep your artwork simple. Don't waste your time using rulers to draw arrows or make perfect squares and circles. If you prewrite on a computer, don't bother using clip art.

■ **Clustering can be an excellent device for organizing ideas but may not help you get started.** Use freewriting or ask questions to start the flow of ideas, then arrange them with clustering techniques.

WRITING ACTIVITY

CLUSTERING

Select one of the following topics. Use a blank sheet of paper to record and arrange your ideas. You may wish to list pros and cons in separate columns or use a simple pie chart to split up a complex or confusing topic. Connect related ideas with arrows. Use different shapes and colors to distinguish contrasting ideas. Remember, clustering is a means to an end. Don't allow your artwork to get in the way of your thinking or take too much time. Neatness does not count.

computer hackers	being laid off	worst/best jobs
role models	airport security	teen pregnancy
violence on TV	singles' bars	fast food
the stock market	poverty	eating disorders
racial profiling	having children	video games

Strategies for Prewriting

1. **Write as often as you can.**
2. **Get in the habit of asking questions and listing ideas and observations.**
3. **Make notes of interesting items you see on television, clip newspaper and magazine articles, and bookmark websites that could serve as writing prompts.**
4. **Review upcoming assignments and make lists of possible topics.**
5. **Experiment with different forms of prewriting and feel free to blend them to develop your own style.**
6. **Save your notes. Ideas that you might discard for one paper might aid you in developing a topic for a future assignment.**

e-writing

Exploring Prewriting Strategies Online

Websites with prewriting resources range from those maintained by academic organizations to those created by individual teachers posting information for their students.

1. Using InfoTrac College Edition (available through your English CourseMate at **www.cengagebrain.com**) or one of your library's databases, enter *prewriting strategies* as a search term to locate articles that may assist you in your writing course and other classes.

2. Using a search engine, such as Yahoo! or Google, enter such terms as *prewriting*, *freewriting*, and *brainstorming* to locate current websites.

3. Familiarize yourself with your library's online databases and resources, such as encyclopedias. Often checking a fact or reference can help trigger ideas for an assignment or prevent you from wasting time.

For Further Reading

Lamm, Kathryn. *10,000 Ideas for Term Papers, Projects, Reports, and Speeches.*

E-Sources

The University of Kansas Writing Center
   http://www.writing.ku.edu/guides
Online Writing Lab at Purdue University
   http://owl.english.purdue.edu/owl/

Access the English CourseMate for this text at **www.cengagebrain.com** for further information on prewriting strategies.

Developing a Thesis

I write because there is some lie I want to expose, some fact to which I want to draw attention, and my initial concern is to get a hearing.

—George Orwell

What Is a Thesis?

Once you discover a topic through prewriting, your next step is developing a thesis. Good writing has a clear purpose. An essay is never just *about* something. Whether the topic is climate change, your first job, high school football, or *A Streetcar Named Desire,* your writing should make a point or express an opinion. The *thesis* is a writer's main or controlling idea. A *thesis statement* presents the writer's position in a sentence or two and serves as the document's mission statement. *A thesis is more than a limited or narrowed topic; it expresses a point of view. It is a declaration, summarizing your purpose.*

Topic	Narrowed Topic	Thesis Statement
gun control	handgun ban	*The city's proposed handgun ban will not prevent gang violence.*
campus housing	rehabbing dorms	*Given the demand for more on-campus housing, the men's dorm, which is fifty years old, should be rehabilitated.*
terrorism	cyber-terrorism	*Federal security agencies must take steps to protect the Internet from cyber-terrorism.*

WRITERS AT WORK

I write in my studio. I've got a little studio in Brooklyn, a couple of blocks from my house—no telephone, nothing there. When I go there, the only thing I ever do there is work, so it's wonderful. I'm like a dog with a conditioned reflex. There is no television, no telephone, nothing. My wife wants me to get a portable telephone. I refuse. I don't want to be tempted. There's an old Jewish belief that you build a fence around an impulse. That's not good enough, you build a fence around the fence, so no telephone.

Norman Mailer, novelist
SOURCE: *Booknotes*

WRITING ACTIVITIES

Develop a thesis statement for each of the following topics. Use prewriting techniques such as asking questions and clustering to explore ideas. Remember, your thesis should state a viewpoint, express an opinion, make an appeal, or suggest a solution, not simply make a factual statement or limit the subject.

1. Driver's licenses for illegal immigrants

2. Universal health care

3. Subprime mortgages

4. The Internet's impact on journalism

5. The aging baby boom generation

6. Welfare reform and child care

7. America's role in the twenty-first century

8. The current job market for college graduates

9. DNA testing and criminal investigations

10. Minimum wage jobs

Elements of a Thesis Statement

Effective thesis statements share the following common characteristics:

■ **They are generally stated in a single sentence.** This statement forms the core of the paper, clearly presenting your point of view. Writing a thesis statement can be a critical part of the prewriting process, helping you move from a list or cluster of ideas to a specific paper. Even if the thesis statement does not appear in the final paper, writing this sentence can focus your ideas and direct your writing.

■ **They express an opinion, not a topic.** What distinguishes a thesis statement from a topic is that it does not announce a subject but expresses a viewpoint. The statement "There is a serious shortage of campus parking" describes a problem, but it does not express an opinion. "Shuttle bus service should be expanded to alleviate the campus parking problem" serves as a thesis statement, clearly asserting a point of view.

■ **They focus the topic.** Part of the job of a thesis statement is to direct the paper, limiting the scope of the writer's area of concentration. "Television is bad for children" states an opinion, but the subject is so broad that any essay would probably just list superficial observations. A thesis such as "Television action heroes teach children that violence is an acceptable method of resolving conflicts" is limited enough to create a far more engaging paper.

- **They indicate the kind of support to follow.** Opinions require proof. "Because of declining enrollment, the cinema course should be canceled" indicates a clear cause-and-effect argument based on factual evidence, leading readers to expect a list of enrollment and budget figures.

- **They often organize supporting material.** The thesis statement "Exercise is essential to control weight, prevent disease, and maintain mental health" suggests that the body of the paper will be divided into three parts.

- **Effective thesis statements are precisely worded.** Because they express the writer's point of view in a single sentence, thesis statements must be accurately stated. General terms, such as *good, bad, serious,* and *important* weaken a thesis. Absolute statements can suggest that the writer is proposing a panacea. "Deadbolt locks should be installed in all dorm rooms to *prevent crime*" implies that a single mechanism is a foolproof method of totally eradicating all crime. "Deadbolt locks should be installed in all dorm rooms to *deter break-ins*" is far more accurate and easier to support.

WRITING ACTIVITIES

Revise the following thesis statements, increasing their precision.

1. The Internet provides students with a lot of educational opportunities.

2. Providing employee health insurance is a challenge for many businesses.

3. Employers should assist employees with small children.

4. Public schools must prepare students for the twenty-first century.

5. Attitudes about fatherhood have changed in the last twenty years.

6. Commercials mislead consumers.

7. Hollywood has given foreigners distorted views of American society.

8. Americans suffer from their lack of understanding of other cultures.

9. Illegal immigration remains a problem for many reasons.

10. Peer pressure can be negative.

Locating the Thesis

To be effective, thesis statements must be strategically placed. The thesis statement does not have to appear in the introduction but can be placed anywhere in the essay.

- **Placing the thesis at the opening starts the essay with a strong statement, providing a clear direction and an outline of the supporting evidence.** However, if the thesis is controversial, it may be more effective to open with supporting details and confront readers' objections before formally announcing the thesis. An essay that opens with the statement "We must legalize heroin" might easily be dismissed by people who would think the writer must be naive or insensitive to the pain of addiction, the spread of AIDS, and other social problems stemming from drug abuse. However, if the essay first demonstrates the failure of current policies and argues that addiction should be treated as a medical rather than a legal issue, more readers might be receptive to the writer's call for legalization.

- **Placing the thesis in the middle of the essay allows a writer to introduce the subject, provide support, raise questions, and guide the reader into accepting a thesis that is then explained or defended.** However, placing the thesis somewhere within the essay may weaken its impact because reader attention is strongest at the opening and closing paragraphs. Writers often highlight a thesis statement in the middle of an essay by placing it in a separate paragraph or using italics.

- **Placing the thesis at the end allows a writer to close the essay with a strong statement.** Delaying the thesis allows the writer to address reader objections and bias, providing narratives, examples, and statistics to support the conclusion. However, postponing the thesis will disappoint some readers who want a clear answer. Delaying the thesis can suggest to some readers that the writer's position cannot stand on its own and depends on a great deal of qualification.

Explicit, Evolving, and Implied Theses

Many textbooks suggest that every essay should have an easily identifiable thesis statement, a sentence you should be able to locate and underline, but this is not always the case. Most writers present explicit thesis statements, but others use a series of sentences to develop their opinions. In some instances, the writer's thesis is not formally stated but only implied or suggested.

Explicit Thesis Statements

Alan M. Dershowitz opens his essay "The 'Abuse Excuse' Is Detrimental to the Justice System" with a boldly stated, explicit thesis statement:

> The "abuse excuse"—the legal tactic by which criminal defendants claim a history of abuse as an excuse for violent retaliation—is quickly becoming a license to kill and maim.

Explicit theses are best used in writing in the modes of argument and persuasion, comparison, and division and classification.

Advantages

- **An explicit thesis statement is clear and concise.** The writer's purpose is stated directly so that readers are not confused.
- **An explicit thesis makes a strong opening or closing statement.**
- **A concise, strongly worded statement is easily understood so that even a casual reader will quickly grasp the writer's main idea.**

Disadvantages

- **Explicit thesis statements can present a narrow interpretation or solution to a complex situation or problem.** In many instances an evolving or implied thesis gives the writer greater freedom to discuss ideas and address possible objections.
- **Explicit theses can easily alienate readers with differing opinions.** An evolving thesis, on the other hand, allows the writer to explain or qualify opinions.

Evolving Thesis Statements

In "Grant and Lee," Bruce Catton compares the two Civil War generals meeting at Appomattox Court House to work out terms for the South's surrender. But instead of stating his thesis in a single sentence, he develops his controlling ideas in a series of statements:

> They were two strong men, these oddly different generals, and they represented the strengths of two conflicting currents that, through them, had come into final collision.

After describing the life and social background of each general, Catton expands his thesis:

> So Grant and Lee were in complete contrast, representing two diametrically opposed elements in American life. Grant was the modern man emerging; beyond him, ready to come on the stage, was the great age of steel and machinery, of crowded cities and a restless burgeoning vitality. Lee might have ridden down from the old age of chivalry, lance in hand, silken banner fluttering over his head. Each man was the perfect champion of his cause, drawing both his strengths and his weaknesses from the people he led.

Catton concludes his essay with a final controlling statement:

> Two great Americans, Grant and Lee—very different, yet under everything very much alike.

Evolving thesis statements are best suited for complex or controversial subjects. They allow you to address an issue piece by piece or present a series of arguments.

Advantages

- **An evolving thesis lets a writer present readers with a series of controlling ideas, allowing them to absorb a complex opinion point by point.**

■ **An evolving thesis can be useful in presenting a controversial opinion by slowly convincing readers to accept less threatening ideas first.**

■ **An evolving thesis can help a writer tailor ideas to suit different situations or contexts.** An evolving thesis can also be organized to address specific reader objections.

Disadvantages

■ **Because the statements are distributed throughout an essay, they can appear scattered and have less impact than a single, direct sentence.**

■ **Evolving theses can make writers appear unsure of their points, as if they are reluctant to state direct opinions.**

Implied Thesis Statements

In describing Holcomb, Kansas, Truman Capote supplies a number of facts and observations without stating a thesis. Although no single sentence can be isolated as presenting the controlling idea, the description is highly organized and is more than a random collection of details.

> The village of Holcomb stands on the high wheat plains of western Kansas, a lonesome area that other Kansans call "out there." Some seventy miles east of the Colorado border, the countryside, with its hard blue skies and desert-clear air, has an atmosphere that is rather more Far Western than Middle West. The local accent is barbed with a prairie twang, a ranch-hand nasalness, and the men, many of them, wear narrow frontier trousers, Stetsons, and high-heeled boots with pointed toes. The land is flat, and the views are awesomely extensive; horses, herds of cattle, a white cluster of grain elevators rising as gracefully as Greek temples are visible long before a traveler reaches them.

Having carefully assembled and arranged his observations, Capote allows the details to speak for themselves and give readers a clear impression of his subject.

Implied thesis statements work best when the writer's evidence is so compelling that it does not require an introduction or explanation. Writers also use an implied thesis to challenge readers by posing an idea or presenting a problem without suggesting an interpretation or solution. Although you may not state a clear thesis statement in writing a description or telling a story, your essay should have a clear purpose, a direction.

Advantages

■ **An implied thesis allows the writer's images and observations to represent his or her ideas.** Implied thesis statements are common in descriptive and narrative writing.

■ **An implied thesis does not dictate an opinion but allows readers to develop their own responses.**

■ **An implied thesis does not confront readers with bold assertions but allows a writer to slowly unfold controlling ideas.**

Disadvantages

■ **Writing without an explicitly defined thesis can lead readers to assume ideas un-intended by the writer.** Capote's description of a small town may provoke both positive and negative responses, depending on the readers' perceptual world.

■ **Writing that lacks a clear thesis statement requires careful reading and critical thinking to determine the writer's purpose.** A strong thesis sentence at the opening or closing of an essay makes the author's goal very clear.

Strategies for Developing Thesis Statements

1. **Develop a thesis statement while planning your essay.** If you cannot state your goal in a sentence or two, you may not have a clear focus regarding your purpose. Even if you decide to use an implied thesis, a clearly worded statement on your outline or top of the page can help keep your writing on track.

2. **Write your thesis statement with your reader in mind.** The goal of writing is not only to express your ideas—but also to share them with others. Choose your words carefully. Be sensitive to your readers' perceptual world. Avoid writing biased or highly opinionated statements that may alienate readers.

3. **Make sure that your thesis statement expresses an opinion.** Don't confuse making an announcement or a factual statement with establishing a thesis.

4. **Determine the best location for your thesis.** If you believe that most of your readers will be receptive to your views, placing the thesis at the opening may be appropriate. If your position is controversial or depends on establishing a clear context of support, delay your thesis by placing it in the middle or at the conclusion.

5. **Make sure your thesis matches your purpose.** Persuasive arguments demand a strongly worded thesis statement, perhaps one that is restated throughout the essay. If your position is complex, you may wish to develop it by making partial thesis statements throughout the essay. If you are not motivating your readers to take specific action, you may wish to use an implied thesis. State your observations or evidence and permit readers to develop their own conclusions.

6. **Test your thesis.** It is not always easy to find people willing to read a full draft of your essay, but you can usually find someone who will listen to a sentence or two. Ask a friend or acquaintance to consider your thesis statement. Is it precise? Does it seem logical? What kind of evidence would be needed to support it? Are there any words or phrases that seem awkward, unclear, or offensive? If your thesis statement seems weak, review your prewriting notes. You may need to further limit your topic or choose a new subject.

7. **Make sure your thesis does more than present a fact, announce a subject, or narrow a topic.** The most common errors writers make in developing thesis statements include simply stating what the paper is about or presenting a narrowed topic:

ANNOUNCEMENTS:	My paper is about racial profiling.
	Snowboarding is a popular sport.
NARROWED TOPICS:	Police departments have been accused of racial profiling.
	Snowboarders are regarded as outlaws by traditional skiers.
IMPROVED THESIS STATEMENTS:	Police departments must develop methods to combat crime and prevent terrorism without resorting to racial profiling.
	Snowboarders and traditional skiers must learn to respect each other on the slopes.

WRITING ACTIVITIES

1. Select three to five topics from pages 751–752 and write thesis statements to guide possible rough drafts. Make sure your statements are opinions, not merely narrowed topics.

2. Skim through the entries in the Reader section of the book and locate thesis statements. Note where they are located and whether they are explicit, implied, or evolving.

3. Select an issue you have thought about over a period of time and write a series of thesis statements illustrating your evolving viewpoints.

e-writing

Exploring Thesis Statements Online

You can use the Web to learn more about developing thesis statements.

1. Using a search engine such as Yahoo! or Google, enter *thesis statement* as a term and review the range of sources. You may wish to print out helpful web pages.

2. Locate one or more newspapers online and scan through a series of recent editorials. Select a few articles on topics you are familiar with and examine the thesis

statements. Which sentence summarizes the editorial's main point or assertion? Where is it placed? Are the thesis statements explicit, evolving, or implied? Are they carefully worded?

3. Using InfoTrac College Edition (available through your English CourseMate at **www.cengagebrain.com**) or one of your library's online databases, search for articles on gun control, abortion, capital punishment, or any other controversial topic. Can you identify the writers' thesis statements? Are they effective?

E-Sources

Indiana University Writing Tutorial Services: How to Write a Thesis Statement
   http://www.indiana.edu/~wts/pamphlets/thesis_statement.shtml

University of Toronto: Using Thesis Statements
   http://www.writing.utoronto.ca/advice/planning-and-organizing/
thesis-statements

University of Wisconsin—Madison, Writing Center: Developing a Thesis Statement
   http://www.wisc.edu/writing/Handbook/Thesis.html

 Access the English CourseMate for this text at **www.cengagebrain.com**—for further information on thesis statements.

Supporting a Thesis

By persuading others, we convince ourselves.

—Junius

What Is Support?

Whether your thesis is explicitly stated or only implied, it must be supported with evidence. Readers will share your views, appreciate your descriptions, understand your narratives, change their opinions, or alter their behavior only if you provide sufficient proof to convince them. Most people associate *evidence* with persuasive or argumentative writing, but all writers—even those composing personal essays or memoirs—provide supporting details for their ideas.

A student proposing a new computer system must provide factual support to create a convincing argument:

> *The college must improve its computer system.* This semester four hundred students did not receive mid-term grades because of a computer breakdown. The college e-mail system, which is critical to the distance learning department, malfunctioned for two weeks, preventing students from electronically submitting research papers. The eight-year-old system simply does not have the speed and capacity needed to serve the faculty, students, and administration. Students were told two years ago that online registration would save the college money and make it possible to sign up for courses from home. But this service has been postponed for another year because the computers can't support it. If the college is to attract students, maintain its programs, and offer new services, it must upgrade its computers.

The same student writing a personal narrative would use supporting details to paint a picture, set a mood, and express a feeling:

> *I spent two years in Paris and hated it!* Most people raise their eyebrows when I say that, but it is true.
>
> My Paris was not the Paris shown in the movies or the Paris seen by tourists. I lived with my mother in a cramped high-rise built for low-income workers. My Paris was a noisy, dark two-room apartment with bad heat, banging pipes, and broken elevators. The hallways were filled with trash and spattered with graffiti. Neighbors blasted us night and day with bad rock music. Punks and druggies harassed my mom every time she left for school. I could not wait for her to finish her degree so we could move back to New Jersey. I never even saw the Eiffel Tower.

WRITERS AT WORK

One day I lost my fountain pen, and I could not find another decent fountain pen. Phyllis Wright has this wonderful store where I live . . . called East End Computers. She is a wonderful woman. I walked in there, and I said, "All right, it's time for me to change my life. I can't find a fountain pen in this town." She really not only taught me how to do it [use a computer], she helped me to do it. Every time I had a problem and I couldn't get my document up, I would call Phyllis Wright. She gave me her home number so I could call her day or night for that period of transition that drives writers crazy. Now I'm all plugged in. Now I have a computer everywhere and a laptop that I take everywhere. I still have a fountain pen. Someone bought me one, but the fountain pen era is over.

Blanche Wiesen Cook, biographer
SOURCE: *Booknotes*

Writers verify their theses using various types of evidence, ranging from personal observations to statistics. Because each type of evidence has limitations, writers usually present a blend of personal observations and testimony, statistics and examples, or facts and analogies. The evidence you select should reflect the writing context and accomplish four goals:

- **Support your thesis.**
- **Address readers' needs and concerns.**
- **Respect the history and values of the discipline or situation.**
- **Suit the nature of the document.**

Types of Evidence

Personal Observations

Personal observations are descriptive details and sensory impressions about a person, place, object, or condition. Writers can support a thesis by supplying readers with specific details. The thesis that "Westwood High School must be renovated" can be supported with observations about leaking roofs, faulty wiring, broken elevators, and defective plumbing.

Advantages

- **Personal observations can be powerful as long as they are carefully selected and well organized.** To be effective, writers must choose words carefully, being aware of their connotations.
- **Personal observations can balance objective facts by adding human interest.**

Disadvantages

- **Because they are chosen by the writer, personal observations are biased.** They often require outside evidence such as facts, statistics, or testimony to be convincing.

■ **Personal observations may be inappropriate in objective reports.** Writers often avoid using first-person references such as *I* or *me* when including evidence they observed in formal documents.

Personal Experiences

Like personal observations, accounts of your own life can be persuasive support. As a college student, you have great authority in discussing higher education. A patient's account of battling a serious disease can be as persuasive as an article by a physician or medical researcher.

Advantages

■ **Personal experiences can be emotionally powerful and commanding because the writer is the sole authority and expert.**

■ **Personal experiences are effective support in descriptive and narrative writing.**

■ **Individual accounts can humanize abstract issues and personalize objective facts and statistics.**

Disadvantages

■ **Personal experience, no matter how compelling, is only one individual's story.** As with personal observations, personal experience can be supported with expert testimony, facts, and statistics.

■ **Personal experience, unless presented carefully, can seem self-serving and can weaken a writer's argument.** Before including your own experiences, consider whether readers will think you are making a selfish appeal, asking readers to accept ideas or take actions that primarily benefit only you.

Examples

Examples are specific events, persons, or situations that represent a general trend, type, or condition. A writer supporting the right to die might relate the story of a single terminally ill patient to illustrate the need for euthanasia. The story of one small business could illustrate an economic trend.

Advantages

■ **Specific cases or situations can dramatize a complex or abstract problem.** They often make effective introductions.

■ **Examples can be used to demonstrate facts and statistics that tend to be static lists.**

■ **Examples allow you to introduce narratives that can make a fact-filled paper more interesting and readable.**

Disadvantages

■ **Examples can be misleading or misinterpreted.** Examples must be representative. Avoid selecting isolated incidents or exceptions to a general condition. For instance, a single mugging, no matter how violent, does not prove that a crime wave is sweeping a college campus.

■ **Because they are highlighted, examples can sometimes be distorted into being viewed as major events instead of illustrations.** Another danger is that examples can create false generalizations and conceal complex subtleties. Examples can be placed in context with statistics or a disclaimer:

> Mary Smith is one of five thousand teachers who participated in last year's strike. Though some of her views do not reflect the opinions of her colleagues, her experiences on the picket line were typical.

Facts

Facts are objective details that are either directly observed or gathered by the writer. The need to renovate a factory can be demonstrated by presenting evidence from inspection reports, maintenance records, and a manufacturer's repair recommendations.

Advantages

■ **Facts provide independent support for a writer's thesis, suggesting that others share his or her conclusions.**

■ **Facts are generally verifiable.** A reader who may doubt a writer's personal observations or experiences can check factual sources.

■ **Because of their objectivity, facts can be used to add credibility to personal narratives.**

Disadvantages

■ **Facts, like examples, can be misleading.** Don't assume that a few isolated pieces of information can support your thesis. You cannot disprove or dismiss a general trend by simply identifying a few exceptions.

■ **Facts, in some cases, must be explained to readers.** Stating that "the elevator brakes are twenty years old" proves little unless readers understand that the manufacturer suggests replacing them after ten years. Lengthy or technical explanations of facts may distract or bore readers.

Testimony (Quotations)

Testimony, the observations or statements by witnesses, participants, or experts, allows writers to interject other voices into their documents, whether in the form of direct quotations or paraphrases.

Advantages

■ **Testimony, like factual support, helps verify a writer's thesis by showing that others share his or her views and opinions.**

- **Testimony by witnesses or participants adds a human dimension to facts and statistics.** Comments by a victim of child abuse can dramatize the problem, compelling readers to learn more and be willing to study factual data.
- **Expert testimony, usually in the form of quotations, enhances writers' credibility by demonstrating that highly respected individuals agree with them.**

Disadvantages

- **Comments by people who observed or participated in an event are limited by the range of their experiences.** An eyewitness to a car accident sees the crash from one angle. Another person, standing across the street, may report events very differently.
- **Witnesses and participants interpret events based on their perceptual worlds and may be less than objective.**
- **Expert testimony can be misleading.** Don't take quotes out of context. Don't assume that you can impress readers by simply sprinkling a paper with quotations by famous people. *Statements by experts must be meaningful, relevant, and accurate.*

Strategies for Using Testimony

Testimony, the statements of others, can be included in your paper in two ways: direct quotes and paraphrases (indirect quotes). Make sure you avoid plagiarism (see pages 7–8) by clearly identifying which words are yours and which are the words of others.

Do not simply cut and paste material into your paper without acknowledging where it came from. Quotations of a few words to a few sentences should be placed in quotation marks. Longer quotations should be placed in indented blocks. These visual markers clearly separate your words from those you have copied from another source.

Original Quote:
The Safe and Sober Program, initiated this year, has clearly worked. Eight students were arrested for drunk driving during the fall semester, compared to fifteen the year before. The number of disorderly conduct charges involving alcohol during Homecoming Week dropped from six last year to just two this year.

Nancy George, The Campus Times Online, *editorial*

Student Paper Using Direct Quote:
Efforts by college administrators and student organizations can reduce binge drinking. Writing in *The Campus Times Online*, Nancy George notes, "The number of disorderly conduct charges involving alcohol during Homecoming Week dropped from six last year to just two this year."

(Continued)

> **Student Paper Using Paraphrase:**
> Efforts by college administrators and student organizations can reduce binge drinking. At Pacific College, the Safe and Sober Program reduced alcohol-related disorderly conduct charges during Homecoming Week by two-thirds (George).
>
> Even if your assignment does not require formal documentation, clearly indicate the source of material you quote or paraphrase.

Analogies (Comparisons)

Analogies compare similar situations, people, objects, or events to demonstrate the validity of the thesis. The thesis "AIDS prevention programs will reduce the incidence of infection" can be supported by pointing to the success of similar programs in combating other infectious diseases.

Advantages

- **Analogies can introduce new topics by comparing them to ones readers find familiar or understandable.**
- **Comparisons can counter alternative theses or solutions by showing their failures or deficiencies in contrast to the writer's ideas.**

Disadvantages

- **Analogy is a weak form of argument.** Because no two situations are exactly alike, analogy is rarely convincing in itself. Arguing that school uniforms reduced violence in one school does not prove it would work in another with different students, teachers, and social challenges.
- **Comparisons depend on readers' perceptual worlds.** Suggesting that an urban planner's design should be adopted because it will transform a city's business district into another Fifth Avenue assumes that readers find Fifth Avenue desirable.

Statistics

Statistics are factual data expressed in numbers and can validate a writer's thesis in dramatic terms readers can readily appreciate. However, you must be careful, because although statistics represent facts and not an opinion, they can be very deceptive. The statement "Last year the number of students apprehended for possessing cocaine tripled" sounds alarming until you learn the arrests went from one to three students at a university with an enrollment of 30,000. Numbers can be used to provide strikingly different perceptions. Suppose the state of California pays half a million welfare recipients $800 a month. A proposal to increase these benefits by 2 percent can be reported as representing $16 a month to the poor or $96 million a year to taxpayers. Both figures are accurate, and one can easily imagine which numbers politicians will use to support or reject the proposal.

Advantages

■ **Statistics can distill a complex issue into a single dramatic statement:**

One out of three American children grows up in poverty.

Each cigarette takes seven minutes off a smoker's life.

Twenty-one thousand instances of domestic violence are reported every week.

■ **Statistics can be easily remembered and repeated to others.**

Disadvantages

■ **Because they are often misused, statistics are often distrusted by readers.** Whenever you quote statistics, be prepared to explain where you obtained them and why they are reliable.

■ **Although statistics can be dramatic, they can quickly bore readers.** Long lists of numbers can be difficult for readers to absorb. Statistics can be made easier to understand if presented in graphs, charts, and diagrams.

Strategies for Using Statistics

In gathering and presenting statistics, consider these questions:

1. **Where did the statistics come from?** Who produced the statistics? Is the source reliable? Statistics released by utility companies or antinuclear organizations about the safety of nuclear power plants may be suspect. If the source might be biased, search for information from additional sources.

2. **When were the statistics collected?** Information can become obsolete very quickly. Determine whether the numbers are still relevant. For example, surveys about such issues as capital punishment can be distorted if they are conducted after a violent crime occurs.

3. **How were the statistics collected?** Public opinion polls are commonly used to represent support or opposition to an issue. A statement such as "90 percent of the student body think Dean Miller should resign" means nothing unless you know how that figure was determined. How many students were polled—ten or a thousand? How were they chosen—at an anti-Miller rally or by random selection? How was the question worded? Was it objective or did it provoke a desired response? Did the polled students reflect the attitudes of the entire student body?

(Continued)

4. **Are the units being counted properly defined?** All statistics count some item—home foreclosures, student dropouts, teenage pregnancies, or AIDS patients. Confusion can occur if the items are not precisely defined. In polling students, for instance, the term *student* must be clearly delineated. Who will be counted? Only full-time students? Undergraduates? Senior citizens auditing an elective art history course? Without a clear definition of *alcoholic* or *juvenile delinquent*, comparing studies will be meaningless.

5. **Do the statistics measure what they claim to measure?** The units being counted may not be accurate indicators. Comparing graduates' SAT scores assumes that the tests accurately measure achievement. If one nation's air force is 500 percent larger than its neighbor's, does it mean that it is five times as powerful? Counting aircraft alone does not take quality, pilot skill, natural defenses, or a host of other factors into account.

6. **Are enough statistics presented?** A single statistic may be accurate but misleading. The statement that "80 percent of Amalgam workers own stock in the company" makes the firm sound employee owned—until you learn that the average worker has half a dozen shares. Ninety percent of the stock could be held by a single investor.

7. **How are the statistics being interpreted?** Numbers alone do not tell the whole story. If one teacher has a higher retention rate than another, does it mean he or she is a better instructor or an easy grader? If the number of people receiving services from a social welfare agency increases, does it signal a failing economy or greater effort and efficiency on the part of an agency charged with aiding the disadvantaged?

WRITING ACTIVITIES

List the types of evidence needed to support the following thesis statements:

1. The city's proposed handgun ban will not prevent gang violence.

2. Consumers will resist shopping on the Web until credit card security is assured.

3. Given the demand for more on-campus housing, the fifty-year-old dorm for men should be rehabilitated.

4. Women must learn to express intolerance toward sexual harassment without appearing humorless or fanatical.

5. Vote for Sandy Mendoza!

Using and Documenting Sources

No matter how dramatic, evidence is not likely to impress readers unless they know its source. Chapter 24 details methods of using academic documentation styles, such as MLA (Modern Language Association) and APA (American Psychological Association) formats. Documentation, usually mandatory in research papers, is useful even in short essays. Even informal notations can enhance your credibility:

> According to a recent *Newsweek* poll, 50 percent of today's first-year students plan to own their own business.

> Half of today's freshmen plan to open their own businesses someday (*Newsweek*, March 10, 2011).

In addition to identifying an outside source, it is important to explain its significance:

> A survey of five thousand heroin addicts conducted by the National Institute of Health revealed . . .

> Mario Perez, who coached teams to four state championships, has stated . . .

Strategies for Evaluating Evidence

Use these questions to evaluate the evidence you have collected to support your thesis.

1. **Does the evidence suit your thesis?** Review the writing context to determine what evidence is appropriate. Personal observations and experiences would support the thesis of an autobiographical essay. However, these subjective elements could weaken the thesis of a business report.

2. **Is the evidence accurate?** It may be possible to find evidence that supports your thesis—but are these quotations, facts, and statistics accurate? Are they current?

3. **Are the sources reliable?** Evidence can be gathered from innumerable sources, but not all proof is equally reliable or objective. Many sources of information have political biases or economic interests and only produce data that support their views. In gathering information about the minimum wage, balance data from labor unions and antipoverty groups with government statistics and testimony from business owners.

4. **Is sufficient evidence presented?** To convince readers, you must supply enough evidence to support your thesis. A few isolated facts or quotations

(Continued)

from experts are not likely to be persuasive. A single extended example might influence readers to accept your thesis about a close friend or relative but would not be likely to alter their views on such issues as immigration, recycling, divorce laws, or public schools. Such topics require facts, statistics, and expert testimony. *Examine your thesis carefully to see whether it can be separated into parts, and determine whether you have adequate proof for each section.*

5. **Is the evidence representative?** To be intellectually honest, writers have to use evidence that is representative. You can easily assemble isolated facts, quotations taken out of context, and exceptional events to support almost any thesis. Books about UFOs, the Bermuda Triangle, or assassination conspiracies are often filled with unsupported personal narratives, quotations from questionable experts, and isolated facts. If you can support your thesis only with isolated examples and atypical instances, you may wish to question your conclusions.

6. **Is the evidence presented clearly?** Although evidence is essential to support your thesis, long quotations and lists of statistics can be boring and counterproductive. Evidence should be readable. Outside sources should blend well with your own writing. *Read your paper out loud to identify awkward or difficult passages.*

7. **Does the evidence support the thesis?** Finally, ask yourself if the evidence you have selected really supports your thesis. You may have found interesting facts or quotations, but that does not mean they should be included in your paper. *If the evidence does not directly support your thesis, it should be deleted.*

WRITING ACTIVITIES

1. If you developed any thesis statements in the exercises on page 55, list the types of sources that would prove the best support.

2. Select a topic from pages 751–752 and list the kind of evidence readers would expect writers to use as support.

e-writing

Exploring Thesis Support Online

You can use the Web to learn more about supporting a thesis.

1. Locate resources about specific types of evidence online or in your library's data-bases by using *statistics* and *personal testimony* as search terms.
2. Search newspapers and journals online and select a few articles and editorials. After identifying the thesis, note how the authors presented supporting evidence.
3. Ask instructors in your various courses to help you locate useful websites in various disciplines.

E-Sources

Paradigm Online Writing Assistant: Supporting Your Thesis
    http://www.powa.org/thesissupport-essays/supporting-your-thesis.html
UC Berkeley Library: Evaluating Web Pages
    http://www.lib.berkeley.edu/TeachingLib/Guides/Internet/Evaluate.html
Johns Hopkins University Libraries: Evaluating Information Found on the Internet
    http://www.library.jhu.edu/researchhelp/general/evaluating/

Access the English CourseMate for this text at **www.cengagebrain.com** for further information on supporting a thesis.

Organizing Ideas

Planning a work is like planning a journey.

—H. J. Tichy

What Is Organization?

Whenever you write, you take readers on a journey, presenting facts, relating stories, sharing ideas, and creating impressions. Readers can follow your train of thought only if you provide them with a clear road map that organizes your thesis and evidence. Even the most compelling ideas will fail to interest readers if placed in a random or chaotic manner. The way you arrange ideas depends on your purpose, the audience, and conventions of the discourse community. Some formal documents dictate a strict format that readers expect you to follow. But in most instances you are free to develop your own method of organization.

As you review the readings in this book, notice how writers organize their essays and provide transitions from one idea to another.

Once you have written a thesis statement and collected supporting material, create a plan for your paper. Prewriting techniques such as brainstorming, writing lists, and clustering can help establish ways to structure your essay. You do not have to develop an elaborate outline with Roman numerals and letters for every paper; a plan can be a simple list of reminders, much like a book's table of contents or a shopping list. A short narrative recalling a recent experience may require only a few notes to guide your first draft.

A complex research paper with numerous sources, however, usually demands a more detailed outline to keep you from getting lost. Sketching out your ideas can help you identify potential problems, spot missing information, reveal irrelevant material, and highlight passages that would make a good opening or final remark.

Informal and Formal Outlines

In most cases, no one sees your outline. It is a means to an end. If prewriting has clearly established the ideas in your mind, you may simply need a few notes to keep your writing on track. The student who worked for an insurance agency for a

WRITERS AT WORK

I had a tape recorder with me and also had a notebook. I'm scribbling furiously, but . . . what ended up being very beneficial . . . is that I had a little tape recorder with me. For example, the night that we were trapped in the mine field— it's pitch black. You can't see to write a note anywhere. I just turned on the tape recorder, and in doing the research for the book, I just listened to hours and hours of these tapes and could reconstruct entire conversations verbatim.

Molly Moore, Gulf War correspondent
SOURCE: *Booknotes*

number of years needs only a few reminders to draft the following comparison of two types of policies:

Whole Life and Term Insurance
Whole Life
— define premiums
— savings & loan options
Term (compare to whole life)
— no savings
— lower rates
Conclusion—last point

A formal outline, however, can serve to refine your prewriting so that your plan becomes a detailed framework for the first draft. Formal outlines organize details and can keep you from drifting off the topic. In addition, they provide a document an instructor or peer reviewer can work with. Few people may be able to decipher the rough notes you make for yourself, but a standard outline creates a clear picture of your topic, thesis, and evidence for others to review and critique. (See the complete essay—based on the following outline—on page 303).

Whole Life and Term Insurance
I.   Introduction: Whole life and term insurance
II. Whole life insurance
   A. General description
      1. History
      2. Purpose
         a. Protection against premature death
         b. Premium payments include savings
   B. Investment feature
      1. Cash value accrual
      2. Loans against cash value

III. Term insurance

    A. General description

        1. History

        2. Purpose

            a. Protection against premature death

            b. Premium payments lower than whole life insurance

    B. Investment feature

        1. No cash value accrual

        2. No loans against cash value

    C. Cost advantage

        1. Lower premiums

        2. Affordability of greater coverage

IV. Conclusion

    A. Insurance needs of consumer

        1. Income

        2. Family situation

        3. Investment goals & savings

        4. Obligations

    B. Investment counselors' advice about coverage

Whether your plan is a simple list or a formal outline, it serves as a road map for the first draft and should focus on three main elements:

Title and introduction
Body
Conclusion

Because new ideas can occur throughout the writing process, your plan does not have to detail each element perfectly. You may not come up with an appropriate title or introduction until final editing. In planning, however, consider the impact you want each part of your paper to make. Consider the qualities of an effective title, introduction, body, and conclusion. Develop as complete a plan as you can, leaving blank spaces for future changes. *Remember, place your most important ideas at the opening or ending of your paper. Do not bury the most important information in the middle of the document, which readers are most likely to skip or skim.*

Writing Titles and Introductions

Titles

Titles play a vital role in creating effective essays. A strong title attracts attention, prepares readers to accept your thesis, and helps focus the essay. If you find developing a title difficult, simply label the paper until you complete the first draft. As you write, you may discover an interesting word or phrase that captures the essence of your essay and would serve as an effective title.

Writers use a variety of types of titles—labels, thesis statements, questions, and creative statements.

Labels

Business reports, professional journals, student research papers, and government publications often have titles that clearly state the subject by means of a label:

> Italian Industrial Production—Milan Sector
>
> Bipolar Disorders: Alternative Drug Therapies
>
> Child Abuse Intervention Strategies

- Labels should be as precisely worded as possible. Avoid general titles that simply announce a broad topic—"*Death of a Salesman*" or "Urban Crime." Titles should reflect your focus—"Willy Loman: Victim of the American Dream" or "Economic Impact of Urban Crime."

Thesis Statements

Titles can state or summarize the writer's thesis:

> We Must Stop Child Abuse
>
> Legalizing Drugs Will Not Deter Crime
>
> Why We Need to Understand Science

- Thesis statements are frequently used in editorials and political commentaries to openly declare a writer's point of view.
- Bold assertions attract attention but can also antagonize readers. If you sense that readers may not accept your thesis, it is better to first build your case by introducing background information or supporting details before stating a point of view.

Questions

Writers use questions to arouse interest without revealing their positions:

> Does Recycling Protect the Environment?
>
> Is There an Epidemic of Child Abuse?
>
> Should This Student Have Been Expelled?

- Questions spark critical thinking and prompt readers to analyze their existing knowledge, values, and opinions.
- Questions are useful for addressing controversial issues, because readers must evaluate the evidence before learning the writer's answer.

Creative Phrases

Writers sometimes use an attention-getting word or creative phrase to attract readers:

> Pink Mafia: Women and Organized Crime
>
> Sharks on the Web: Consumer Fraud on the Internet
>
> Climbing the Ebony Tower: Tenure in Black Colleges

- Creative titles, like questions, grab attention and motivate people to read items they might ignore. Magazine writers often use clever, humorous, or provocative titles to stimulate interest.

- Creative titles are usually unsuited to formal documents or reports. Creative wording may appear trivial, inappropriate, or biased and should be avoided in objective writing.

Introductions

Introductions should arouse attention, state what your essay is about, and prepare readers for what follows. In addition to stating the topic, the introduction can present background information and provide an overview of the entire essay. A student explaining the different types of Hispanic students on her campus uses the first paragraph to address a misconception and then describes how she will use classification to develop the rest of her essay.

> Students, faculty, and administrators tend to refer to "Hispanics" as if all Latino and Latina students belonged to a single homogeneous group. Actually, there are four distinct groups of Hispanic students. Outsiders may only see slight discrepancies in dress and behavior, but there are profound differences which occasionally border on suspicion and hostility. Their differences are best measured by their attitude toward and their degree of acceptance of mainstream American values and culture.

If you don't have a strong introduction in mind, use a thesis statement (see next section) to focus the first draft. In reviewing your initial version, look for quotes, facts, statements, or examples that would make a strong first impression. Avoid making general opening statements that serve as diluted titles: "This paper is about a dangerous trend happening in America today."

Writers use a number of methods to introduce their essays. You can begin with a thesis statement, a striking fact or statistic, or a quotation, among other possibilities.

Open with a Thesis Statement

> The "abuse excuse"—the legal tactic by which criminal defendants claim a history of abuse as an excuse for violent retaliation—is quickly becoming a license to kill and maim. More and more defense lawyers are employing this tactic and more and more jurors are buying it. It is a dangerous trend, with serious and widespread implications for the safety and liberty of every American.
>
> *Alan Dershowitz, "The 'Abuse Excuse' Is Detrimental to the Justice System"*

- Opening with a thesis creates a strong first impression so even a casual reader quickly understands the message.

■ Like a title summarizing the writer's thesis, however, introductions that make a clear assertion may alienate readers, particularly if your topic or position is controversial. You may wish to present evidence or explain reasons before openly announcing your thesis.

Begin with Facts or Statistics

One out of every five new recruits in the United States military is female. The Marines gave the Combat Action Ribbon for service in the Persian Gulf to 23 women. Two female soldiers were killed in the bombing of the USS Cole.

The Selective Service registers for the draft all male citizens between the ages of 18 and 25.

What's wrong with this picture?

Anna Quindlen, "Uncle Sam and Aunt Samantha:
It's Simple Fairness: Women as Well as Men Should Be Required to Register for the Draft"

■ The fact or statistic you select should be easy to comprehend and stimulate reader interest.

Use a Quotation

In 1773, on a tour of Scotland and the Hebrides Islands, Samuel Johnson visited a school for deaf children. Impressed by the students but daunted by their predicament, he proclaimed deafness "one of the most desperate of human calamities." More than a century later Helen Keller reflected on her own life and declared that deafness was a far greater hardship than blindness. "Blindness cuts people off from things," she observed. "Deafness cuts people off from people."

Edward Dolnick, "Deafness as Culture"

■ Quotations allow you to present another voice, giving a second viewpoint. You can introduce expert opinion, providing immediate support for the upcoming thesis.

■ Select relevant quotations. Avoid using famous sayings by such people as Shakespeare or Benjamin Franklin unless they directly relate to your subject.

Open with a Brief Narrative or Example

At first, Robert Maynard thought they were harmless—albeit crude—electronic postings. Most closed with the same poem: "Lord, grant me the serenity to accept the things I cannot change . . . and the wisdom to hide the bodies of the people I had to kill." One claimed that Maynard's employees were liars. Others that his wife, Teresa, was unfaithful. But when the messages, posted on an Internet newsgroup, did not stop, Maynard went to court.

Kevin Whitelaw, "Fear and Dread in Cyberspace"

■ A short narrative personalizes complex topics and helps introduce readers to subjects that they might not initially find interesting.

■ Narratives should be short and representative. An engaging example may distort readers' understanding and should be balanced with facts and statistics to place it in context.

Pose a Question

> Think for a minute. Who were you before this wave of feminism began?
>
> *Gloria Steinem, "Words and Change"*

- ■ An opening question, like one posed in the title, arouses attention by challenging and engaging readers, prompting them to consider your topic.
- ■ Questions can introduce a discussion of controversial topics without immediately revealing your opinion.

Organizing the Body of an Essay

Once you introduce the subject, there are three basic methods of organizing the body of the essay: *chronological, spatial,* and *emphatic.* Just as writers often have unique composing styles, they often have different ways of viewing and organizing their material. The way you organize the body of the essay should reflect your thesis and your train of thought. Within these general methods of organization, you may include portions using different modes. For example, a spatially organized essay may contain chronological sections.

Chronological: Organizing by Time

The simplest and often the most effective way of structuring an essay is to tell a story, relating events as they occurred. Narrative, process, cause-and-effect, and example essays commonly follow a chronological pattern, presenting evidence on a timeline. Biographies, history books, accident reports, and newspaper articles about current events are often arranged chronologically.

A student discussing the causes of the Civil War might explain the conflict as the result of a historical process, the outcome of a chain of events.

THESIS: The American Civil War resulted from a growing economic, cultural, and ideological division between North and South that could not be resolved through peaceful compromise.

Outline

I. 1776 historical background
    A. Jefferson's deleted anti-slavery statement in Declaration of Independence
    B. Seeds of eventual clash
II. 1820s economic conflict
    A. Growth of Northern commercial and industrial economy
    B. Growth of Southern agrarian economy
III. 1830–1840s political feuds stemming from conflicting interests
    A. Northern demand for tariffs to protect infant industries
    B. Southern desire for free trade for growing cotton exports

(Continued)

IV. 1850s ideological conflict
  A. Growing abolitionist movement in North
    1. John Brown
    2. Underground Railroad
  B. Southern defense of slavery
    1. Resentment of abolitionist actions in South
    2. Resistance to westward expansion and free states
V. 1860s movement to war
  A. Election of Lincoln
  B. Southern calls for secession
  C. Fort Sumter attack, start of Civil War

■ Readers are accustomed to reading information placed in chronological order. Using a narrative form allows writers to demonstrate how a problem developed, relate an experience, or predict a future course of action.

■ Chronological organization does not have to follow a strict timeline. Dramatic events can be highlighted by using flash-forwards and flashbacks (see pages 188–189).

■ Arranging evidence in a chronological pattern can mislead readers by suggesting cause-and-effect relationships that do not exist.

Spatial: Organizing by Division

Writers frequently approach complex subjects by breaking them down into parts. Comparison, division, and classification essays are spatially arranged. Instead of using chronology, another student explaining the causes of the Civil War might address each cause separately.

THESIS: The American Civil War was caused by three major conflicts between the North and the South: economic, cultural, and ideological.

Outline

I. Economic conflict
  A. Northern commercial and industrial economy
    1. Demand for tariffs to protect infant industries
    2. Need for skilled labor
  B. Southern agrarian economy
    1. Desire for free trade for cotton exports
    2. Dependence on slave labor
II. Cultural conflict
  A. Northern urban business class
  B. Southern landed aristocracy

(Continued)

III. Ideological conflict
   A. Growing abolitionist movement in North
      1. John Brown
      2. Underground Railroad
   B. Southern defense of slavery
      1. Resentment of abolitionist actions in South
      2. Resistance to westward expansion and free states

■ Spatial organization can simplify complex issues by dividing them into separate elements. By understanding the parts, readers can appreciate the nature of the whole.

■ Spatial organization is useful if you are addressing multiple readers. Those with a special interest can quickly locate where a specific issue is discussed. In a chronological paper, this information would be distributed throughout the essay and require extensive searching.

Emphatic: Organizing by Importance

If you believe that some ideas are more significant than others, you can arrange information by importance. Because readers' attention is greatest at the beginning and end of an essay, open or conclude with the most important points. A writer could decide that simply enumerating the causes of the Civil War fails to demonstrate the importance of what he or she considers the driving reason for the conflict. The student who believes that slavery was the dominant cause of the war could organize a paper in either of two patterns.

Advantages: Most Important to Least Important

■ **Starting with the most important idea places the most critical information in the first few paragraphs or pages.** This can be useful for long, detailed papers or documents that you suspect may not be read in their entirety.

■ **You are likely to devote less space and detail to minor ideas, so the reading will become easier to follow and will counter reader fatigue.**

Disadvantages: Most Important to Least Important

■ **The principal disadvantage of this method is that the paper loses emphasis and can trail off into insignificant details.** An effective conclusion that refers to the main idea can provide the paper with a strong final impression.

■ **In some instances, important ideas cannot be fully appreciated without introductory information.**

THESIS: Although North and South were divided by cultural, economic, and ideological conflicts, slavery was the overwhelming issue that directly led to secession and war.

Outline *(Most Important to Least Important)*

I. Slavery, most important cause of Civil War
   A. Jefferson compromise in 1776
   B. Abolitionist movement in North
      1. Expansion of abolitionist newspapers
      2. Establishment of Underground Railroad
      3. Protests and riots over Fugitive Slave Act
      4. *Uncle Tom's Cabin* & popular culture
      5. International resentment over slavery
   C. Growing Southern dependence on slavery
      1. Growth of militant press
      2. Rise of King Cotton
      3. Intellectual defenses of slavery
      4. Need for cheap labor
      5. Resentment of Northern attacks on slavery
II. Economic Conflict
   A. Northern economy
      1. Commercial, financial, industrial interests
      2. Factory owners
      3. Rise of New York as financial center
   B. Southern economy
      1. Agricultural interests
      2. Landowners
      3. Resentment of Northern financial power
III. Ideological Conflict
   A. Northern philosophy
      1. Desire for Western expansion to add free states
      2. Need for stronger federal government
   B. Southern philosophy
      1. Desire for Southern expansion to add slave states
      2. Need to assert states' rights
IV. Foreign Trade
   A. Northern demand for tariffs
   B. Southern need for free trade

Outline *(Least Important to Most Important)*

I. Foreign Trade
   A. Northern demand for tariffs
   B. Southern demand for free trade
II. Ideological conflict
   A. Northern philosophy
      1. Desire for Western expansion to add free states
      2. Need for stronger federal government
   B. Southern philosophy
      1. Desire for Southern expansion to add slave states
      2. Need to assert states' rights
III. Economic conflict
   A. Northern economy
      1. Commercial, financial, industrial interests
      2. Factory owners
      3. Rise of New York as financial center
   B. Southern economy
      1. Agricultural interests
      2. Landowners
      3. Resentment of Northern financial power
IV. Slavery, most important cause of Civil War
   A. Jefferson compromise in 1776
   B. Abolitionist movement in North
      1. Expansion of abolitionist newspapers
      2. Establishment of Underground Railroad
      3. Protests and riots over Fugitive Slave Act
      4. *Uncle Tom's Cabin* & popular culture
      5. International resentment over slavery
   C. Growing Southern dependence on slavery
      1. Growth of militant press
      2. Rise of King Cotton
      3. Intellectual defenses of slavery
      4. Need for cheap labor
      5. Resentment of Northern attacks on slavery

Advantages: Least Important to Most Important

- **Papers concluding with the most important idea create intensity, building a stronger and stronger case for the writer's thesis.**
- **Concluding with the most important information leaves readers with a dominant final impression.**

Disadvantages: Least Important to Most Important

- **Readers' attention diminishes over time, so that the ability to concentrate weakens as you present the most important ideas.** Because you are likely to devote more space to the significant points, the sentences become more complex and the paragraphs longer, making the essay more challenging to read toward the end. Subtitles, paragraph breaks, and transitional statements can alert readers to pay particular attention to your concluding remarks.
- **Readers who are unable to finish the paper will miss the most important ideas.**

Writing Conclusions

Not all essays require a lengthy conclusion. A short essay does not need a separate paragraph that simply repeats the opening. But all writing should end with an emphatic point, final observation, or memorable comment.

Summarize the Thesis and Main Points

A long, complex essay can benefit from a summary that reminds readers of your thesis and principal considerations:

> Public understanding of science is more central to our national security than half a dozen strategic weapon systems. The sub-mediocre performance of American youngsters in science and math, and the widespread adult ignorance and apathy about science and math, should sound an urgent alarm.
>
> *Carl Sagan, "Why We Should Understand Science"*

- Ending with a summary or restatement of the thesis leaves readers with your main point.
- Summaries in short papers, however, can be redundant and weaken rather than strengthen an essay.

End with a Question

Just as an introductory question can arouse reader interest, so concluding with a question can prompt readers to consider the essay's main points or challenge readers to consider a future course of action:

> So the drumbeat goes on for more police, more prisons, more of the same failed policies. Ever see a dog chase its tail?
>
> *Wilbert Rideau, "Why Prisons Don't Work"*

Some writers pose a last question and provide an answer to reinforce their thesis:

> Can such principles be taught? Maybe not. But most of them can be learned.
>
> *William Zinsser, "The Transaction"*

- Questions can be used to provoke readers to ponder the issues raised in the essay, guiding them to take action or reconsider their views.

- Questions lead readers to pause and consider the writer's points. Readers may be tempted to skim through an essay, but a final question provides a test—prompting them to think about what they have just read.

Conclude with a Quotation

A quotation allows writers to introduce a second opinion or conclude with remarks by a noted authority or compelling witness:

> I once had the opportunity to describe father's life to the late, great Jewish American writer Bernard Malamud. His only comment was, "Only in America!"
>
> *José Antonio Burciaga, "My Ecumenical Father"*

- Select quotations that are striking, relevant, and that emphasize the main points of the essay.

- Avoid irrelevant or generic quotations by famous people.

End with a Strong Image

Narrative and descriptive essays can have power if they leave readers with a compelling fact or scene:

> When the others went swimming, my son said he was going in, too. He pulled his dripping trunks from the line where they had hung all through the shower and wrung them out. Languidly, and with no thought of going in, I watched him, his hard little body, skinny and bare, saw him wince slightly as he pulled up around his vitals the small, soggy, icy garment. As he buckled the swollen belt, suddenly my groin felt the chill of death.
>
> *E. B. White, "Once More to the Lake"*

- Choose an image that will motivate readers to consider the essay's main points.

- Concluding images and statements should be suited to the conventions of the discourse community and the nature of the document.

Conclude with a Challenging Statement

Writers of persuasive essays frequently end with an appeal, prediction, warning, or challenge aimed directly at the reader:

> Ally yourself with us while you can—or don't be surprised if, one day, you're asking one of *us* for work.
>
> *Suneel Rataan, "Why Busters Hate Boomers"*

- Direct challenges are effective if you want readers to take action. Make sure that any appeal you use is suited to both your goal and your audience.

- Avoid making statements that are hostile or offensive. Consider possible extended audiences. If you are writing as the agent of others, determine if the remark you make reflects the attitudes, values, and tone of those you represent.

Moving from Prewriting to Planning

The plan you develop builds upon your prewriting, pulling the relevant ideas into meaningful order. Having read and discussed several essays concerning criminal justice, a student decided to write a short essay debating the merits of a current legal issue. At first she listed topics, then used clustering, freewriting, and questioning to narrow her topic and develop her thesis.

After reviewing her prewriting notes, the student created an outline organizing her essay spatially, presenting positive and then negative effects of victim impact statements. To give her paper a strong conclusion, she decided to end the paper with her thesis.

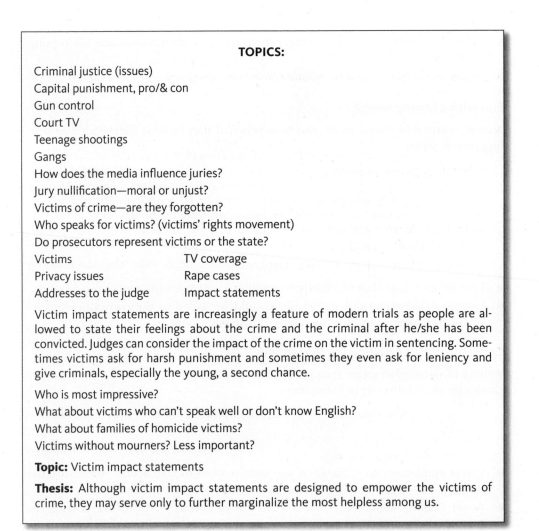

TOPICS:

Criminal justice (issues)
Capital punishment, pro/& con
Gun control
Court TV
Teenage shootings
Gangs
How does the media influence juries?
Jury nullification—moral or unjust?
Victims of crime—are they forgotten?
Who speaks for victims? (victims' rights movement)
Do prosecutors represent victims or the state?

Victims	TV coverage
Privacy issues	Rape cases
Addresses to the judge	Impact statements

Victim impact statements are increasingly a feature of modern trials as people are allowed to state their feelings about the crime and the criminal after he/she has been convicted. Judges can consider the impact of the crime on the victim in sentencing. Sometimes victims ask for harsh punishment and sometimes they even ask for leniency and give criminals, especially the young, a second chance.

Who is most impressive?
What about victims who can't speak well or don't know English?
What about families of homicide victims?
Victims without mourners? Less important?

Topic: Victim impact statements

Thesis: Although victim impact statements are designed to empower the victims of crime, they may serve only to further marginalize the most helpless among us.

OUTLINE

I. Introduction
    A. Background of victim impact statements
    B. Definition of victim impact statements
II. Goals of victim impact statements (pro)
    A. Victims granted a voice
    B. Therapeutic benefits for victims
    C. Recommendations for sentencing
III. Negative effects of victim impact statements (con)
    A. Inarticulate victims ignored
    B. Benefits limited to the affluent
IV. Conclusion

Thesis: Victim impact statements marginalize the poor and helpless.

WRITING ACTIVITIES

1. Write a brief plan for the following topics. Choose one of the three basic methods of organization for each.

   Topic: Television violence

   Chronological | Spatial | Emphatic

   Topic: Texting while driving

   Chronological | Spatial | Emphatic

   Topic: America's role in the twenty-first century

   Chronological | Spatial | Emphatic

2. Review the following prewriting notes and assemble the ideas into an effective outline. (You may use more than one organizational method.)

   Topic: Telemarketing Fraud

   Thesis: State and federal agencies must take greater steps to stem the rapid increase in telemarketing fraud.

NOTES

Thousands of victims defrauded of their life savings

Failure of police and DAs to investigate and prosecute

History of telemarketing fraud

Case of Nancy Sims—defrauded of $75,000 in investment scam

Statements by former telemarketer who admitted preying on the elderly

(Continued)

> Need to change attitudes that fraud is "nonviolent crime"
> Telemarketing scams use long distance to avoid local victims
> Failure of existing state and federal laws
> Telemarketing scams rarely lead to convictions or harsh sentences

PLANNING CHECKLIST

After you have completed your plan, consider these questions.

✔ **Does your plan fulfill the needs of the writing task?** Review notes, comments, or instructor's guidelines to make sure you have clearly understood the assignment. Are there standard formats that should be followed, or are you free to develop your own method of organization? Does your plan address the needs of readers?

✔ **Is your thesis clearly stated?** Does your thesis state a point of view, or is it simply a narrowed topic?

✔ **Have you developed enough evidence?** Is the thesis clearly supported by examples, details, facts, quotations, and examples? Is the evidence compelling and clearly stated? Are the sources accurate? Will readers accept your evidence? Should outside sources be documented?

✔ **Have you selected an appropriate method of organization?** Will readers be able to follow your train of thought? Are transitions clearly indicated?

✔ **Does your plan help overcome common problems?** Review previous assignments or comments instructors have made about your writing in the past. Does your plan provide guidelines for a stronger thesis or more organized support?

✔ **Does your opening arouse attention and introduce readers to your topic?**

✔ **Does your conclusion end the paper with a strong point or memorable image?**

✔ **Does your plan give you a workable guideline for writing your first draft?** Does it include reminders, references, and tips to make your job easier? Do you use a format that you can easily amend? *(Note: If writing on paper, leave space between points so you have room for new ideas.)*

Strategies for Overcoming Problems in Organization

If you have problems organizing your ideas and developing a plan for your paper, review your prewriting.

1. **Examine your thesis and goal.** The subject and purpose of your writing can suggest an organizational method. Would your ideas be best expressed by telling a story or categorizing them? Are some ideas more important than others?

2. **Use prewriting strategies to establish a pattern.** Make a list of your main ideas. Use clustering to draw relationships between points. What pattern best pulls these ideas together?

3. **Discuss your paper with your instructor or fellow students.** You may be so focused on details that you cannot obtain an overall view of your paper. Another person may be able to examine your notes and suggest a successful pattern.

4. **Start writing.** Although writing without a plan may make you feel like starting a journey without a map, plunging in and starting a draft may help you discover a way of organizing ideas. Although you are writing without a plan, try to stay on target. Focus on your goal. If the introduction gives you trouble, start with the body or conclusion. Developing connections between a few ideas may help you discover a method of organizing your entire essay.

e-writing

Exploring Organization Online

You can use the Web to learn more about organizing an essay.

1. Using a search engine, enter such terms as *organizing an essay, topic outline, sentence outline,* or *writing introductions* to locate current sites of interest.

2. Using InfoTrac College Edition (available through your English CourseMate at **www.cengagebrain.com**) or one of your library's databases, look up recent editorials or brief articles and notice how authors organized their ideas. Did the writers use a chronological or a spatial method? Where did they place the thesis and the most important evidence? How did they begin and end the article? Could any parts be improved to make the article easier to read or more effective?

E-Sources

Paradigm Online Writing Assistant: Introductions and Conclusions
 http://www.powa.org/thesissupport-essays/introductions-and-conclusions.html
Purdue Online Writing Lab: Four Main Components for Effective Outlines
 http://owl.english.purdue.edu/owl/resource/544/01/

 Access the English CourseMate for this text at **www.cengagebrain.com** for further information on organizing ideas.

Developing Paragraphs

Just as the sentence contains one idea in all its fullness, so the paragraph should embrace a distinct episode; and as sentences should follow one another in harmonious sequence, so the paragraphs must fit on to one another like the automatic couplings of railway carriages.

—Winston Churchill

What Are Paragraphs?

Most students can explain the goal of an essay and define the meaning of a sentence. But many are unsure how to describe paragraphs or even when to make them. In writing, they often fail to use paragraphs at all or impulsively indent every few sentences just to break up their essay.

A paragraph is more than a cluster of sentences or a random break in a block of text. **Paragraphs are groups of related sentences unified by a single idea. Like chapters in a book, they organize details and have a clear goal.** Paragraphs are used to introduce a subject, explain a point, tell a story, compare ideas, support a thesis, or summarize a writer's main points.

The importance of paragraphs can be demonstrated by removing them from a text. Printed without paragraphs, Walter Lord's foreword to *A Night to Remember* is difficult to comprehend and becomes an unimaginative jumble of facts and numbers:

WRITERS AT WORK

I don't allow anybody around while I'm writing. My wife manages to live with me, and my son and our dog, but I like to be let alone when I'm working. I see these Hollywood movies where the man gets up in the middle of the night and dashes off a few thousand words, and his little wife comes in to make sure he's comfortable and everything. That's all foolishness. It would never be anything like that. In fact, I'm privately convinced that most of the really bad writing the world's ever seen has been done under the influence of what's called inspiration.

Shelby Foote, historian
SOURCE: *Booknotes*

Sam Diephuis/jupiterimages

Maria Toutoudaki/jupiterimages

In 1898 a struggling author named Morgan Robertson concocted a novel about a fabulous Atlantic liner, far larger than any that had ever been built. Robertson loaded his ship with rich and complacent people and then wrecked it one cold April night on an iceberg. This somehow showed the futility of everything, and in fact, the book was called *Futility* when it appeared that year, published by the firm of M. F. Mansfield. Fourteen years later a British shipping company named the White Star Line built a steamer remarkably like the one in Robertson's novel. The new liner was 66,000 tons displacement; Robertson's was 70,000. The real ship was 882.5 feet long; the fictional one was 800 feet. Both vessels were triple screw and could make 24–25 knots. Both could carry about 3,000 people, and both had enough lifeboats for only a fraction of this number. But, then, this didn't seem to matter because both were labeled "unsinkable." On April 12, 1912, the real ship left Southampton on her maiden voyage to New York. Her cargo included a priceless copy of the *Rubaiyat of Omar Khayyam* and a list of passengers collectively worth two hundred fifty million dollars. On her way over she too struck an iceberg and went down on a cold April night. Robertson called his ship the *Titan;* the White Star Line called its ship the *Titanic.* This is the story of her last night.

Presented as Lord wrote it, the foreword is far more striking:

In 1898 a struggling author named Morgan Robertson concocted a novel about a fabulous Atlantic liner, far larger than any that had ever been built. Robertson loaded his ship with rich and complacent people and then wrecked it one cold April night on an iceberg. This somehow showed the futility of everything, and in fact, the book was called *Futility* when it appeared that year, published by the firm of M. F. Mansfield.

Fourteen years later a British shipping company named the White Star Line built a steamer remarkably like the one in Robertson's novel. The new liner was 66,000 tons displacement; Robertson's was 70,000. The real ship was 882.5 feet long; the fictional one was 800 feet. Both vessels were triple screw and could make 24–25 knots. Both could carry about 3,000 people, and both had enough lifeboats for only a fraction of this number. But, then, this didn't seem to matter because both were labeled "unsinkable."

On April 12, 1912, the real ship left Southampton on her maiden voyage to New York. Her cargo included a priceless copy of the *Rubaiyat of Omar Khayyam* and a list of passengers collectively worth two hundred fifty million dollars. On her way over she too struck an iceberg and went down on a cold April night.

Robertson called his ship the *Titan;* the White Star Line called its ship the *Titanic.* This is the story of her last night.

Each paragraph signals a shift, breaking up the text to highlight the parallels between the fictional ocean liner and the real one. The conclusion dramatizes the eerie similarity between the ships' names by placing the final two sentences in a separate paragraph.

Although it is important to provide breaks in your text, choppy and erratic paragraph breaks interrupt the flow of ideas and create a disorganized list of sentences:

I was born in New Orleans and grew up in a quiet section of Metairie. I had a lot of friends and enjoyed school a lot.

I played football for two seasons. In my sophomore year I won an award at the Louisiana Nationals.

The games are held in Baton Rouge and allow high school athletes from across the state to compete in a number of events.

I came in second out of over fifty high school quarterbacks.

The award guaranteed me a slot on my school's varsity team when I started my junior year. But that summer my Dad was transferred to Milwaukee.

In August we moved to Bayside, a north shore suburb. Our house was larger, and we had a wonderful view of Lake Michigan.

The move was devastating to me personally. I missed my friends. I found out that I would not even be allowed to try out for football until my senior year.

The coach was impressed with my ability, but he told me all positions had been filled.

Improved:

I was born in New Orleans and grew up in a quiet section of Metairie. I had a lot of friends and enjoyed school a lot. I played football for two seasons. In my sophomore year I won an award at the Louisiana Nationals. The games are held in Baton Rouge and allow high school athletes from across the state to compete in a number of events. I came in second out of over fifty high school quarterbacks. The award guaranteed me a slot on my school's varsity team when I started my junior year.

But that summer my Dad was transferred to Milwaukee. In August we moved to Bayside, a north shore suburb. Our house was larger, and we had a wonderful view of Lake Michigan.

The move was devastating to me personally. I missed my friends. I found out that I would not even be allowed to try out for football until my senior year. The coach was impressed with my ability, but he told me all positions had been filled.

WRITING ACTIVITY

Read this passage and indicate where you would make paragraph breaks. See page 359 for the original essay.

The car ahead of you stops suddenly. You hit the brakes, but you just can't stop in time. Your front bumper meets the rear end of the other car. *Ouch!* There doesn't seem to be any damage, and it must be your lucky day, because the driver you hit agrees that it's not worth hassling with insurance claims and risking a premium increase. So after exchanging addresses, you go your separate ways. Imagine your surprise when you open the mail a few weeks later only to discover a letter from your "victim's" lawyer demanding $10,000 to cover car repairs, pain, and suffering. Apparently the agreeable gentleman decided to disagree, then went ahead and filed a police report blaming you for the incident and for his damages. When automobiles meet by accident, do you know how to respond? Here are 10 practical tips that can help you avoid costly legal and insurance hassles.

Developing Paragraphs

Experiment with different ways to develop paragraphs to determine which way best fits your writing context.

Creating Topic Sentences

A topic sentence serves as the thesis statement of a paragraph, presenting the writer's main point or controlling idea. Like a thesis statement, the topic sentence announces the subject and indicates the writer's stance or opinion. The text of the paragraph explains and supports the topic sentence.

Writing about the status of France following the First World War, Anthony Kemp uses strong topic sentences to open each paragraph and organize supporting details:

> **The French won World War I—or so they thought.** In 1918, after four years of bitter conflict, the nation erupted in joyful celebration. The arch-enemy, Germany, had been defeated and the lost provinces of Alsace and Lorraine had been reunited with the homeland. The humiliation of 1870 had been avenged and, on the surface at least, France was the most powerful nation in Europe. Germany was prostrate, its autocratic monarchy tumbled and the country rent by internal dissension.
>
> *topic sentence*
> *supporting details*
>
> **The reality was different.** The northern provinces, as a result of the fighting, had been totally devastated and depopulated. The treasury was empty and saddled with a vast burden of war debt. The French diplomat, Jules Cambon, wrote prophetically at the time, "France victorious must grow accustomed to being a lesser power than France vanquished."
>
> *topic sentence*
> *supporting details*
>
> **The paradox was that Germany had emerged from the war far stronger.** France had a static population of some 40 million, but was confronted by 70 million Germans whose territory had not been ravaged and who had a higher birthrate. The Austro-Hungarian Empire had been split up into a number of smaller units, none of which could pose a serious threat to Germany. Russia, once the pillar to the Triple Entente, forcing Germany to fight on two fronts, had dissolved into internal chaos. The recreation of an independent Poland after the war produced a barrier between Russia and Germany that meant the old ally of France no longer directly threatened German territory.
>
> *topic sentence*
> *supporting details*

The topic sentence does not always open a paragraph. Like an essay's thesis statement, the topic sentence can appear in the middle or end. Often a writer will present supporting details, a narrative, or a description before stating the topic sentence, as in the following passage:

> The airline industry has suffered dramatic losses in the last two years. Lucrative business travel has ebbed, and overseas tourist bookings have dropped by a third. In addition, rising fuel prices and an inability to increase fares have eroded the profit margin on most domestic

flights. Reflecting the ongoing concern with terrorism, insurance costs have soared. Four of the largest airlines have announced plans to lay off thousands of employees. **The federal government must take steps to save airlines from bankruptcy.**

Not all paragraphs require an explicit topic sentence, but all paragraphs should have a controlling idea, a clear focus or purpose. By including enough details, Truman Capote lets the facts speak for themselves to create a clear impression about the lonely desolation of a small Kansas town:

> Down by the depot, the postmistress, a gaunt woman who wears a rawhide jacket and denims and cowboy boots, presides over a falling-apart post office. The depot itself, with its peeling sulphur-colored paint, is equally melancholy; the Chief, the Super Chief, the El Capitan go by every day, but these celebrated expresses never pause there. No passenger trains do—only an occasional freight. Up on the highway, there are two filling stations, one of which doubles as a meagerly supplied grocery store, while the other does extra duty as a café—Hartman's Café, where Mrs. Hartman, the proprietress, dispenses sandwiches, coffee, soft drinks, and 3.2 beer. (Holcomb, like all the rest of Kansas, is "dry.")

> *Truman Capote, "Out There," pages 167–168*

Using Modes

Just as writers organize essays using modes such as narration and definition, they can use the same patterns of development to unify paragraphs. In writing a comparison, you can use definition, cause and effect, or classification to organize individual paragraphs. You can also number points to make your train of thought easier to follow.

In *Race Matters*, Cornel West uses several modes to analyze views of African American society:

topic sentence
division
definition

contrast
definition

topic sentence
transition
examples

contrast

> **Recent discussions about the plight of African Americans—especially those at the bottom of the social ladder—tend to divide into two camps.** On the one hand, there are those who highlight the *structural* constraints on the life chances of black people. Their viewpoint involves a subtle historical and sociological analysis of slavery, Jim Crowism, job and residential discrimination, skewed unemployment rates, inadequate health care, and poor education. On the other hand, there are those who stress the *behavioral* impediments on black upward mobility. They focus on the waning of the Protestant ethic—hard work, deferred gratification, frugality, and responsibility—in much of black America.
>
> **Those in the first camp—the liberal structuralists—call for full employment, health, education, and child-care programs, and broad affirmative action practices.** In short, a new, more sober version of the best of the New Deal and the Great Society: more government money, better bureaucrats, and an active citizenry. Those in the second camp—the conservative behaviorists—promote self-help programs, black business expansion, and nonpreferential job practices. They support vigorous "free market" strategies that depend on fundamental changes in how black people act and live. To put it bluntly, their projects rest largely upon a cultural revival of the Protestant ethic in black America.
>
> *(Continued)*

Unfortunately, these two camps have nearly suffocated the crucial debate that should be taking place about the prospects for black America. This debate must go far beyond the liberal and conservative positions in three fundamental ways. First, we must acknowledge that structures and behavior are inseparable, that institutions and values go hand in hand. How people act and live are shaped—though in no way dictated or determined—by the larger circumstances in which they find themselves. These circumstances can be changed, their limits attenuated, by positive actions to elevate living conditions.

topic sentence
transition

use of numbered points

Second, we should reject the idea that structures are primarily economic and political creatures—an idea that sees culture as an ephemeral set of behavioral attitudes or politics; it is rooted in institutions such as families, schools, churches, synagogues, mosques, and communication industries (television, radio, video, music). Similarly, the economy and politics are not only influenced by values but also promote particular cultural ideals of the good life and good society.

topic sentence
supporting detail

Third, and most important, we must delve into the depths where neither liberals nor conservatives dare to tread, namely, into the murky waters of despair and dread that now flood the streets of black America. To talk about the depressing statistics of unemployment, infant mortality, incarceration, teenage pregnancy, and violent crime is one thing. But to face up to the monumental eclipse of hope, the unprecedented collapse of meaning, the incredible disregard for human (especially black) life and property in much of black America is something else.

topic sentence
supporting detail

The liberal/conservative discussion conceals the most basic issue now facing black America: the nihilistic threat to its very existence. This threat is not simply a matter of relative economic deprivation and political powerlessness—though economic well-being and political clout are requisites for meaningful black progress. It is primarily a question of speaking to the profound sense of psychological depression, personal worthlessness, and social despair so widespread in black America.

thesis statement example

Emphasizing Transitions

Just as writers use exclamation points to dramatize a sentence, a paragraph break can serve to highlight a transition or isolate an important idea that might be buried or overshadowed if placed in a larger paragraph. In some instances writers will use a one- or two-sentence paragraph to dramatize a shift or emphasize an idea:

> He could remember a time in his early childhood when a large number of things were still known by his family name. There was a Zhivago factory, a Zhivago bank, Zhivago buildings, a Zhivago necktie pin, even a Zhivago cake which was a kind of *baba au rhum,* and at one time if you said "Zhivago" to your sleigh driver in Moscow, it was as if you had said: "Take me to Timbuctoo!" and he carried you off to a fairy-tale kingdom. You would find yourself transported to a vast, quiet park. Crows settled on the heavy branches of firs, scattering the hoarfrost; their cawing echoed and re-echoed like crackling wood. Pure-bred dogs came running across the road out of the clearing from the recently constructed house. Farther on, lights appeared in the gathering dusk.
>
> And then suddenly all that was gone. They were poor.
>
> *Boris Pasternak,* Doctor Zhivago

Organizing Dialogue

Dialogue can be difficult to follow unless paragraph breaks show the transition between speakers. Paragraph breaks make dialogue easier to follow and allow you to avoid repeating "he said" or "I said." In "The Fender-Bender," Ramón "Tianguis" Pérez reproduces a conversation that occurred after a minor traffic accident:

> I get out of the car. The white man comes over and stands right in front of me. He's almost two feet taller.
>
> "If you're going to drive, why don't you carry your license?" he asks in an accusatory tone.
>
> "I didn't bring it," I say, for lack of any other defense.
>
> I look at the damage to his car. It's minor, only a scratch on the paint and a pimple-sized dent.
>
> "I'm sorry," I say. "Tell me how much it will cost to fix, and I'll pay for it; that's no problem." I'm talking to him in English, and he seems to understand.
>
> "This car isn't mine," he says. "It belongs to the company I work for. I'm sorry, but I've got to report this to the police, so that I don't have to pay for the damage."
>
> "That's no problem," I tell him again. "I can pay for it."

Paragraph Style

A writer's style or the style of a particular document is shaped by the length of the paragraphs as well as the level of vocabulary. Newspaper articles, which are meant to be skimmed, use simple words, short sentences, and brief paragraphs. Often a paragraph in a newspaper article will contain only two or three sentences. E-mail and memos also use short paragraphs to communicate quickly. Longer and more detailed writing tends to have paragraphs containing 50 to 250 words. No matter what their length, however, paragraphs should be well organized and serve a clear purpose.

Strategies for Developing Paragraphs

1. **Use topic sentences to organize supporting details.**
2. **Use modes to unify paragraphs.**
3. **Use paragraphs to highlight transitions.**
4. **Use paragraphs to distinguish speakers in dialogue.**

WRITING ACTIVITIES

1. In the following excerpt, indicate paragraph breaks to distinguish speakers. See pages 245–246 for the original version.

   Both cops got out. The older one checked out the rental plates. The younger one wanted to see my driver's license. "Where's your hotel?" he asked. Right over there, I said, the Maria Cristina Hotel on Rio Lerma Street. "I don't know any hotel by that name," he said. "Prove it. Show me something from the hotel." I fumbled through my wallet, finally producing a card-key from the hotel. The dance between the cops and me had begun. "I see," the young policeman said. "What are you doing in Mexico?" I'm a journalist, I said. I'd been reporting in Queretaro state. "You know," he said, "for making that illegal turn, we're going to have to take away your driver's license and the plates from the car." I said, What? Why can't you just give me a ticket? He then walked away and asked the other, older, policeman, "How do you want to take care of this?" The veteran officer then took over. "The violation brings a fine of 471 pesos," he told me. "But we still have to take your plates and license. You can pick them up at police headquarters when you pay the fine. Or, I can deliver them to you tomorrow at your hotel, but only after you pay."

2. Select one or more of the subjects listed and write a paragraph about it. Your paragraph may or may not have a topic sentence—but it should have a controlling idea. It should have a clear purpose and focus and not simply contain a number of vaguely related ideas. After drafting your paragraph, review it for missing details or irrelevant material. Underline your topic sentence or list your controlling thought.

   - Describe your first car.
   - Compare high school and college instructors.
   - Explain with one or more reasons why you are attending college.
   - State one or more reasons why you admire a certain actor, singer, athlete, or politician.

3. Develop paragraphs using the topic sentences provided. Use each topic sentence as a controlling idea to guide your selection of supporting details and examples.

   Living off campus provides students with many opportunities.

   However, off-campus housing poses many challenges to young adults.

   Distractions and unexpected responsibilities can interfere with studying.

   Students who plan to live off campus should think carefully before signing a lease.

4. Write a paragraph supporting each of the following topic sentences:

   College students must develop self-discipline to succeed.

   The central problem in male–female relationships is a failure to communicate.

   Three steps must be taken to curb teenagers from smoking.

   Proper nutrition is essential for maintaining good health.

5. Develop a conversation between two people and use paragraphs to indicate shifts between the speakers.

e-writing

Exploring Paragraphs Online

You can use the Web to learn more about developing paragraphs.

1. Using a search engine, enter terms such as *paragraph structure* and *topic sentence* to locate current websites of interest.

2. Using InfoTrac College Edition (available through your English CoureMate at **www.cengagebrain.com**) or one of your library's databases, look up recent editorials or brief articles and notice how authors developed paragraphs. Did they use paragraph breaks to signal important transitions, group related ideas, and make the text easier to follow?

   Were individual paragraphs organized by specific modes such as comparison, process, or cause and effect? How many had topic sentences you could underline?

E-Sources

University of North Carolina–Chapel Hill, Writing Center: Paragraph Development
   http://www.unc.edu/depts/wcweb/handouts/paragraphs.html

 Access the English CourseMate for this text at **www.cengagebrain.com** for further information on developing paragraphs.

Writing the First Draft

Try simply to steer your mind in the direction or general vicinity of the thing you are trying to write about and start writing and keep writing.

—Peter Elbow

What Is a First Draft?

The goal of a first draft is to capture your ideas on paper and produce a rough version of the final essay. A first draft is not likely to be perfect and will probably include awkward sentences, redundant passages, irrelevant ideas, and misspelled words—but it gives you something to build on and refine.

There is no single method of transforming your outline into a completed draft, but there are techniques that can improve your first efforts.

WRITERS AT WORK

The key to turning out good stuff is rewriting. The key to grinding it out is consistency. It sounds silly, but if you write four pages a day, you've written 1,200 pages in a year—or 1,400, whatever it is. You accumulate the stuff. So what I normally do is give myself quotas. They'll vary depending on the depth and complexity of the subject, but somewhere between three and five pages—that's my day's writing. I've got to do it every day. I can't go out and work on my farm until I've done my day's writing, and working on my farm is so pleasurable. So that's my incentive. I hold myself hostage, so to speak, and it gets done.

Forrest McDonald, historian
SOURCE: *Booknotes*

Strategies for Writing the First Draft

1. **Review your plan.** Examine your outline, prewriting notes, and any instructions to make sure your plan addresses the needs of the writing assignment. If you have developed a formal outline, use it as a road map to keep your writing on track.

2. **Focus on your goal.** As you write, keep your purpose in mind. What is your objective—to entertain, inform, or persuade?

3. **Write to your reader.** Consider the readers' perceptual world. What information do readers need to accept your thesis? How will they respond to your ideas? How can your paper arouse their interest, build on their current knowledge, or address their objections?

4. **Visualize the completed document.** Consider the writing context and what the final product should look like to guide decisions about word choice, sentence structure, and paragraph length.

5. **Support your thesis.** Include sufficient evidence that is accurate, relevant, and easily understood.

6. **Amend your plan if needed.** In some cases you will be able to follow a detailed outline point by point, turning words into sentences and adding supporting detail to transform a single line into a half page. In other instances, you will discover new ideas while writing. **Be willing to make changes, but keep your goal, your reader, and the nature of the document in mind to keep your writing on course.**

7. **Start writing.** The most important thing in writing a first draft is getting your ideas on paper.
   - Start with the easiest parts. Don't feel obligated to write the introduction first.
   - Give yourself room for changes. You can easily insert text on a computer, but if you are writing on paper, leave wide margins for last-minute additions.
   - Don't edit as you write. Pausing to look up facts or check spelling can interrupt your train of thought, but you can make notes as you write to identify items for future revisions. Underline words you think might be misspelled or misused. Make notes in parentheses to signal missing details.
   - Break the paper into manageable parts. Instead of attempting to write a complete draft, you may find it more effective to focus on one section, especially if your paper is long and complex.
   - If you get stuck, return to passages you have written and revise them. Keep writing.

8. **Read your work aloud.** Hearing your words can help you evaluate your writing and test the logic of your ideas.

9. **Lower your standards.** Keep writing even if your ideas seem clumsy or repetitive. Don't expect to write flawless copy; this is a rough draft.

10. **Save everything you write.** Ideas that may seem unrelated to your topic could prove to be valuable in future drafts or other assignments.
    - Make sure you save your work on a flash drive if working on a computer. If you print a hard copy, you may wish to double- or triple-space the text for easier editing.

11. **Avoid plagiarism.** If you insert material from other sources, highlight these passages in another color for future reference. Clearly distinguish your words and ideas from the words and ideas of others. **Record source information needed for documentation** (see pages 7–8).

Making Writing Decisions

In writing the first draft, you will make a series of decisions. In expressing your ideas, you will choose words, construct sentences, and develop paragraphs. The more thought you put into these decisions, the better your rough draft will reflect what you want to say and the less rewriting it will require.

Choosing the Right Words

Words have power. The impact of your writing greatly depends on the words you choose. In writing your first draft, select words that represent your stance and will influence readers. Because the goal of the first draft is to record your ideas, don't stop writing to look up words; instead, underline items for further review.

Use Words Precisely

Many words are easily confused. Should a patient's heart rate be monitored *continually* (meaning at regular intervals, such as once an hour) or *continuously* (meaning without interruption)? Is the city council planning to *adapt* or *adopt* a budget? Did the mayor make an *explicit* or *implicit* statement?

Your writing can influence readers only if you use words that accurately reflect your meaning. There are numerous pairs of frequently confused words:

allusion	an indirect reference
illusion	a false or imaginary impression
conscience (noun)	a sense of moral or ethical conduct
conscious (adjective)	awake or aware of something

principle	a basic law or concept
principal	something or someone important, as in a school *principal*
affect (verb)	to change or modify
effect (noun)	a result

See pages 746–748 for a list of commonly confused or misused words.

Use Specific Words

Specific words communicate more information and make clearer impressions than abstract words, which express only generalized concepts.

Abstract	**Specific**
motor vehicle	pickup truck
modest suburban home	three-bedroom colonial
individual	boy
protective headgear	helmet

Specific words make a greater impact on readers, as these examples show:

ABSTRACT: Wherever we went, malnourished individuals lined the road in serious need of assistance.

SPECIFIC: Wherever we walked, starving children lined the road like skeletons silently holding empty bowls with bony fingers.

As you write, try to think of effective images and specific details that will suit your purpose and your reader.

Use Verbs that Create Action and Strong Images

Linking verbs (such as *is* and *are*) join ideas but do not suggest action or present compelling images. Like abstract nouns, generalized verbs, such as *move, seem,* and *appear,* make only vague impressions. Use verbs that express action and create strong images.

Weak Verbs	**Strong Verbs**
The landlord *expressed* little interest in his tenants and *did not repair* the building.	The landlord *ignored* his tenants and *refused to repair* the building.
The firefighters *moved* quickly to the accident scene and then *moved* slowly through the debris *to look* for victims.	The firefighters *raced* to the accident scene and then *crept* slowly through the debris *searching* for victims.

Use an Appropriate Level of Diction

The style and tone of your writing are shaped by the words you choose. Your goal, your reader, the discourse community, and the document itself usually indicate the kind of language that is appropriate. Informal language that might be acceptable when texting a coworker may be unsuited to a formal report or article written for publication.

FORMAL: Sales representatives are required to maintain company vehicles at their own expense. (employee manual)

STANDARD: Salespeople must pay for routine maintenance of company cars. (business letter)

INFORMAL: Remind the reps to change their oil every 3,000 miles. (e-mail memo)

Slang expressions can be creative and attention-getting, but they may be inappropriate and detract from the credibility of formal documents.

Appreciate the Impact of Connotations

All words *denote,* or indicate, a particular meaning. The words *home, residence,* and *domicile* all refer to where someone lives. Each has the same basic meaning or *denotation,* but the word *home* evokes personal associations of family, friends, and favorite belongings. *Domicile,* on the other hand, has a legalistic and official tone devoid of personal associations.

Connotations are implied or suggested meanings. Connotations reflect a writer's values, views, and attitudes toward a subject. A resort cabin can be described as a *rustic cottage* or a *seedy shack.* The person who spends little money and shops for bargains can be praised for being *thrifty* or ridiculed for being *cheap.* The design of a skyscraper can be celebrated as being *clean* and *streamlined* or criticized for appearing *stark* and *sterile.*

The following pairs of words have the same *denotation* or basic meaning but their *connotations* create strikingly different impressions:

young	inexperienced
traditional	old-fashioned
brave	ruthless
casual	sloppy
the homeless	bums
residential care facility	nursing home
unintended landing	plane crash
uncompromising	stubborn
torture	enhanced interrogation
junkies	the chemically dependent

In selecting words, be sure that your connotations are suited to your task, role, and readers. *Avoid terms your readers may find inappropriate or offensive.*

Writing Effective Sentences

Writing well is more than a matter of avoiding grammatical errors such as fragments and run-ons. Sentences express thoughts. Your sentences should be clear, logical, and economical. There are several techniques that can increase the power of your sentences.

WRITING ACTIVITIES

1. Review papers you have written in previous classes and examine your use of words. Read passages out loud. How does your writing sound? Are there abstract terms that could be replaced by specific words? Are there connotations that detract from your goal? Does the level of diction fit the assignment?

2. Write a description of your hometown, using as many specific words as possible to provide sensual impressions. Avoid abstract words like *pleasant* or *noisy* and offer specific details.

3. Use connotations to write a positive and a negative description of a controversial personality such as a politician, celebrity, or sports figure.

4. Translate the following negative description into a positive one by substituting key words:

   > Frank Kelso is a reckless, money-grubbing gossip who eagerly maligns celebrities. He is impulsive, stubborn, and insulting. He refuses to show restraint and will exploit anyone's personal misfortune to get ahead while claiming to serve his readers' desire for truth.

Emphasize Key Words

Words placed at the beginning and end of sentences receive more attention than those placed in the middle.

Cumulative sentences open with the main idea or key word:

Computer literacy is mandatory for today's high school students.

Alcoholism and drug addiction are contributing causes of child neglect.

Periodic sentences conclude with a key word or major idea:

For today's high school student, success demands *computer literacy*.

Child neglect often stems from two causes: *alcoholism and drug addiction*.

Both cumulative and periodic sentences are more effective than those that bury important words in the middle:

In today's world *computer literacy* is mandatory for high school students to succeed.

The problem of child neglect often has *alcoholism and drug addiction* as contributing causes.

Use Parallel Structures to Stress Equivalent Ideas

You can demonstrate that ideas have equal value by placing them in pairs and lists:

Coffee and tea are favorite beverages for dieters.

Wilson, Roosevelt, and Johnson managed domestic reform while waging war.

His doctor suggested that *diet and exercise* could *lower his blood pressure and reduce his risk of stroke.*

Subordinate Secondary Ideas

Secondary ideas that offer background information should be subordinated or merged into sentences that stress primary ideas. Combining ideas into single sentences allows writers to demonstrate which ideas they consider significant.

PRIMARY IDEA: *Nancy Chen was accepted into Yale Law School.*

SECONDARY IDEA: Nancy Chen did not learn English until she was twelve.

COMBINED VERSIONS: Although she did not learn English until she was twelve, *Nancy Chen was accepted into Yale Law School.*

Nancy Chen, who did not learn English until she was twelve, *was accepted into Yale Law School.*

Secondary ideas can be placed at the beginning, set off by commas in the middle, or attached to the end of a sentence:

PRIMARY IDEA: *Bayport College will close its doors.*

SECONDARY IDEAS: Bayport College has served this community for a hundred years.

Bayport College was forced to declare bankruptcy.

Bayport College will close on June 15.

COMBINED VERSIONS: On June 15, *Bayport College,* forced to declare bankruptcy, *will close its doors* after serving this community for a hundred years.

After serving this community for a hundred years, *Bayport College,* forced to declare bankruptcy, *will close its doors* on June 15.

Forced to declare bankruptcy, *Bayport College,* which served this community for a hundred years, *will close its doors* on June 15.

Stress the Relationship between Ideas

You can make your train of thought easier for readers to follow if your sentences stress how one idea affects another. **Coordinating conjunctions—**words that join ideas—demonstrate relationships:

> **and**   joins ideas of equal importance:
>
>> The president urged Americans to conserve oil, **and** he denounced Congress for failing to pass an energy bill.
>
> **or**   indicates choice, suggesting that only one of two ideas is operative:
>
>> The university will raise tuition **or** increase class size.
>
> **but**   indicates a shift or contrast:
>
>> The company lowered prices, **but** sales continued to slump.
>
> **yet**   also demonstrates a contrast, often meaning *nevertheless:*
>
>> He studied for hours **yet** failed the exam.
>
> **so**   implies cause and effect:
>
>> Drivers ignored the stop sign, **so** authorities installed a traffic light.

In addition to coordinating conjunctions, there are transitional expressions that establish the relationship between ideas.

TRANSITIONAL EXPRESSIONS

To establish time relationships:

before	*after*	*now*	*then*
today	*further*	*once*	*often*

To demonstrate place relationships:

above	*below*	*over*	*under*
around	*inside*	*outside*	*nearby*
next	*beyond*	*to the left*	

To indicate additions:

again	*also*	*moreover*	*too*
furthermore		*in addition*	

To express similarities:

alike	*likewise*	*in the same way*

To stress contrasts:

after all	*different*	*on the other hand*
although	*however*	*still*
unlike	*in contrast*	

To illustrate cause and effect:

as a result	*because*	*therefore*

To conclude or summarize:

finally	*in conclusion*	*in short*

When you write the first draft, try to stress the relationships between ideas as clearly as you can. If trying to determine the best way to link ideas slows your writing down, simply underline related items to flag them for future revision and move on to the next point.

Understand How Structure Affects Meaning

Just as the connotations of words you choose shape meaning, so does the structure of your sentences. The way you word sentences can create both dramatic effects and make subtle distinctions. Although the basic facts are the same in the following sentences, notice how altering the words that form the subject (in boldface) affects their meaning:

Dr. Green and a group of angry patients are protesting the closing of the East Side Clinic.

(*This sentence suggests the doctor and patients are of equal importance.*)

Dr. Green, flanked by angry patients, **is** protesting the closing of the East Side Clinic.

(*This sentence emphasizes the role of the doctor. The singular verb "is protesting" highlights the actions of a single person. Set off by commas, the "angry patients" are not even considered part of the subject.*)

Angry patients, supported by Dr. Green, **are** protesting the closing of the East Side Clinic.

(*In this version the angry patients are emphasized, and the doctor, set off by commas, is deemphasized, reduced to the status of a bystander.*)

Despite protests by Dr. Green and angry patients, **the East Side Clinic** is being closed.

(*This wording suggests the protests are futile and that the closing of the clinic is inevitable.*)

The closing of the East Side Clinic has sparked protests by Dr. Green and angry patients.

(*This sentence indicates a cause-and-effect relationship, implying that the final outcome may be uncertain.*)

WRITING ACTIVITIES

1. Combine the following sets of items into single sentences that emphasize what you consider the most important idea.
   a. Alcatraz is located on an island in San Francisco Bay.
      Alcatraz is one of the most famous prisons in American history.
      Alcatraz was closed in 1963.
      Alcatraz is now a tourist attraction.
   b. Arthur Conan Doyle created Sherlock Holmes.
      Arthur Conan Doyle modeled his detective after Dr. Bell.
      Dr. Bell was famous for his diagnostic ability.
      Arthur Conan Doyle was an eye specialist.
   c. Dr. James Naismith was born in Canada.
      He was a YMCA athletic director.
      He invented the game of basketball.
      Naismith wanted to develop a new recreation.

2. Combine the following sets of facts into a single sentence and write three versions for each, placing emphasis on different elements.
   a. The student council proposed a freeze on tuition.
      The faculty accepted the student proposal.
      The alumni accepted the student proposal.
   b. The city was devastated by an earthquake.
      The public responded with calm determination.
      The mayor urged citizens to help authorities.

(*Continued*)

c. Job interviews are stressful.
Applicants fear rejection.
Interviewers fear hiring the wrong employee.

3. Select a topic from the list on pages 751–752 and freewrite for ten minutes. Let the draft cool and then analyze your use of sentences. Do they emphasize primary ideas? Are minor ideas given too much significance? Are the relationships between ideas clearly expressed?

Writing Paragraphs

Paragraphs are the building blocks of an essay. If writing the entire paper seems like a confusing or overwhelming task, focus on writing one paragraph at a time.

Use Topic Sentences or Controlling Ideas to Maintain Focus

It is easy to become sidetracked when you write a first draft. You can keep your writing focused by using a topic sentence as a goal for each paragraph. If you have not created an outline, you might organize your paragraphs by writing down possible topic sentences:

The United States must reduce its national debt.

Cutting debt will require Americans to make painful sacrifices.

The solutions we select will change the way our government operates at home and abroad.

Let each topic sentence dictate the details you include in each paragraph. Even if you do not plan to include a topic sentence, make sure your paragraph has a controlling idea and a clear purpose.

Use the Modes to Organize Paragraphs

Generally, outlines and notes list *what* you want to write but not *how* to express or organize the ideas. As you develop paragraphs, consider using one or more of the modes. In writing a narrative about moving into your first apartment, for instance, you might use *cause and effect* in one paragraph to explain why you decided to get your own apartment and *comparison* in another paragraph to show how your initial expectations about living alone contrasted with the reality. Later paragraphs in this narrative might be organized by using *process* or *classification*.

Note New Ideas Separately

As you write a first draft, new ideas may come to you. If they do not directly relate to the paragraph you are writing, jot them down on a separate piece of paper or in a different computer file apart from your essay. This way they will not clutter up the paragraph you are working on but remain available for future versions. You might use different fonts or colors to distinguish ideas.

Note Possible Paragraph Breaks

Some people find it difficult to make paragraph breaks in the first draft. Narrative and descriptive essays, for example, often seem like a seamless stream of events or details. Because the main goal of the first draft is to get your thoughts on paper, don't agonize over making paragraph breaks. As you write, you might insert a paragraph symbol (¶) or even a pair of slashes (//) to indicate possible breaks.

Moving from Plan to First Draft

A writer's plan serves as a guide for the first draft, a framework or blueprint that is expanded into a rough version of the final essay. The student writing about victim impact statements used her outline as a guideline for her first draft. In writing her draft, she introduced new ideas, departing from the original plan. At this stage, she does not worry about spelling—the purpose of writing the first draft is not to produce flawless prose, but to get ideas down on paper.

Outline

I. Introduction
    A. Background of victim impact statements
    B. Definition of victim impact statements
II. Goals of victim impact statements (pro)
    A. Victims granted a voice
    B. Therapeutic benefits for victims
    C. Recommendations for sentencing
III. Negative effects of victim impact statements (con)
    A. Inarticulate victims ignored
    B. Benefits limited to the affluent
IV. Conclusion

Thesis: Victim impact statements marginalize the poor and helpless.

First Draft

Across America today more and more victims of crime are being allowed to address the court in terms of making what is called a victim impact statment. This written or oral presentation to the court allows victims to express their feelings to the judge after someone has been convicted of a crime.

Advocates of victim impact statements point to key advantages. First, these statements give victims' a voice. For years, victims have felt helpless. Prosecutors represent the state, not the crime victim. Victims have been dismayed when prosecutors have arranged pleas bargains without their knowledge. Some victims are still recovering from their injuries when they learn the person who hurt them has plead to a lesser charge and received probation.

Therapists who work with victims also say that being able to address the court helps with the healing process. Victims of violent crime can feel powerless and vulnerable. Instead of suffering in silence, they are given the chance to addres the criminal, to clear their chests, and get on with the rest of their lives.

(Continued)

Impact statements allows judges to consider what sentences are aproppriate. In one case a judge who planned to fine a teenager for shoplifting excepted the store owners suggestions to waive the fine if the defendent completed his GED.

But giving victims a change to speak raises some issues. What about the victim who is not articulate, who doesn't even speak English? In murder cases the victim's relatives are given a chance to speak? Does this mean that a middle class professional victim with a circle of grieving friends and family members will be granted more signifiacne than the homeless murder victim who leaves no one behind?

Victim impact statements may help empower victims who are educated, personally impressive, and socially promient. But they may also allow forgotten victims to remain voiceless.

Strategies for Overcoming Problems in the First Draft

In writing a first draft, you may encounter problems. Remember, your goal is to sketch out your main ideas, not to write flawless prose. Write as well as you can in the first draft—but keep in mind that your objective is to get your ideas on paper.

1. **Getting started.** You may find yourself unable to write. Perhaps the task seems imposing, your outline too complex, your thoughts unclear.
   - See pages 17–18 for overcoming writer's block.
   - Freewrite on your topic to loosen up and get in the mood to write.
   - Break your essay into parts and start with the easiest section.
   - Flesh out your plan. Write a new version, turning words into phrases and expanding them into full sentences. Let the draft emerge from the outline.

2. **Running out of time.** Often you will be writing well, discovering new thoughts as you go. If you cannot write fast enough to capture these ideas or if you run out of time, make notes. A rough draft does not have to be stated in complete sentences.

3. **Writing in circles.** Even with the best map, you can sometimes get lost and find yourself repeating ideas, discovering that on page 3 you are restating your introduction.
   - Stop writing and reread your introduction. Does it clearly set up the rest of the essay? Does it try to say too much? An introduction indicates upcoming ideas, but it does not have to summarize every point.
   - List your main ideas or use a diagram to create a pattern you can follow.

4. **Running out of ideas.** Sometimes you may find yourself running out of ideas on the first page of a five-page essay.
   - Review your goal and plan. Are there details that could be added to support your points? Do not add extra ideas just to increase the length of your paper. Whatever you write should relate to your thesis.

- If you can't think of anything else, stop writing and put the draft aside. Do other work, read something about your topic, and let the draft cool. Return to it later and try adding more details. You may find it beneficial to start fresh with a new draft rather than working with an unsuccessful attempt.

Use key words from your essay as search terms for a quick Internet search. See if the results can stimulate additional ideas of your own.

5. **Your draft becomes too long.** You might find that the writing goes very well. One idea leads to another. Details and examples come easily. Then you discover that at this rate you will need fifteen pages to cover all the points you planned to discuss in a five-page paper.
   - Read your draft aloud. Are you recording interesting ideas, developing needed support, or merely summarizing the obvious or repeating yourself?
   - Continue writing, concentrating on capturing main points and realizing that much of what you write will be deleted.
   - Narrow the scope of your paper. You may have to limit your subject and refine your thesis. Look over what you have written and determine what section would make the best topic for a more sharply defined essay.

e-writing

Exploring Writing the First Draft Online

You can explore the Web to learn more about writing first drafts.

1. Using a search engine, enter such terms as *writing process* and *writing first drafts* to locate current sites of interest.
2. Write the draft of an e-mail to a friend. Relate an interesting story about something that happened recently at school or at work. Write a full draft if you can, but do not send it.

E-Sources

University of Chicago Writing Program: Preparing to Write and Drafting the Paper
   http://writing-program.uchicago.edu/resources/collegewriting

Online Writing Lab at Purdue University: Avoiding Plagiarism
   http://owl.english.purdue.edu/owl/resource/589/01/

 Access the English CourseMate for this text at **www.cengagebrain.com** for further information on writing a first draft.

Revising and Rewriting

Rewriting is the essence of writing well . . .

—William Zinsser

What Is Revision?

After completing the first draft, you may be tempted to start rewriting immediately—to reword awkward sentences, add a quote or statistic, or look for missing commas. But revision is more than correcting mistakes and inserting missing details. *Revision* means "to see again." Before you begin to start rewriting, it is important to examine your draft the way your readers will.

Developing a Revising Style

Most writers follow a standard pattern for revising. They begin by examining the larger elements, reading through the draft for content and rewriting the paragraphs, before making corrections at the sentence and word levels. In revising, ask yourself key questions about the goals of your writing:

■ **Is my thesis clear?**

■ **Is my thesis adequately supported?**

■ **Does my draft suit the writing context?**

   Does it meet the needs of the assignment and my reader?

   Does it reflect the methods, style, and approach expected in the discipline or situation?

   Does my essay follow the format expected in this kind of document?

WRITERS AT WORK

I sometimes write in bars in the afternoons. I go out and find a corner of a bar. If the noise is not directed at me—in other words, there's not a phone ringing or a baby crying or something—I quite like it if the jukebox is on and people are shouting the odds about a sports game. I just hunch over a bottle in the corner. I write in longhand anyway, so I can do it anywhere—sometimes in airport terminals. Then when I've got enough [written] down, I start to type it out, editing it as I go. I don't use any of the new technology stuff.

Christopher Hitchens, editor
SOURCE: *Booknotes*

Strategies for Revising

1. **Let your writing "cool."** Before you can look at your draft objectively, set it aside. Attempting to revise a text immediately after writing is difficult because many of your ideas are still fresh in your mind. Take a walk, check your e-mail, or work on other assignments before attempting to review the text.

2. **Print your draft.** Although some students are skilled at revising on a computer, many find it easier to work with hard copy. Printing the draft can allow you to spread out the pages and see the entire text. Double- or even triple-space the document to provide room for notes and corrections.

3. **Examine your draft globally.** Revising is not editing. Don't immediately start by correcting spelling and punctuation. Instead, focus on the larger elements of the draft.
   - **Is the thesis clearly stated?**
   - **Is the supporting evidence sufficient?**
   - **Is the paper logically organized?**
   - **Does the introduction arouse interest and prepare readers for what follows?**
   - **Does the conclusion leave readers with a strong final impression, question, or challenge?**
   - **Are sections off topic or redundant?**
   - **Does this draft meet the needs of the writing assignment?**
   - **What are the strong and weak points of the essay? What problems should be given priority?**

4. **Examine your paper with a reader's eye.** Consider your readers' perceptual world. What existing knowledge, experiences, values, or attitudes will shape their responses to your paper?

(Continued)

5. **Analyze your critical thinking.** In the rush of creating a first draft, it can be easy to make lapses in critical thinking. New ideas spring to mind, and you may make connections that lack logical foundation. Review "Common Errors in Critical Thinking" on pages 39–41.

6. **Consider the nature of the document.** Documents often dictate specific styles and formats. The brief sentences and short paragraphs expected in an e-mail are inappropriate for a research paper. The subjective impressions that add color to a personal essay are unsuited to a business report.

7. **Read your draft aloud.** Hearing how your draft sounds increases your ability to evaluate your draft for clarity, logic, and tone. Awkward sentences, illogical statements, redundant passages, and missing details are far easier to *hear* than see.

8. **Revise and rewrite.** If you are fortunate, your first attempt will be well written enough to require only minor revisions. But many writers, especially those working on complex or challenging assignments, usually discover enough flaws to require extensive revising.

   - If your first attempt is very unsatisfactory, it may be easier to return to your plan and start a fresh draft. Try writing from a different angle, starting with a new introduction, using different examples, selecting different words and images. Often it will take you less time to write a new draft than to repair an existing one.

   - If you placed images or visual aids in your draft, review their use. Do photographs support your points or simply supply illustrations? Avoid images that will distract or offend readers. Make sure that graphs, charts, and diagrams are accurate and do not oversimplify or distort data. Do you explain where they came from and their significance?

   - **Examine your use outside sources.** If you have included words, facts, numbers, or ideas from other sources, do you acknowledge them? Are direct quotes placed in quotation marks or indented blocks to distinguish them from your own writing? Are paraphrases—indirect quotes—identified?

Strategies for Peer Review

Writers can greatly benefit from editors, people who can offer a fresh perspective on their work and objective analysis of their writing. Professional writers receive reactions from editors and reviewers who analyze their work for factual errors, lapses in judgment, and mechanical mistakes. Many instructors encourage students to engage in peer review.

Your Role as Writer

1. **Let others read your work "cold."** If you preface their reading by telling them what you are trying to say, they will have a harder time evaluating your work objectively.

2. **If you ask people outside of your composition class to read your paper, however, explain the assignment first.** People cannot provide advice if they read your draft in a vacuum. The more they know about your goal and the intended audience, the more valuable their responses will be.

3. **Ask specific questions.** If you simply ask, "Do you like it?" or "Is my paper any good?" you are likely to receive polite compliments or vague assurances that your work is "okay." To get helpful advice, ask peers specific questions, such as "Is my thesis clear?" or "Do I need more evidence to make my point?"

4. **Ask your peers to identify the paper's strong and weak points.**

Your Role as Editor

1. **Understand the role of editors.** An editor is not a writer. Your job as an editor is not to tell others how you would write the paper but to help a writer craft his or her document. Work with the writer to identify errors and suggest improvements.

2. **Understand the writer's goal and the assignment.** If you are not familiar with the assignment, ask to see any directions the student received from his or her instructor. Does the paper meet the instructor's requirements?

3. **Review the document globally, and then look at specifics.**
   - Does the topic suit the assignment?
   - Does it need to be more clearly focused or limited?
   - Does the paper have a clear thesis?
   - Is the thesis effectively supported with details?
   - Are there irrelevant details that can be deleted?
   - Do paragraphs adequately organize the paper? Could the paragraph structure be more effective?
   - Can you detect sentences that are unclear, illogical, or awkward?
   - Does the paper need proofreading for spelling and grammar errors? As a peer editor, your job is not to correct mechanical errors but to indicate to the writer whether the paper needs proofreading.

4. **Be positive.** Make constructive, helpful comments. Don't simply point out errors, indicate how they might be corrected or avoided.

5. **Ask questions.** Instead of stating that a sentence or paragraph does not make sense, ask the writer what he or she was trying to say. Asking questions can prompt a writer to rethink what he or she wrote, remember missing details, or consider new alternatives.

Revising Elements of the First Draft

Although you can correct errors in spelling and punctuation at any point, your main objective in revising an essay is to study the larger elements, especially the paragraphs.

Look at the Big Picture

Review the Entire Essay

Read the paper aloud. How does it sound? What ideas or facts are missing, poorly stated, or repetitive? Highlight areas that need improvement and delete paragraphs that are off topic or redundant.

- How does your draft measure up against your goal?
- What prevents this draft from meeting the needs of the writing assignment?
- What are the most serious defects?
- Have you selected an appropriate method of organizing your essay? Would a chronological approach be better than division? Should you open with your strongest point or reserve it for the conclusion?

Examine the Thesis

Most important, focus on the thesis or controlling idea of the essay. Does your paper have a clear thesis, a controlling idea—or is it simply a collection of facts and observations? Does the essay have a point?

- If your paper has a thesis statement, read it aloud. Is it clearly stated? Is it too general? Can it be adequately supported?
- Where have you placed the thesis? Would it be better situated elsewhere in the essay? Remember, the thesis does not have to appear in the opening.
- If the thesis is implied rather than stated, does the essay have a controlling idea? Do details and your choice of words provide readers with a clear impression of your subject?

Review Topic Sentences and Controlling Ideas

Each paragraph should have a clear focus and support the thesis.

- Does each paragraph have a clear purpose?
- Do all the paragraphs support the thesis?
- Are there paragraphs that are off topic? You may have developed some interesting ideas, recalled an important fact or quote, or told a compelling story—but if these don't directly relate to the thesis, they do not belong in this essay.

Review the Sequence of Paragraphs

While writing, you may have discovered new ideas or diverted from your plan, altering the design of the essay. Study your topic sentences and determine whether their order serves your purpose.

- Should paragraphs be rearranged to maintain chronology or to create greater emphasis?
- Does the order of paragraphs follow your train of thought? Should some paragraphs be preceded by those offering definitions and background information?

Revise the Introduction

The opening sentences and paragraphs of any document are critical. Because you cannot always predict how you will change the body of the essay, you should always return to the introduction and examine it before writing a new draft.

INTRODUCTION CHECKLIST

✔ Does the introduction clearly announce the topic?

✔ Does the opening paragraph arouse interest?

✔ Does the opening paragraph limit the topic and prepare readers for what follows?

✔ If the thesis appears in the opening, is it clearly and precisely stated?

✔ Does the language of the opening paragraph set the proper tone for the paper?

✔ Does the introduction address reader concerns, correct misconceptions, and provide background information so that readers can understand and appreciate the evidence that follows?

Revise Supporting Paragraphs

The paragraphs in the body of the essay should support the thesis, develop ideas, or advance the chronology.

PARAGRAPH CHECKLIST

✔ Does the paragraph have a clear focus?

✔ Is the controlling idea supported with enough evidence?

✔ Is the evidence easy to follow? Does the paragraph follow a logical organization? Would a different mode be more effective in unifying the ideas?

✔ Are there irrelevant ideas that should be deleted?

✔ Are there clear transitions between ideas and between paragraphs?

✔ Do paragraph breaks signal major transitions? Should some paragraphs be combined and others broken up?

Revise the Conclusion

Not all essays require a separate paragraph or group of paragraphs to conclude the writing. A narrative may end with a final event. A comparison may conclude with the last point.

WRITERS AT WORK

If I wake up and I've got a deadline looming, it's just awful.

To get through it, you just make coffee. You make a lot of coffee, and you sit down in front of the [computer] screen and you just type out a word. Then you go and talk on the telephone. You go get some more coffee, you come back, and you make yourself type out [a] sentence.

Then, if you're at home, you rearrange your ties or you clean off your dresser. Then you go back and do it again. You make another phone call. And pretty soon your editor's on the phone saying, "Where is my copy? I need your column." So then you sit down, and you just do it.

Andrew Ferguson, editor
SOURCE: *Booknotes*

Strategies for Editing

1. **Read your paper aloud.** Missing and misspelled words, awkward and redundant phrases, and illogical constructions are easier to hear than see.

2. **Use peer editing.** It is far easier to detect errors in someone else's writing. Switch papers with another student if you can. Read this student's paper aloud if possible, noting mistakes and areas needing revision.

3. **Use the spell-checker and other computer tools.** Most word-processing programs include a spell-checker, which detects items it does not recognize as words.
   - Spell-check systems have limitations. They will not find missing words or always distinguish between homonyms such as *their* and *there*. In addition, they will not be able to detect errors in unusual proper names such as *Kowalski* or *Aix-la-Chapelle*.

4. **Edit backward.** An effective way of spotting errors is to start with the last line and read backward, moving from the conclusion to the introduction. Working in reverse order isolates sentences so that you can evaluate them out of context.

5. **Focus on identifying and correcting habitual errors.** Students often have habitual errors. You may frequently make spelling errors, forget needed commas, or continually confuse *its* and *it's*.
   - Review previously written papers and instructor comments to identify errors you are likely to repeat.

Correcting Grammar

Common Grammar Errors

When editing drafts, look for these common grammar errors.

Fragments

Fragments are incomplete sentences. Sentences require a subject and a verb and must state a complete thought:

Tom works until midnight.	**sentence**
Tom working until midnight	**fragment** (incomplete verb)
Works until midnight.	**fragment** (subject missing)
Because Tom works until midnight.	**fragment** (incomplete thought)

Notice that even though the last item has a subject, *Tom,* and a verb, *works,* it does not state a complete thought.

See pages 698–700 for more on fragments.

Run-ons and Comma Splices

Run-ons and comma splices are incorrectly punctuated compound sentences. Simple sentences (independent clauses) can be joined correctly to create compound sentences in two ways:

1. Link with a **semicolon (;)**
2. Link with a **comma (,) + and, or, yet, but,** or **so**

I was born in Chicago, but I grew up in Dallas.	**correct**
I studied French; Jan took Italian.	**correct**
We have to take a cab my battery is dead.	**run-on**
Jim is sick, the game is canceled.	**comma splice**

See pages 700–702 for more about run-ons and comma splices.

Subject and Verb Agreement

Subjects and verbs must match in number. Singular subjects use singular verbs, and plural subjects use plural verbs.

The boy *walks* to school.	**singular**
The boys *walk* to school.	**plural**
The cost of drugs *is* rising.	**singular** (the subject is *cost*)
Two weeks *is* not enough time.	**singular** (amounts of time and money are singular)
The jury *is* deliberating.	**singular** (group subjects are singular)
The teacher or the students *are* invited.	**plural** (when two subjects are joined with *or,* the subject nearer the verb determines whether it is singular or plural)

See pages 706–709 for more on subject and verb agreement.

Pronoun Agreement

Pronouns must agree or match the nouns they represent. Singular nouns require singular pronouns, and plural nouns require plural pronouns.

Everyone should cast *his* or *her* vote.	**singular**
The children want *their* parents to call.	**plural**

The most misused pronoun is *they*. *They* is a pronoun and should clearly refer to a noun. Avoid unclear use of pronouns as in "Crime is rising. Schools are failing. *They* just don't care." Who does *they* refer to? The citizens? City officials?

See pages 710–712 for more on pronoun agreement.

Dangling and Misplaced Modifiers

To prevent confusion, modifiers—words and phrases that add information about other words—should be placed near the words they modify.

Rowing across the lake, the moon rose over the water.	**dangling** (who was *rowing*? The *moon?*)
Rowing across the lake, *we* saw the moon rise over the water.	**correct**
She drove the car to the house which was rented.	**misplaced** (which was rented, the car or the house?)
She drove the car to the rented house.	**correct**

See pages 719–721 for more about dangling and misplaced modifiers.

Faulty Parallelism

Pairs and lists of words and phrases should match in form.

Jim is tall, handsome, and an athlete.	**not parallel** (list mixes adjectives and a noun)
Jim is tall, handsome, and athletic.	**parallel** (all adjectives)
We need to paint the bedroom, shovel the walk, and the basement must be cleaned.	**not parallel** (The last item does not match with *to paint* and *shovel.*)
We need to paint the bedroom, shovel the walk, and clean the basement.	**parallel** (all verb phrases)

See pages 703–705 for more on faulty parallelism.

Awkward Shifts in Person

Avoid illogical shifts in person.

We climbed the tower and you could see for miles.	**illogical shift from *we* to *you***
We climbed the tower and we could see for miles.	**correct**

If a student works hard, you can get an A.

illogical shift from *student* **to** *you*

If you work hard, you can get an A.

correct

Awkward Shifts in Tense

Avoid illogical shifts in tense (time).

Hamlet hears from a ghost; then he avenged his father.

awkward shift from present to past

Hamlet heard from a ghost; then he avenged his father.

correct (both past)

Hamlet hears from a ghost; then he avenges his father.

correct (both present)

Improving Sentence Structure

Editing Sentences

Along with editing the grammar of your draft, examine the sentences in each paragraph. Read each sentence separately to make sure it expresses the thoughts you intended.

SENTENCE CHECKLIST

✔ Does the sentence support the paragraph's controlling idea? Could it be eliminated?

✔ Are key ideas emphasized through specific words and active verbs (see pages 102–104)?

✔ Are secondary ideas subordinated (see page 105)?

✔ Are the relationships between ideas clearly expressed with transitional expressions (see page 106)?

✔ Do the tone and style of the sentence suit your reader and the nature of the document?

Be Brief

Sentences lose their power when cluttered with unnecessary words and phrases. When writing the rough draft, it is easy to slip in expressions that add nothing to the meaning of the sentence.

ORIGINAL: I was running late and went racing home to get ready to pack for our trip.

It was starting to get dark, so we went out and looked for a cab.

You have a lot of smokers out there who are desperate to quit.

IMPROVED: I was late and raced home to pack for our trip.

It was getting dark, so we looked for a cab.

A lot of smokers are desperate to quit.

Phrases that begin with *who is* or *which were* can often be shortened:

ORIGINAL: Viveca Scott, who was an ambitious business leader, doubled profits, which stunned her stockholders.

He sold tickets he got as premiums which was illegal.

IMPROVED: Viveca Scott, an ambitious business leader, stunned her stockholders by doubling profits.

He illegally sold premium tickets.

Delete Wordy Phrases

Even skilled writers use wordy phrases in trying to express themselves in a first draft. When editing, locate phrases that can be replaced with shorter phrases or single words:

Wordy	Improved
at that period of time	then
at the present time	now
in the near future	soon
winter months	winter
round in shape	round
blue colored	blue
for the purpose of informing	to inform
render an examination of	examine
make an analysis	analyze
in the event of	if

Delete Needless Detail and Superfluous Sentences

Unimportant details can be deleted. Avoid sentences that simply present a single detail.

ORIGINAL: It was October 24, 2011. It was the day I would learn if my football career was over. I had to have a CAT scan at Columbia. I got in my car and drove to Columbia Hospital. I found a place to park and went inside. I made it just in time, so I did not have to wait long.

IMPROVED: On October 24, 2011, I went to Columbia Hospital for a CAT scan that would determine if my football career was over.

Eliminate Redundancy

Repeating or restating words and ideas can have a dramatic effect, but it is a technique that should be used sparingly and only when you wish to emphasize a specific point.

REDUNDANT: The computer has revolutionized education, revolutionizing delivery systems, course content, and teaching methods.

He took his medicine, but poor nutrition, bad eating habits, his lack of exercise, and sedentary lifestyle hampered his recovery.

IMPROVED: The computer has revolutionized educational delivery systems, course content, and teaching methods.

He took his medicine, but his bad eating habits and sedentary lifestyle hampered his recovery.

Limit Use of Passive Voice

Most sentences state ideas in *active voice*: the subject performs the action of the verb. In *passive voice* the order is reversed and the sentence's subject is acted on:

Active	Passive
Mr. Smith towed the car.	The car was towed by Mr. Smith.
The hospital conducted several tests.	Several tests were conducted by the hospital.
The mayor's office announced a new round of budget cuts.	A new round of budget cuts was announced by the mayor's office.

Passive voice is used when the actor is unknown or less important than the object:

My car was stolen.
The door was locked.
His chest was crushed by a rock.

Passive voice, however, can leave out critical information:

After the plane crash, several photographs were taken.

(*Who took the photographs—investigators, reporters, the airline, survivors, bystanders?*)
Use passive voice *only* when it emphasizes important elements in a sentence.

Vary Your Use of Sentence Types

You can keep your writing interesting and fresh by altering types of sentences. Repeating a single kind of sentence can give your writing a monotonous predictability. A short sentence isolates an idea and gives it emphasis, but a string of choppy sentences explaining minor details robs your essay of power. Long sentences can subordinate minor details and show the subtle relationships between ideas, but they can become tedious for readers to follow.

UNVARIED: Mary Sanchez was elected to the assembly. She worked hard on the budget committee. Her work won her respect. She was highly regarded by the mayor. People responded to her energy and drive. She became popular with voters. The mayor decided to run for governor. He asked Mary Sanchez to manage his campaign.

VARIED: Mary Sanchez was elected to the assembly. Her hard work on the budget committee won her respect, especially from the mayor. Voters were impressed by her drive and energy. When the mayor decided to run for governor, he asked Mary Sanchez to manage his campaign.

WRITING ACTIVITIES

Edit the following sentences to eliminate wordy and redundant phrases and emphasize main ideas.

1. In many ways students must learn to teach themselves to be successful.

2. American automobiles, once threatened by imports from Japan and other countries, are entering and competing in the global car market.

3. Illness and disease can be prevented through proper diet, appropriate exercise, and moderation in the consumption of alcohol.

4. In my personal opinion, the calculus course is too tough for the majority of freshmen students.

5. The exams were distributed by the professor after a brief introduction.

Edit the sentences in the following paragraph to reduce clutter and increase clarity and variety:

The English Department originally opened the writing lab three years ago. This lab was designed to aid and assist students taking freshman composition courses. The lab was at first staffed by four paraprofessionals with extensive experience in teaching writing and editing. The dean of liberal arts cut the lab budget, reducing funds. Now only two part-time graduate students are available in the lab to help students. Neither has teaching or editing experience. The students are no longer getting the assistance they need to improve their writing. The lab is no longer crowded and hardly used. Often students are found using the computers to send e-mail to friends. Some students with nothing to do drop in to play solitaire or minesweeper, killing time between classes. This should change.

Maintaining Style

Editing Words

Your writing will improve when you make careful decisions about *diction*, the choice of appropriate words.

DICTION CHECKLIST

✔ Are the words accurate? Have you chosen words that precisely reflect your thinking? (See pages 101–103.)

✔ Have you chosen the right word from easily confused pairs like *affect* and *effect, there* and *their,* and *weather* and *whether?* (See pages 746–748.)

✔ Is the level of diction appropriate? Do your words suit the tone and style of the document? (See pages 102–103.)

✔ Do connotations suit your purpose or do they detract from your message? (See page 103.)

✔ Are technical terms clearly defined?

✔ Do you use specific rather than abstract words?

Replace General or Abstract Words with Specific Ones

GENERAL: My grandmother was a very *special* person. Her death *affected* me *greatly*. I was sixteen years old at the time. Her loss made me *feel bad,* and I *acted out negatively.*

SPECIFIC: My grandmother was a *generous, caring, wise* person. When I was sixteen, she died suddenly, leaving me feeling *sad, lost,* and *angry.* I *skipped school, quit the basketball team,* and *failed three classes.*

Avoid Sexist Language

Sexist language either ignores the existence of one gender or promotes negative attitudes about men or women.

■ **Replace sexist words with neutral terms.**

Sexist	Nonsexist
mankind	humanity, people
policeman	police officer
Frenchmen	the French
manmade	synthetic
everyman	everyone
fireman	firefighter
chairman	chairperson, chair

■ **Avoid nouns with "female" endings or adjectives.** Although the words *actress* and *waitress* are still used, other words designating female professionals are largely considered obsolete:

Sexist	Nonsexist
poetess	poet
authoress	author
lady lawyer	lawyer
woman judge	judge

■ **Avoid using male pronouns when nouns refer to both genders.** The single noun *man* takes the single male pronoun *he*. If you are writing about a boys' school, it is appropriate to substitute "he" for the noun "student." But if the school includes both males and females, both should be represented:

Every student should try *his or her* best.
All students should try *their* best.

Plural nouns take the pronouns *they* and *their*, avoiding wordy *he or she* and *his or her* constructions.

Avoid Clichés

Clichés are worn-out phrases. Once creative or imaginative, these phrases, like jokes you have heard more than once, have lost their impact. In addition, clichés allow simplistic statements to substitute for genuine thought.

white as snow	light as a feather	acid test
perfect storm	in the thick of it	on pins and needles
evil as sin	dead heat	crushing blow
viable option	bottom line	all that jazz
crack of dawn	calm before the storm	dog-tired

WRITING ACTIVITY

Edit the diction in the following sentences to avoid sexism, clichés, awkward phrases, and misused words.

1. Every student should bring his books to class.

2. He jogged at the crack of dawn every morning.

3. The university has listed three mandatory requirements for future revision.

4. We had better get down to brass tacks if we want to get a fresh start.

5. Threatened by drug dealers, the witness required continual security.

6. This dispute must be settled by an uninterested judge.

7. He could manage to explain a difficult problem with childish simplicity.

8. The computer company began to flounder in debt.

9. The president's speech contained several illusions to the New Deal.

10. A voter should use his best judgment.

Proofreading

Proofreading examines writing for mechanical errors and evaluates the physical appearance—the *look*—of the finished document.

Strategies for Proofreading

1. **Make a last check for errors in the text.** Read the paper through to make last-minute corrections in grammar, spelling, usage, punctuation, and capitalization.
   - Double-check details, such as names, dates, addresses, and prices, for accuracy.
2. **Use the appropriate format.** College instructors often dictate specific styles and requirements about paging, margins, spacing, and cover sheets. Business, government, and professional documents may have precise guidelines.
3. **Use standard formats.** If you are not given specific instructions, follow these standard guidelines.
   - Use standard-size 8½- × 11-inch white paper.
   - Remove any perforated edges.
   - Use standard typeface or fonts. Avoid script or fonts smaller than ten point. Use fonts larger than fourteen point only for titles and headings.
   - Double-space your text, leaving ample margins.
   - Use a title page or header listing your name, instructor's name, course, date, and assignment.
4. **Keep copies of all your papers.** Papers do get lost. Always make a copy in case your instructor fails to get your assignment. Save documents on flash drives or e-mail them to yourself.

Fixing Common Mechanical Errors

Spelling and Usage Errors

Spell-checkers do not distinguish between words like *its* and *it's* or *affect* and *effect*.
Get in the habit of using a dictionary and see pages 749–751 and 746–748.

Punctuation

Use **commas** to separate items in a list, set off introductory and nonrestrictive elements, and join clauses in complex and compound sentences:

We bought pens, pencils, paper, and ink.
After losing the game, we met with the coach to discuss strategy.
My brother, who was born in Manhattan, took us to 21.
Because it was hot, the game was canceled.
We bought the plane tickets, but Hector paid for the hotel.

Use **semicolons** to separate independent clauses in compound sentences:

> I flew to San Francisco; Juan took the train.

Use **apostrophes** to indicate contractions and possessives:

> Don't let Carlo's truck leave the garage.

See pages 723–736 for more on punctuation.

Capitalization

Capitalize proper nouns such as names of products, organizations, geographical places, and people:

> Buick   Yale University   Chicago   Rocky Mountains   Jim Wilson   Jane

Capitalize titles when used before a name:

> We called for a doctor just as Dr. Green walked in.

Capitalize *East, North, West, South* when they refer to regions, not directions:

> We drove south to the airport and grabbed a flight to the East.

See pages 737–739 for more about capitalization.

WRITING ACTIVITY

Edit and proofread the following essay, correcting errors in spelling, capitalization, and punctuation.

Most American Muslims are not Arab and most Americans of Arab decent are Christian not Muslim. People of south Asian decent—those with roots in Pakistan, India, Bangladesh, and Afghanistan—make up 34 percent of American Muslims, according to the polling organization Zogby international. Arab-Americans constitute only 26 percent while another 20 percent are native-born American blacks most of whom are converts. The remaining 20 percent come from Africa, Iran, Turkey, and elsewhere.

Muslims have no equivalent to the catholic pope and his cardinals. The faith is decentralized in the extreme and some beliefs and practices vary depending on region and sect. In America, Muslims do not think and act alike any more than Christians do. That said all observant Muslims acknowledge Islam's "five pillars": faith in one God, prayer, charity, fasting during Ramadan, and pilgrimage to Mecca. Muslims are also united in the way they pray. The basic choreography of crossing arms bowing kneeling and prostrating oneself is more or less the same in mosques everywhere.

The two major subgroups of Muslims, Sunni and Shiite, are found in the United States in roughly their global proportions: 85 percent Sunni, 15 percent Shiite. Ancient history still animates the rivalry, which began in the struggle for Muslim leadership after the Prophet Muhammad's death in 632. Shiites believe that Muhammad intended for only his blood descendents to succeed him. Muhammad's beloved cousin and son-in-law Ali was the only male relative who qualified. Ali's followers became known as Shiites, a derivation of the Arabic phrase for "partisans of Ali." Things did not go smoothly for them. The larger body of early Muslims known as Sunnis a word related to Sunnah, or way of the Prophet, had a more flexible nation of who should succed Muhammad. In 661, an extremist asassinated Ali near Najaf in what is now Iraq. Nineteen years later Sunnis killed his son, Hussein, not far away in Karbala. These deaths permanently divided the aggreved Shiite minority from the Sunni majority.

(See the proper text on page 178 to check your answers.)

Strategies for Overcoming Problems in Editing and Proofreading

1. **Sentences remain awkward.** Even after revising and editing, a sentence may still be awkward or garbled.
   - Think about the idea you were trying to express and write a new sentence without looking at your paper. Try restating your ideas with different words.
   - Use peer review if possible.
2. **Sentences contain redundant phrases and repeated words.**
   - Search a thesaurus for alternative words.
   - Examine your text to see whether subtitles or other devices could substitute for repeating phrases.
   - Read your paper aloud or use peer review to detect needless or awkward repetitions.
3. **You are unable to determine the final format of the document.** Even when your text is perfected, you may find yourself unable to decide whether your paper should be single- or double-spaced, whether diagrams or charts should be included, or whether citations should appear at the bottom of the page, within the text, or at the end.
   - Review instructions for guidelines or talk with your instructor.
   - Examine any existing examples for guidance.
   - Review official sources such as *The Chicago Manual of Style* or *The MLA Handbook.*

---

e-writing

Exploring Editing Online

You can use the Web to learn more about editing.

1. Using a search engine, enter such terms as *editing drafts* and *editing process* to locate current sites of interest.
2. If you wrote an e-mail to a friend in Chapter 10, review and edit your revised draft. Can you locate any grammar errors such as fragments, run-ons, or dangling modifiers? Have you used standard forms of punctuation and capitalization?

For Further Reading

Fulwiler, Toby, and Alan R. Hayakawa. *The College Writer's Reference.*

Sabin, William A. *The Gregg Reference Manual.*

Stilman, Anne. *Grammatically Correct: The Writer's Essential Guide to Punctuation, Spelling, Style, Usage, and Grammar.*

Sutcliffe, Andrea, ed. *The New York Public Library Writer's Guide to Style and Usage.*

Wilson, Kenneth G. *The Columbia Guide to Standard American English.*

E-Sources

Answers.com—online dictionary and encyclopedia
> **http://www.answers.com**

Dictionary of Difficult Words
> **http://www.talktalk.co.uk/reference/dictionaries/difficultwords/**

Thesaurus
> **http://thesaurus.com/**

Capital Community College: Guide to Grammar and Writing
> **http://grammar.ccc.commnet.edu/grammar/index.htm**

 Access the English CourseMate for this text at **www.cengagebrain.com** for further information about editing and proofreading.

Becoming a Critical Reader
Reading with a Writer's Eye

If reading is to accomplish anything more than passing time, it must be active.

—Mortimer Adler

What Is Critical Reading?

As a student you are accustomed to reading for information. Studying for examinations, you review textbooks, highlighting facts, dates, statistics, quotations, and concepts that you expect to be tested on. Engrossed in a novel, you read for plot, paying little attention to the author's syntax and literary techniques as you follow the story.

As a composition student, however, you need to read critically; you need to read with a "writer's eye." Tourists in Rome marvel at the ancient ruins; an architectural student examines how the columns support the roof. Moviegoers gasp at car chases, but filmmakers study the director's use of camera angles and special effects. The audience in a comedy club laughs as a comic spins out a series of one-liners, while a would-be performer analyzes her timing and delivery.

To increase your skills as a writer, you need to read like a writer, examining *how* something is written. Reading gives you the opportunity to watch other writers at work. When you read, note the way other writers use words, form sentences, and develop paragraphs. Focus on techniques that you can use in your own assignments:

- **How did the author limit the subject?**
- **Where did the writer place the thesis statement?**
- **What kind of support is used?**
- **How did the writer organize ideas?**
- **What sentence opens the essay?**
- **What thought, image, question, or fact did the author choose for the conclusion?**

In short, learn to read like a writer.

How to Read with a Writer's Eye

When you pick up a magazine, you rarely read every article. Flipping through the pages, you allow your eyes to guide you. A headline, a photograph, a chart, or a famous name makes you pause and begin reading. If you become bored, you skip to the next article. Reading textbooks, you skim over familiar material to concentrate on new information.

In a composition course, however, you should read *all* the assigned selections carefully. Reading as a writer, you examine familiar works differently than do readers seeking information. Even if you know a particular essay well, study it closely, observing how it is constructed. As a writer, you read to learn, seeing the writing as a model demonstrating strategies that you can use in your own work.

Like writing, critical reading occurs best in stages.

First Reading

1. **Look ahead and skim selections.** Do not wait until the night before a class discussion to tackle your assigned reading. Skim through upcoming readings to get a general impression. If you think about the authors and their topics, you can approach essays more critically.

2. **Study the headnote and introduction.** Consider the author, the issue, and the writing context. What readers does the writer seem to be addressing? What can you observe about the discourse community?

3. **Suspend judgment.** Try to put your personal views aside as you read. Even if you disagree with the author's choice of topic, tone, or opinion, read the essay objectively. You can still learn useful writing techniques even if you reject an author's thesis.

4. **Consider the title.** Titles often provide clues about the author's attitude toward his or her subject. Does the title label the essay, state a thesis, pose a question, or use a creative phrase to attract attention?

5. **Read the entire work.** Just as in writing the first draft, it is important to complete the entire selection in one sitting if possible. Do not pause to look up an unfamiliar word at this stage. Instead, try to get the big picture.

6. **Focus on understanding the writer's main point.** If possible, summarize the writer's thesis in your own words.

7. **Jot down your first impressions.** What do you think of this work? Do you like it? If so, why? If you find it dull, disturbing, or silly, ask yourself why. What is lacking? How did the author fail in your eyes?

Put the essay aside, allowing it to cool. If possible, let two or three days pass before returning to the assignment. If the assignment is due the next day, read the selection early in the day and then turn to other work or run an errand, so that you can come back to it with a fresh outlook.

Second Reading

1. **Review your first impressions.** Determine whether your attitudes are based on biases or personal preferences rather than the writer's ability. Realize that an essay that supports your views is not necessarily well written. If you disagree with

the author's thesis, try to put your opinions aside to objectively evaluate how well the writer presented his or her point of view. Don't allow your personal views to cloud your critical thinking. Appreciating an author's writing ability does not require you to accept his or her opinion.

2. **Read with a pen in your hand.** Make notes and underline passages that strike you as interesting, odd, offensive, or disturbing. Reading with a pen will prompt you to write, to be an active reader rather than a passive consumer of words.

3. **Look up unfamiliar words.** Paying attention to words can increase your vocabulary and enhance your appreciation of connotations.

4. **Analyze passages you found difficult or confusing during the first reading.** In many instances a second reading can help you understand complex passages. If you still have difficulty understanding the writer's point, ask why. Would other readers also have problems comprehending the meaning? Could ideas be stated more directly?

5. **Review the questions at the end of the selection.** When available, the questions can help you focus on a closer, more analytical reading of the work.

   This book's questions are arranged in three groups:

   - *Understanding Context*
     What is the writer's purpose?
     What is the thesis?
     What audience is the writer addressing?
     What is the author trying to share with his or her readers?

   - *Evaluating Strategy*
     How effective is the title?
     How does the writer introduce the essay?
     What evidence supports the thesis?
     How does the writer organize ideas?
     Where does the author use paragraph breaks?
     Is the writer's approach subjective or objective?
     How does the writer address possible objections or differing opinions?
     How does the writer conclude the essay?
     Does the author use any special techniques?

   - *Appreciating Language*
     How does the writer use words?
     What does the language reveal about the intended readers?
     What connotations do the words have?
     How do the words establish the writer's tone?

6. **Summarize your responses in a point or two for class discussion.** Consider how you will express your opinions of the essay to fellow students. Be prepared to back up your remarks by citing passages in the text.

7. **Most important, focus on what this essay can teach you about writing.** How can this writer's style, way of organizing ideas, or word choice enrich your own writing?

Though you may not wish to imitate everything you see, you can learn techniques to enhance your writing and overcome problems.

8. **Consider how writers resolve problems that you have encountered.** If you have trouble making an outline and organizing ideas, study how the essays in this book are arranged. If your instructor returns papers with comments about vague thesis statements and lack of focus, examine how the writers in this book generate controlling ideas.

Before Class Discussion

1. **Before class discussion of an assigned essay, review the reading and your notes.** Identify your main reactions to the piece. What do you consider the essay's strongest or weakest points?

2. **Ask fellow students about their reactions to the writing.** Determine whether their responses to the writer's thesis, tone, approach, and technique match yours. If their reactions differ from yours, review your notes to get a fresh perspective.

3. **Be prepared to ask questions.** Ask your instructor about unfamiliar techniques or passages that you find confusing.

Read the following essay by Emily Prager and study how it has been marked during a critical reading. Notice how the student used the essay to generate ideas for upcoming assignments.

Emily Prager (1952–) graduated from Barnard College with a degree in anthropology. She has written pieces for *National Lampoon* as well as several screenplays. Prager has also appeared in several films. For four years she was a star on *The Edge of Night,* a popular soap opera. She has published three books of fiction: *A Visit from the Foot-Binder and Other Stories, Clea and Zeus Divorce*, and *Eve's Tattoo*.

Our Barbies, Ourselves

Source: "Our Barbies, Ourselves" by Emily Prager. Copyright © 1991 by Emily Prager. By permission.

Notice how Prager uses a variety of modes, including comparison, description, narration, and cause and effect, to develop her essay about the Barbie doll. As you read the piece, consider her choice of topics. Is a popular toy a fitting subject to prompt thoughts about gender roles? Is it too trivial? Does Prager give a doll too much significance?

1 I read an astounding obituary in *The New York Times* not too long ago. It concerned the death of one Jack Ryan. A former husband of Zsa Zsa Gabor, it said, Mr. Ryan had been an inventor and designer during his lifetime. A man of eclectic creativity, he designed Sparrow and Hawk missiles when he worked for the Raytheon Company, and, the notice said, when he consulted for Mattel he designed Barbie.

2 If Barbie was designed by a man, suddenly a lot of things made sense to me, things I'd wondered about for years. I used to look at Barbie and wonder, What's wrong with this picture? What kind of woman designed this doll? Let's be honest: Barbie looks like someone who got her start at the Playboy Mansion. She could be a regular guest on *The Howard Stern Show*. It is a fact of Barbie's design that her breasts are so out of proportion to the rest of her body that if she were a human woman, she'd fall flat on her face.

3 If it's true that a woman didn't design Barbie, you don't know how much saner that makes me feel. Of course, that doesn't ameliorate the damage. There are millions of women who are subliminally sure that a thirty-nine-inch bust and a twenty-three-inch waist are the epitome of lovability. Could this account for the popularity of breast implant surgery?

4 I don't mean to step on anyone's toes here. I loved my Barbie. Secretly, I still believe that neon pink and turquoise blue are the only colors in which to decorate a duplex condo. And like so many others of my generation, I've never married, simply because I cannot find a man who looks as good in clam diggers as Ken.

5 The question that comes to mind is, of course, Did Mr. Ryan design Barbie as a weapon? Because it *is* odd that Barbie appeared about the same time in my consciousness as the feminist movement—a time when women sought equality and small breasts were king. Or is Barbie the dream date of a weapons designer? Or perhaps it's simpler than that: Perhaps Barbie is Zsa Zsa if she were eleven inches tall. No matter

modern ideal
of a hard
body?

what, my discovery of Jack Ryan confirms what I have always felt: <u>There is something indescribably masculine about Barbie—dare I say it, phallic.</u> For all her giant breasts and high-heeled feet, she lacks a certain softness. If you asked a little girl what kind of doll she wanted for Christmas, I just don't think she'd reply, "Please, Santa, I want a hard-body."

Barbie as role 6
model?

Barbie = adult
not baby or
child doll

On the other hand, you could say that Barbie, in feminist terms, is definitely her own person. With her condos and fashion plazas and pools and beauty salons, <u>she is definitely a liberated woman</u>, a gal on the move. And she has always been sexual, even totemic. Before Barbie, American dolls were flat-footed and breastless, and ineffably dignified. They were created in the image of little girls or babies. Madame Alexander was the queen of doll makers in the fifties, and her dollies looked like Elizabeth Taylor in *National Velvet*. They represented the kind of girls who looked perfect in jodhpurs, whose hair was never out of place, who grew up to be Jackie Kennedy—before she married Onassis. Her dolls' boyfriends were figments of the imagination, figments with large portfolios and three-piece suits and presidential aspirations, figments who could keep dolly in the style to which little girls of the fifties were programmed to become accustomed. . . . And perhaps what accounts for Barbie's vast popularity is that she was also a sixties woman: into free love and fun colors, anti-class, and possessed of real, molded boyfriend, Ken, with whom she could chant a mantra.

Ken sexless in 7
comparison to
Barbie

questions

Barbie's fate

Conclusion
and final
observation

But there were problems with Ken. <u>I always felt weird about him.</u> He had no genitals, and, even at age ten, I found that ominous. I mean, here was Barbie with these humongous breasts, and that was OK with the toy company. And then, there was Ken, with that truncated, unidentifiable lump at his groin. I sensed injustice at work. Why, I wondered, was Barbie designed with such obvious sexual equipment and Ken not? Why was he treated as if it were more mysterious than hers? Did the fact that it was treated as such indicate that somehow his equipment, his essential maleness, was considered more powerful than hers, more worthy of the dignity of concealment? And if the issue in the mind of the toy company was obscenity and its possible damage to children, I still object. How do they think I felt, knowing that no matter how many water beds they slept in, or hot tubs they romped in, or swimming pools they lounged by under the stars, Barbie and Ken could never make love? No matter how much sexuality Barbie possessed, she would never turn Ken on. He would be forever withholding, forever detached. <u>There was a loneliness about Barbie's situation that was always disturbing.</u> And twenty-five years later, movies and videos are still filled with topless women and covered men. <u>As if we're all trapped in Barbie's world and can never escape.</u>

STUDENT NOTES

First Reading

Barbie as symbol of male domination?

What about G.I. Joe and boys?

Is Prager really serious about this?

Barbie as paradox—a toy that presents a sexist Playboy image of women but a toy that is independent and more "liberated" than traditional baby dolls.

Tone: witty but serious in spots, raises a lot of issues but doesn't really discuss many.

Second Reading

Thesis: The Barbie doll, the creation of a male weapons designer, has shaped the way a generation of women defined themselves. (Get other opinions.)

Body: spins off a number of topics and observations, a list of associations, suited for general readers

Approach: a mix of serious and witty commentary, writer appears to entertain as much as inform or persuade

Organization: use of modes critical to keeping the essay from becoming a rambling list of contradictory ideas. Good use of description, comparison, cause and effect

Conclusion: "trapped in Barbie's world," good ending

Prewriting—Possible Topics

Description—childhood toys—models of cars and planes? games—Monopoly (preparing kids for capitalism?)

Comparison/contrast—boy and girl toys and games, playing house vs. playing ball (social roles vs. competition, teamwork)

Cause and effect—we are socialized by our toys and games in childhood, affecting how men and women develop (needs support—Psych class notes)

Example—My daughter's old Beanie Baby?

Using the Reader

The Reader portion of *The Sundance Writer* is organized in nine modes focusing on writers' goals. The readings in each section illustrate how writers achieve their purpose in different contexts. Each chapter opens with an explanation of the goal or mode. The opening readings in each chapter are brief, clear-cut examples of the mode and can serve as models for many of your composition assignments. Later readings are longer and more complex and demonstrate writing tasks in a range of disciplines and writing situations. Chapters end with samples of applied writings taken from business, industry, and government to illustrate how the mode is used beyond the classroom.

In addition to reading entries assigned by your instructor, perhaps the best way to improve your writing is to flip through the Reader and review how different writers state a thesis, support an argument, open an essay, organize ideas, and present a conclusion. Focus on how other writers cope with the problems you encounter in your writing.

Strategies for Critical Reading

As you read entries in the reader, ask yourself these questions:

1. **What is the writer's purpose?** Even writers pursuing the same goal—to tell a story or explain a process—have slightly different intentions. What is the goal of the writing—to raise questions, motivate readers to take action, or change people's perceptions?

2. **What is the thesis?** What is the writer's main idea? Is the thesis explicitly stated, developed throughout the essay, or only implied? Can you state the thesis in your own words?

3. **What evidence does the writer provide to support the thesis?** Does the writer use personal observations, narratives, facts, statistics, or examples to support his or her conclusions?

4. **How does the writer organize the essay?** How does he or she introduce readers to the topic, develop ideas, arrange information, and conclude the essay? How does the writer use modes?

5. **Who are the intended readers?** What does the original source of the document tell you about its intended audience? Does the writer direct the essay to a particular group or a general readership? Are technical or uncommon terms defined? What knowledge does the writer seem to assume readers already possess?

6. **How successful is the writing—in context?** Does the writer achieve his or her goals while respecting the needs of the reader and the conventions of the discipline or situation? Are there particular considerations that cause the writer to break the "rules of good writing"? Why?

7. **What can you learn about writing?** What does this writer teach you about using words, writing sentences, developing paragraphs? Are there any techniques you can use in future assignments?

e-writing

Exploring Reading Online

The Web offers extensive opportunities to read a variety of articles and documents in a range of professions and disciplines and from different organizations.

1. Using InfoTrac College Edition (available through your English CourseMate at **www.cengagebrain.com**) or one of your library's databases, enter a search for the term *critical reading* to access current articles about the reading process.
2. Become familiar with library databases to locate reading material that can assist you not only in composition but also in all your college courses.

E-Sources

York University Counselling and Development Centre: Reading Skills for University
http://www.yorku.ca/cdc/lsp/skillbuilding/reading.html
Study Guides and Strategies
http://www.studygs.net/
Dartmouth Academic Skills Center: Reading Your Textbooks Effectively and Efficiently
http://www.dartmouth.edu/~acskills/success/reading.html

Access the English CourseMate for this text at **www.cengagebrain.com** for further information about critical reading.

Description
Presenting Impressions

What Is Description?

Description captures impressions of persons, places, objects, or ideas. It records what we see, hear, feel, taste, and smell. Description is probably the most basic task that writers encounter. Whether you are writing a short story or a sales proposal, your success depends on your ability to effectively share impressions. Good description not only provides information but brings subjects to life through sensory details. Almost all writing requires a skilled use of description. Before you can narrate events, establish a cause-and-effect relationship, or develop a persuasive argument, you must provide readers with a clear picture of your subject. Dramatists open plays with set descriptions. Homicide detectives begin reports with descriptions of the crime scene. Before proposing an airport expansion, the writers of a government study must first describe congestion in the existing facility.

The way writers select and present details depends on context, particularly their purpose and the needs of their readers.

Objective and Subjective Description

There are two basic types of description. **Objective description** attempts to create an accurate, factual record, free of personal interpretation or bias. In contrast, **subjective description** emphasizes a writer's personal reactions, opinions, and values.

Objective Description

Objective description focuses on facts and observable details. Textbooks, newspaper articles, business reports, and professional journals include objective description. Although objective description may avoid highly charged emotional appeals or creative imagery, it is not necessarily lifeless. Objective description is effective when the writer's purpose is to present readers with information required to make an evaluation or decision. In many instances objective description does not attempt to arouse interest or attract attention, because it is often written in response to reader demand. *The New Illustrated Columbia Encyclopedia*, for example, includes this description of Chicago:

> The third largest city in the country and the heart of a metropolitan area of almost 7 million people, it is the commercial, financial, industrial, and cultural center for a vast region and a great midcontinental shipping port. It is a port of entry; a major Great Lakes port, located at the junction of the St. Lawrence Seaway with the Mississippi River system; the busiest air center in the country; and an important rail and highway hub.

- Objective description is best suited for providing reference material for a diverse audience seeking reliable, factual information.

- Objective description avoids figurative language that is subject to interpretation. A personal essay or real-estate brochure might describe a home as being a "snug cottage" or "stylish condo." But an insurance underwriter would demand specific facts about its location, size, and construction.

- If you are writing as an employee or agent of others, objective description allows you to avoid personalizing a document that must express the views of others.

- Objective description is useful when you are writing to a critical or hostile audience that may demand explanations or justifications of subjective characterizations.

- Objective description is effective when the evidence you are presenting is compelling and dramatic. A description of a plane crash or a famine can be totally factual yet emotionally wrenching to readers. Objective description can be powerful and influential.

Subjective Description

In contrast to objective description, subjective description creates impressions through sensory details and imagery. Short stories, novels, personal essays, advertising copy, memoirs, and editorials use highly personal sensory details and responses to create an individual's sense of the subject. The writer's perceptual world guides the writing. Instead of photographic realism, subjective description paints scenes, creates moods, or generates emotional responses. Providing accurate information is less important than giving readers a feel for the subject. In a subjective description of a car, the color, shape, ride, and memories it evokes for the owner are more important than facts about horsepower, resale value, and fuel efficiency.

Attempting to capture his view of Chicago, John Rechy gives the city a personality, comparing it to an expectant mother:

> You get the impression that once Chicago was like a constantly pregnant woman, uneasy in her pregnancy because she has miscarried so often. After its rise as a frontier town, plush bigtime madams, adventurers, and soon the titanic rise of the millionaires, the city's subsequent soaring population—all gave more than a hint that Chicago might easily become America's First City. But that title went unquestionably to New York. Brazenly, its skyscrapers, twice as tall as any in the Midwest city, symbolically invaded the sky. Chicago, in squat self-consciousness, bowed out. It became the Second City.

Rechy uses imagery and unconventional syntax to create a highly personalized view of the city. In the context of his essay, written for a literary magazine, impression is more important than accuracy. Dates and statistics are irrelevant to his purpose. The goal in subjective description is to share a vision, not provide information.

- Subjective description emphasizes the writer's personal impressions rather than accurate reporting. It is best suited for writers who are acting independently, giving readers their personal insights.

- Subjective description relies heavily on the writer's selection and presentation of details. The choice of words and their connotations is critical in achieving the writer's goal.

- Subjective description is widely used when the goal is to entertain and persuade readers rather than to provide information. Humorists, columnists, political commentators, essayists, and advertising copywriters use subjective writing to shape readers' opinions of their subject.

Blended Description

Most description is not purely objective or subjective. Many writers blend subjective elements into objective reporting. Even when trying to be neutral and unbiased, reporters and historians generally cannot avoid being influenced by their personal values and attitudes. Popular nonfiction writers include subjective touches to humanize their writing and enhance the appeal of their work. Best-selling biographers, for instance, frequently employ subjective details to make remote historical figures and events more contemporary and more accessible to readers.

In his description of Chicago's State Street, Russell Miller blends elements of objective realism and subjective impressions to create a striking portrait:

> Summer 1983. State Street, "that great street," is a dirty, desolate, and depressing street for most of its length. It runs straight and potholed from the Chicago city line, up through the black ghettos of the South Side, an aching wasteland of derelict factories pitted with broken windows, instant slum apartment blocks, vandalized playgrounds encased in chain-link fencing, and vacant lots where weeds sprout gamely from the rubble and the rusting hulks of abandoned automobiles. Those shops that remain open are protected by barricades of steel mesh. One or two men occupy every doorway, staring sullenly onto the street, heedless of the taunting cluster of skyscrapers to the north.

In this description, objective details such as "vandalized playgrounds" are interwoven with expressions granting human emotions to inanimate objects so that wastelands are "aching" and skyscrapers "taunting." Blended descriptions such as this one are useful in strengthening subjective accounts with factual details.

- Blended descriptions are found in newsmagazines, literary criticism, and most nonfiction books. The degree and intensity of subjective elements depend on the context and may have to conform to stylistic guidelines established by editors.

- If you are writing as the agent of others or part of a larger organization, examine the use of subjective words carefully. Avoid connotations and characterizations that may offend or displease those you represent. Peer review can help you determine whether you have achieved the right blend of objective and subjective description.

Dominant Impressions

Whether their goal is to produce an objective, subjective, or blended description, writers generally strive to create a **dominant impression** that expresses their thesis or main point. A good description is not a collection of random facts or a list of everything you can remember about a subject, but a focused, organized presentation of key details that gives readers a specific, clear understanding or feeling.

The description of a room, for instance, can concentrate on one detail:

> Although I live three hundred miles from the ocean, my apartment has a seagoing motif. Beneath a sweeping seascape, a large antique aquarium dominates the living room, its colorful tropical fish flashing among rocks and shells I brought back from Florida. Miniature schooners, windjammers, and ketches line the windowsill. The ornate glass cabinet intended for china houses my collection of Hawaiian seashells.

By highlighting a single distinctive feature, the student creates a more memorable description of her apartment than one that lists all of its contents.

The Language of Description

Diction—the choice of words—is important in all writing, but it has a special role in description. Whether your description is objective, subjective, or a blend, the words you select should be accurate, appropriate, and effective. In choosing words, consider your purpose, readers, and discipline. *Review Chapter 10 to make sure that you have used words accurately and have been particularly sensitive to their connotations.*

WRITING ACTIVITY

Select sample descriptions from a variety of sources—readings from this chapter, other textbooks, magazine articles, brochures, mail-order catalogs, and newspaper advertisements—and review their use of objective and subjective details.

1. Can you detect subjective description in newsmagazines such as *Time or Newsweek?* Is there a difference between the news stories and personal essays and political commentary pieces?

2. Do you observe different blends of subjective elements in online sources such as CNN, Salon, TMZ, and The Huffington Post?

3. Circle the subjective details used in ads that describe products.

4. Can you detect subjective description in any of your textbooks?

5. How does the writer's stance affect the blend of objective and subjective elements?

6. What details and words do writers use to create dominant impressions? Do they serve as thesis statements?

WRITING ACTIVITIES

1. Read the following pair of descriptions of a village:

   The Yucca tribe lives in dire poverty. Their homes consist of rude shacks clustered around a rotting wooden platform that serves as a stage for primitive rituals. The village has no paved streets, no electricity, no running water. They subsist on fish and roots they dig from the ground with crude sticks. The village women spend their days fashioning coarse garments from tree bark and leaves. Their children wander aimlessly about the village without supervision. Their chief, an illiterate old man, resents the intrusion of outsiders who threaten his hold over his people.

   The Yucca tribe lives simply. Their homes consist of small cottages grouped around an altar that serves as the center of their religious worship. The village has no crime, pollution, or violence. They live on natural fish and vegetables they harvest using the tools of their ancestors. Their children play freely with no fear of traffic or molestation. Their chief, steeped in tradition, resents the intrusion of outsiders who threaten to erode their culture.

   ■ How do these passages differ? How does word choice affect your impression of the village and its inhabitants?
   ■ What do word choices reveal about the attitudes and values of the writer?
   ■ Do you consider these objective, subjective, or blended descriptions?

2. Review a number of advertisements in women's magazines. What words and images are used to sell products to women? Would these connotations appeal to men?

3. Consider words used by advocates on both sides of a controversial issue—abortion, capital punishment, affirmative action, or sexual harassment. Can you draw parallel lists of words and phrases that reflect the views of opposing groups? Why, for instance, do both pro-life and pro-choice groups talk about "rights"?

4. Analyze several popular television commercials. What connotations are used? Do they have any logical connection to the products or services being sold?

Strategies for Writing Description: Prewriting and Planning

Critical Thinking and Prewriting

1. **Use brainstorming and lists to generate possible topics.** Choose subjects you are familiar with—people you know, places you have visited, items you work with.
   ■ You may find it easier to write about a person you met once than a close friend, or a city you toured on vacation rather than your hometown. Sometimes a subject may have so many memories and complex associations that it is difficult to develop a clear focus for a short paper.

2. **Narrow your list of possible topics and generate details.** Use clustering and freewriting to develop details about your subject.

3. **Use senses other than sight.** Most writers immediately think of description as being visual. But descriptions can be enriched by including impressions of taste, touch, smell, and hearing.
   - Experiment by building a description based on nonvisual impressions. Describe your job or neighborhood, for instance, by sound rather than sight.

Planning

1. **Determine your purpose.** What is your goal—to entertain a general audience or provide information to colleagues, employees, your boss, or customers? What are the most important details needed to support your thesis?
   - Even if no formal thesis statement appears in the text, your description should have a controlling idea or focus. *Ask yourself what is the most important thing readers should know about your subject.*

2. **Define your role.** If you are expressing personal opinion or observations, you are free to add subjective details. You may include yourself in the description, referring to your actions and observations in the first person. If you are writing as a representative of others, however, an objective impersonal approach is more appropriate.

3. **Consider your reader.** Which type of description best suits your audience— subjective impressions or objective facts? What needs and expectations do your readers have? What details, facts, statistics, or observations will help them appreciate your topic and share your impression?

4. **Review the nature of the discourse community.** Determine whether you should use technical or specialized terminology. If you are writing within a profession, academic discipline, government agency, or corporation, use standard methods of presenting information, such as choosing an appropriate format.

5. **Select key details.** Having determined the context, choose points that will reflect your purpose and impress your readers, and follow any guidelines dictated by the assignment or discourse community. Descriptions should have focus.

6. **Organize details.** Good descriptions should be logically organized. You may arrange details spatially by describing a house room by room or a city neighborhood by neighborhood. You can present ideas in the order of their importance. If your essay includes both objective and subjective description, these can be blended or placed in separate paragraphs.
   - Use modes like comparison and contrast, narration, or process to organize details.

Strategies for Writing Description: Writing the First Draft

Writing the First Draft

1. **Describe people and objects in action.** Descriptions of people and objects can become stilted lists of facts. You can bring your subject to life by introducing short narratives or showing people in action. In writing description, follow the creative writer's advice to *show*, not *tell*.

Original

Mr. Bryant was the best boss I ever worked for. He supervised the payroll office. He was smart, generous, and patient. He knew the payroll office like the back of his hand. He had a fantastic eye for detail and a great memory. He appeared to have memorized the most complicated IRS regulations and could master any new accounting software in less than an hour. He was a great teacher and trainer. He was always available if anyone in the office had problems with a complex situation. He had excellent communications skills. I never saw him lose his temper no matter how mad employees got when the company made mistakes on their paychecks. He would simply and calmly explain policies and do his best to rectify any errors. He always gave his staff and the employees more than anyone expected. People came away from payroll usually wishing the rest of the company could be run the same way.

Improved

The payroll office came alive the moment Al Bryant stormed in, usually bearing a carton of donuts and a bag of carrot sticks for his employees. Unlike the other supervisors, he rarely used his private office but spent his day roving past our cubicles, answering our questions, showing us shortcuts, and tackling problems we couldn't figure out. Highly patient, he never lost his temper when an employee banged at the door, waving an incorrect check. Instead, he offered the employee a donut and grabbed the nearest computer. He punched in data like a speed typist while juggling a telephone receiver, checking pay schedules, consulting IRS guidelines, and asking the employee about his or her family. He worked with the precision of a surgeon and the speed of a race car driver, bobbing and weaving behind the computer as he sliced through a week of paperwork. Glancing at the clock, he would start to hum, going into overdrive, making it his personal mission to cut a new paycheck before the employee's break was over.

2. **Use dialogue to add action to descriptions involving people.** Allowing people to speak for themselves is more interesting and effective than simply describing their comments.

3. **Avoid unnecessary detail or static descriptions.** Avoid writing descriptions that are cluttered with unimportant facts like dates and addresses or place unnecessary emphasis on organizational arrangements:

On the left-hand wall is a bookcase. *To the right of the bookcase* is a stereo. *Around the corner of* the stereo stands an antique aquarium with tropical fish. *Above the aquarium* is a large seascape painting. Model ships line the windowsill. A cabinet *to the right of the window* is filled with seashells.

4. **Keep the length of your paper in mind as you write the first draft.** If you are writing a 500-word essay describing your hometown and discover that by the second page you have covered only two of a dozen items on your outline, you may wish to review your plan.
   - Revise your outline, expanding or limiting your topic. It is better to describe a single New York neighborhood in detail than to attempt to create an impression of the entire city that becomes only a bland list of generalities.

Strategies for Writing Description: Revising and Editing

Revising

1. **Review your plan and read your draft, focusing on its overall impact.**
   - Does it capture the true essence of your topic?
   - Is the draft too general, too vague? Should the topic be narrowed?
   - Does the paper generate interest by telling a story, highlighting details that would otherwise be overlooked, or does it read like a shopping list of facts?
2. **Examine the information you have included.**
   - Are there minor details that should be deleted?
   - Can the description be improved by adding essential or interesting details that you overlooked in the first draft?
   - Did you include impressions from senses other than sight?
3. **Does the paper create a dominant impression?**
   - Does your paper have a clear focus? Can you state a thesis?
   - Can ideas be rearranged to add emphasis, suspense, or interest?
4. **Is the description clearly organized?**
   - Does the paper's opening arouse interest?
   - Are details logically arranged? Do you use other modes to tell a story, create a pattern, or establish contrasts?
   - Does the paper end with a strong image, thought, or question that will leave a lasting impression on readers?
5. **Does your paper maintain a consistent point of view?** Avoid shifting from third to first person.
   - Determine whether you should change your role in the description. Would it be better stated from an objective or subjective viewpoint? Should you appear in the essay?
6. **Can you add action and dialogue to enliven the description?**

(Continued)

7. **Can you blend other modes into the description to make it more interesting or easier to follow?**
   - Could the description be revised by adding narrative elements to tell a story?
   - Would comparison and contrast or cause and effect help present the details?

8. **If possible, use peer review to gain an additional perspective.**
   - Ask a friend or fellow student to read your draft. Ask your readers whether your paper creates a vivid picture of your subject. Ask what elements could be added to make the essay more effective.

Editing and Proofreading

1. **Read the paper aloud.** Listen to your sentences.
   - Are there awkward or repetitive phrases that could be revised or deleted?
   - Are the sentences varied in length and complexity, or do they fall into a redundant, humdrum pattern?

2. **Examine your choice of words.**
   - Is your diction fresh and inventive or bland and general?
   - Do you use specific words?
   - Can clichés be replaced with original statements?
   - Do you use words accurately?
   - Do your connotations create the impressions you intend?

3. **Use a dictionary and thesaurus to examine word choice.**

STUDENT PAPER

This descriptive paper was written in response to the following assignment in a composition course:

> Briefly describe a current social or technological trend that is changing the way we live. Document the use of outside sources.

FIRST DRAFT WITH INSTRUCTOR'S COMMENTS

better title?
Using the Web to Build a Career

run-on   *Vague*
All over the country people are unemployed and new graduates cannot get jobs in the field

they want to enter. It is easy to get discouraged. After a year of looking for work, people

(Continued)

are afraid of their skills eroding or being so out of touch, that when the economy does turn

wordy

around and jobs come back that employers will look at these people and not consider them.

A lot of these people are using the Internet to not just look for jobs or post their résumés

Who?/slang

but demonstrate their skills online. A guy on TV last week said people are becoming blog-

sp

gers to stay current and build a network in there field. One guy was an unemployed quality

control engineer from GM. He used Facebook to connect with other quality control experts.

He created a blog, linking to current articles, and discussing technical problems. He got a

discourse going with other engineers, posting pictures and videos. He made up YouTube

awkward   *sp*

lectures that small companies used in training. Basically, he became like a free consulstant

slang

and the go-to guy in his field. He had factories in India and Canada asking for his advice. He

picked up a few consulting jobs. But the main thing when a job came up, he a lot more than a

résumé to show people what he could do.

which article?   *exact quote?*

People right out of college, an article online said, should retool their social networking

profile to create a credible professional package that demonstrates skills and abilities. In

wordy

looking for jobs, people right out of school should like continue to do research and build a

website that is like an ongoing class project showing their practical knowledge in their field.

They should cut and paste facts and become a source they email to people. In a way they

give away some of what they learned for free. A finance major, for example, did a whole

informal

website on how to invest for retirement and got 10,000 hits and then got a bunch of attor-

neys and accountants to contribute and link to her site. So when she interviewed for a job at

comma?

a bank/she didn't just have a résumé but thousands of potential customers.

(Continued)

People always complained you can't get a job without experience and you can't get

sp
expeirence without a job. But now people are using the Internet to build what people call

good word
shadow jobs. If you can't fix cars, sell insurance, plan weddings, or run a ~~restuarant~~ *sp* like you

want for real to make money, you do it online to show off your skills, build a network, and

get experience you need to be an asset in a tough job market.

REVISION NOTES

You have identified an important and interesting topic and provide specific details. Your description needs to be refined through revision and editing:

* Document the outside sources you refer to. Make sure exact quotes are placed in quotation marks.

* Revise the introduction to be more direct and precise.

* Delete wordy phrases such as "look at these people and not consider them."

* Edit for spelling and run-ons.

*Delete informal and slang phrases unsuited for a college paper.

REVISED DRAFT

Hector Ruiz   September 15, 2011
English 201-038

Casting a Cyber Shadow

Job seekers have been using the Internet to locate jobs and email résumés for twenty years. Today, downsized executives and new graduates are using the Web to create a shadow career, a kind of virtual internship to demonstrate their skills, gain experience, and build a presence online they can sell to employers. When job searches during a recession can take years, professionals worry about losing skills, becoming out of touch, and appearing stale to employers. New graduates, unable to find entry level positions, fear being trapped in marginal jobs and losing out to the next graduating class. Without relevant experience, the class of '11 is less attractive than brand new graduates, untainted by a minimum wage track record.

Speaking last week on the *Today Show,* Brad Manning, a New York career consultant, pointed out that a lot of job seekers are creating "shadow careers" online. Instead of just posting their résumés on Facebook, they are demonstrating their skills online by blogging

(Continued)

about issues, posting videos, answering questions, proposing ideas, and often providing free consultation services. A quality control engineer laid off after fifteen years at General Motors created his own technical journal, posting pictures, articles, and videos about quality control issues. Factories in India and Canada began using his videos to train new employees. In applying for jobs, he could prove that he was an expert in his field and that his skills had not eroded.

New college graduates who cannot find jobs in their careers now use social networking sites and blogs to create their own shadow jobs, creating an imaginary internship in which they demonstrate their skills. "After graduation," Nancy Pearlman suggests, "it's time to clear your Facebook page of spring break photos and create a credible professional package that demonstrates your skills and abilities." She points out that a finance major who ended up working in retail sales to pay her rent created a website on investing for retirement. By taking her academic knowledge and putting it in plain language, she attracted over ten thousand hits. She answered questions and began a running discourse with attorneys and accountants, who contributed articles to her site. When she interviewed for a job at a bank, she did not arrive with just a résumé but a list of a two hundred potential clients and a proven ability to handle day-to-day problems. Pearlman, who teaches online networking, reminds students to make their websites polished and professional. "They can't be a scrapbook of cut and paste articles and blogger-ese," she notes, "but clearly unified, credible, formal presentations that resemble corporate websites."

Shadow careers sometimes turn into consulting businesses with their creators abandoning the job search to form their own companies. In most cases, however, these websites allow job seekers to actually work in their fields, link with professionals, demonstrate an ability to solve problems, gather information, and connect with potential customers. In a competitive job market employers want recent "real world" experience. The down-sized executive or college graduate waiting tables has to bring more to an interview than a résumé or a two-year-old degree to stand out. A well-packaged blog can overshadow months of unemployment or unrelated entry level work to make an applicant the talented, proven professional organizations need in a challenging marketplace.

Works Cited

Manning, Brad. Interview with Matt Lauer. *The Today Show*. NBC. WNBC, New York.
28 Jan. 2011. Television.
Pearlman, Nancy. "Putting Facebook to Work." *Career News*. Career News,
21 May 2011. Web. 15 Sep. 2011.

QUESTIONS FOR REVIEW AND REVISION

1. How interesting do you find this essay? How successfully did the student describe his subject?
2. Can you describe a "shadow career" in your own words?

3. What is the student's goal in this essay? What does he want readers to know?

4. How effective is the ending? Does it sum up the point of the essay?

5. Descriptions do not always have an identifiable thesis statement. How would you state the student's thesis?

6. Where did the student use other modes, such as comparison or example, to build his description? Why are they important?

7. Did the student follow the instructor's comments? Could you suggest other improvements?

8. Did the student document the paper properly? (See pages 554–563).

9. Read the paper aloud. Are there any sentences that could be revised for clarity?

WRITING SUGGESTIONS

1. Write a description of a social or technological trend you are familiar with. How has texting changed the way people communicate? Do you observe new types of friendships or communities emerging from social networking?

2. *Collaborative writing:* Discuss this essay with a group of students. Have each member volunteer opinions on its strengths and weaknesses. Do members suggest revisions or a need for added detail?

Suggested Topics for Writing Description

General Assignments

Write a description of any of the following topics. Your description may include other modes. Determine whether your description should rely on objective observations and factual detail or subjective impressions. When you select words to describe your topic, be conscious of their connotations. Above all, keep in mind what you are trying to share with your reader.

- Your first apartment
- The people who gather in a place you frequent—a coffee shop, store, nightclub, library, or student union
- Your best or worst boss or professor
- The most desirable or least desirable place to live in your community
- The most dangerous situation you have faced
- The worst day you have had in recent memory
- The type of man or woman you find attractive
- The most serious environmental problem in your region
- The best or worst party you have attended
- Holiday shopping at the mall
- Starting a new job

- Cramming for final exams
- Completing the chore you hate the most
- The most serious problem you face today
- Student attitudes about a specific subject: terrorism, racism, crime, jobs, television
- Violence in America

Writing in Context

1. Imagine that your college has asked you to write a description of the campus for a brochure designed to recruit students. Write a three- or four-paragraph description that is easy to read and creates a favorable impression. Consider what would appeal to high school seniors or adults returning to school.

2. Assume you are writing a column for an alternative student newspaper. Develop a short, satiric, or sarcastic description of the campus, the administration, or the student body. Draw witty comparisons to create humor and use inventive word choices.

3. Write an open letter to the graduating class of your high school describing college life. You may wish to compare college to high school to prepare students for the problems and challenges they will encounter.

4. Imagine you are trying to sell your car. Write two short ads, one designed for a campus flyer and the other for a newspaper.

Strategies for Reading Description

As you read the descriptions in this chapter, keep these questions in mind:

Context

1. **What is the author's goal—to inform, enlighten, share personal observations, or provide information demanded by others?** What is the writer's role? Is he or she writing from a personal or professional stance?

2. **What is the intended audience—general or specific readers?** How much knowledge does the author assume readers have? Are technical terms defined? Does the description appear to have a special focus?

3. **What is the nature of the discourse community?** What does the source of the document—newsmagazine, corporation, personal essay, or book—reveal about the context?

(Continued)

Strategy

1. **What details does the writer select?** Does he or she appear to be deliberately emphasizing some items while ignoring or minimizing others?
2. **Does the description establish a dominant impression?** What method does the writer use to create it?
3. **How much of the description is objective and how much is subjective?**
4. **How does the author organize details?** Is there any particular method of grouping observations?
5. **Does the writer include sensory impressions other than visual details?**

Language

1. **What level of language does the writer use?** Are technical terms explained?
2. **What role do connotations have in shaping the description?** How do they support the writer's goal?

READING TO LEARN

As you read the descriptions in this chapter, note techniques you can use in your own writing.

■ **"The Bomb" by Lansing Lamont** blends objective and subjective details about the world's first atomic bomb, bringing a metallic object to life by describing it as a "bloated black squid" with "guts" and a "heart."

■ **"Out There" by Truman Capote** creates a dominant impression about the lonesome isolation of a Kansas town that is so small the streets have no names.

■ **"Border Story" by Luis Alberto Urrea** describes both the US–Mexican border and the illegals trying to cross it. By using the word "you" to describe the illegals, he puts his readers in their place.

■ **"American Islam" by Paul M. Barrett** uses example, narration, and comparison to build a factual description of Muslims in America that dispels common misconceptions.

■ **The job announcement by Bayou Printing** selects key words to describe both the company and the ideal candidate it seeks.

Lansing Lamont was born in New York City and was educated at Harvard College and the Columbia School of Journalism. He was a national political correspondent for *Time* magazine from 1961 to 1968. He became deputy chief of *Time*'s London bureau and later served as the magazine's Ottawa bureau chief. His best-selling book *Day of Trinity* (1965) told the story behind the development of the atom bomb during World War II. His second book *Campus Shock* (1979) examined American college life in the 1970s.

The Bomb

Source: "The Bomb" from *Day of Trinity* by Lansing Lamont, pp. 11–12. Copyright © 1985 by Lansing Lamont. By permission.

In this section from Day of Trinity *Lamont describes the first atomic bomb before its detonation in the New Mexico desert in July 1945. Note how Lamont includes both objective facts and subjective impressions of the bomb.*

1   The bomb rested in its cradle.

2   It <u>slept</u> upon a steel-supported oakwood platform, inside a sheet-metal shack 103 feet above the ground: a <u>bloated black squid girdled with cables and leechlike detonators</u>, each tamped with enough explosive to spark simultaneously, within a millionth of a second, the final conflagration. <u>Tentacles</u> emerged from the <u>squid</u> in a harness of wires connecting the detonators to a shiny aluminum tank, the firing unit.   *subjective animal imagery*

3   Stripped of its coils, the bomb weighed 10,000 pounds. Its teardrop dimensions   *objective facts* were 4½ feet wide, 10½ feet long. Its guts contained two layers of wedge-shaped high-explosive blocks surrounding an inner core of precisely machined nuclear ingots that lay, as one scientist described them, like diamonds in an immense wad of cotton. These ingots were made from a metal called plutonium.

4   At the <u>heart</u> of the bomb, buried inside the layers of explosive and plutonium, lay the ultimate <u>key</u> to its success or failure, a metallic sphere no bigger than a ping-pong ball that even twenty years later would still be regarded a state secret: the initiator.

5   Within five seconds the initiator would trigger the sequence that hundreds of shadows had gathered to watch that dawn. The bomb would either fizzle to a premature death or shatteringly christen a new era on earth.

6   Weeks, months, years of toil had gone into it.

7   The nation's finest brains and leadership, the cream of its scientific and engineering force, plus two billion dollars from the taxpayers, had built the squat monster on the tower for this very moment. Yet it had been no labor of love. There was not the mildest affection for it.

8   Other instruments of war bore dashing or maidenly names: Britain's "Spitfires"; the "Flying Tigers"; the "Gravel Gerties" and "Gypsy Rose Lees" that clanked across North Africa or blitzed bridgeheads on the Rhine; even the Germans' "Big Bertha" of World War I; and, soon, the Superfortress "Enola Gay" of Hiroshima, deliverer of an atomic bundle called "Little Boy."

9   The test bomb had no colorful nickname. One day its spawn would be known as "Fat Man" (after Churchill). But now its identity was cloaked in a welter of impersonal

terms: "the thing," "the beast," "the device," and its Washington pseudonym, "S-1." The scientists, most of whom called it simply "the gadget," had handled it gently and daintily, like the baby it was—but out of respect, not fondness. One wrong jolt of the volatile melon inside its Duralumin frame could precipitate the collision of radioactive masses and a slow, agonizing death from radiation. Or instant vaporization.

use of witness quotation 10   The monster engendered the sort of fear that had caused one young scientist to break down the evening before and be escorted promptly from the site to a psychiatric ward; and another, far older and wiser, a Nobel Prize winner, to murmur, as he waited in his trench, "I'm scared witless, absolutely witless."

UNDERSTANDING CONTEXT

1. What dominant impression does Lamont make?
2. How did the scientists feel about the bomb they created?
3. What impact does the final quotation have?
4. *Critical thinking:* Lamont notes that, unlike other weapons of WWII, the bomb was not given a colorful nickname. What does this imply? How does it set this weapon apart from the others that bore heroic or even whimsical names?

EVALUATING STRATEGY

1. How does Lamont blend objective details and subjective impressions?
2. How does Lamont demonstrate how the scientists felt about the weapon?

APPRECIATING LANGUAGE

1. What words create Lamont's dominant impression?
2. What role does animal imagery play in the description? How does it make the bomb appear as a "monster"?

WRITING SUGGESTIONS

1. Write a short description of an object like a car, house, or computer, and use subjective impressions to bring it to life by comparing it to a person or animal. You might describe an old car as a "beast" or a guitar as a "best friend."
2. *Collaborative writing:* Work with a group of students and write a short essay describing the threat of nuclear terrorism. What would happen if terrorists were able to place a nuclear weapon in a large American city? How would the nation and the public respond to a sudden, unexpected explosion that claimed a hundred thousand lives?

Truman Capote (1924–1985) was born in New Orleans and first gained prominence as a writer of short stories. At the age of twenty-four he produced his first novel, *Other Voices, Other Rooms*, which achieved international attention. His other works include *Breakfast at Tiffany's* and *A Tree of Night*. In 1965 he published *In Cold Blood*, which became an immediate best seller. Based on extensive research and interviews, *In Cold Blood* tells the story of a 1959 mass murder of a Kansas farm family and the fate of the killers. Although nonfiction, Capote's book reads much like a novel. *In Cold Blood* helped shape a new school of journalism that uses the stylistic touches of fiction to relate actual events.

Out There

The opening pages of In Cold Blood *describe the small town of Holcomb, Kansas, where the murders occurred. Capote spent a great deal of time in Holcomb and describes it almost as if it had been his own hometown. Notice how Capote blends objective facts with subjective impressions.*

1 The village of Holcomb stands on the high wheat plains of western Kansas, a lonesome area that other Kansans call "out there." Some seventy miles east of the Colorado border, the countryside, with its hard blue skies and desert-clear air, has an atmosphere that is rather more Far Western than Middle West. The local accent is barbed with a prairie twang, a ranch-hand nasalness, and the men, many of them, wear narrow frontier trousers, Stetsons, and high-heeled boots with pointed toes. The land is flat, and the views are awesomely extensive; horses, herds of cattle, a white cluster of grain elevators rising as gracefully as Greek temples are visible long before a traveler reaches them.

2 Holcomb, too, can be seen from great distances. Not that there is much to see— simply an aimless congregation of buildings divided in the center by the main-line tracks of the Santa Fe Railroad, a haphazard hamlet bounded on the south by a brown stretch of the Arkansas (pronounced "Arkan-sas") River, on the north by a highway, Route 50, and on the east and west by prairie lands and wheat fields. After rain, or when snowfalls thaw, the streets, unnamed, unshaded, unpaved, turn from the thickest dust into the direst mud. At one end of the town stands a stark old stucco structure, the roof of which supports an electric sign—Dance—but the dancing has ceased and the advertisement has been dark for several years. Nearby is another building with an irrelevant sign, this one in flaking gold on a dirty window— Holcomb Bank. The bank closed in 1933, and its former counting rooms have been converted into apartments. It is one of the town's two "apartment houses," the second being a ramshackle mansion known, because a good part of the local school's faculty lives there, as the Teacherage. But the majority of Holcomb's homes are one-story frame affairs, with front porches.

3 Down by the depot, the postmistress, a gaunt woman who wears a rawhide jacket and denims and cowboy boots, presides over a falling-apart post office. The depot

Sam Diephuis/jupiterimages

itself, with its peeling sulphur-colored paint, is equally melancholy; the Chief, the Super Chief, the El Capitan go by every day, but these celebrated expresses never pause there. No passenger trains do—only an occasional freight. Up on the highway, there are two filling stations, one of which doubles as a meagerly supplied grocery store, while the other does extra duty as a café—Hartman's Café, where Mrs. Hartman, the proprietress, dispenses sandwiches, coffee, soft drinks, and 3.2 beer. (Holcomb, like all the rest of Kansas, is "dry.")

4   And that, really, is all. Unless you include, as one must, the Holcomb School, a good-looking establishment, which reveals a circumstance that the appearance of the community otherwise camouflages: that the parents who send their children to this modern and ably staffed "consolidated" school—the grades go from kindergarten through senior high, and a fleet of buses transport the students, of which there are usually around three hundred and sixty, from as far as sixteen miles away—are, in general, a prosperous people. Farm ranchers, most of them, they are outdoor folk of very varied stock—German, Irish, Norwegian, Mexican, Japanese. They raise cattle and sheep, grow wheat, milo, grass seed, and sugar beets. Farming is always a chancy business, but in western Kansas its practitioners consider themselves "born gamblers," for they must contend with an extremely shallow precipitation (the annual average is eighteen inches) and anguishing irrigation problems. However, the last seven years have been years of droughtless beneficence. The farm ranchers in Finney County, of which Holcomb is a part, have done well; money has been made not from farming alone but also from the exploitation of plentiful natural-gas resources, and its acquisition is reflected in the new school, the comfortable interiors of the farmhouses, the steep and swollen grain elevators.

5   Until one morning in mid-November of 1959, few Americans—in fact, few Kansans—had ever heard of Holcomb. Like the waters of the river, like the motorists on the highway, and like the yellow trains streaking down the Santa Fe tracks, drama, in the shape of exceptional happenings, had never stopped there. The inhabitants of the village, numbering two hundred and seventy, were satisfied that this should be so, quite content to exist inside ordinary life—to work, to hunt, to watch television, to attend school socials, choir practice, meetings of the 4-H Club. But then, in the earliest hours of that morning in November, a Sunday morning, certain foreign sounds impinged on the normal nightly Holcomb noises—on the keening hysteria of coyotes, the dry scrape of scuttling tumbleweed, the racing, receding wail of locomotive whistles. At the time not a soul in sleeping Holcomb heard them—four shotgun blasts that, all told, ended six human lives. But afterward the townspeople, theretofore sufficiently unfearful of each other to seldom trouble to lock their doors, found fantasy re-creating them over and again—those somber explosions that stimulated fires of mistrust in the glare of which many old neighbors viewed each other strangely, and as strangers.

UNDERSTANDING CONTEXT

1. How much of Capote's description can be considered objective, how much subjective?
2. Capote includes a great deal of factual detail—the name of a highway, the number of students in the high school, and Holcomb's population. Why are these facts important in establishing an impression of the town?
3. What does Capote attempt to capture about this town?

EVALUATING STRATEGY

1. *Critical thinking:* A key element in the opening of any book is to get people's attention and motivate them to continue reading. How does Capote generate interest by describing a nondescript town?
2. What is the impact of the closing lines?

APPRECIATING LANGUAGE

1. How does the language of Capote's description differ from that of an encyclopedia or newspaper article?
2. *In Cold Blood* has sold millions of copies. What elements in Capote's style make his story about a crime in a small Kansas town so popular? What phrases strike you as being colorful or interesting?

WRITING SUGGESTIONS

1. Rewrite a recent article from the local newspaper, adding subjective details to arouse human interest for a national audience. Include observations about your community to give readers a feel for the location.
2. Using Capote's description as a resource, write a purely objective one-paragraph description of Holcomb, Kansas.
3. Write a one-line thesis statement for "Out There."

Luis Alberto Urrea

Luis Alberto Urrea was born in Tijuana to a Mexican father and American mother. He grew up in San Diego and attended the University of California. After graduation and a brief career as a movie extra, Urrea worked with a volunteer organization that provides food, clothing, and medical supplies to the poor of northern Mexico. In 1982 he taught writing at Harvard. His most recent novel, *Into the Beautiful North,* was published in 2010.

Border Story

Source: From *Across the Wire: Life and Hard Times on the Mexican Border* by Luis Alberto Urrea, copyright © 1993 by Luis Alberto Urrea. Photographs © 1993 by John Lueders-Booth. By permission.

In this description of the Mexican–American border from Across the Wire: Life and Hard Times on the Mexican Border *(1993), Urrea uses the device of second person to place his reader in the scene. By making "you" the "illegal," he seeks to dramatize and humanize the plight of the poor seeking a new life in the United States.*

1 At night, the Border Patrol helicopters swoop and churn in the air all along the line. You can sit in the Mexican hills and watch them herd humans on the dusty slopes across the valley. They look like science fiction crafts, their hard-focused lights raking the ground as they fly.

2 Borderlands locals are so jaded by the sight of nightly people-hunting that it doesn't even register in their minds. But take a stranger to the border, and she will *see* the spectacle: monstrous Dodge trucks speeding into and out of the landscape; uniformed men patrolling with flashlights, guns, and dogs; spotlights; running figures; lines of people hurried onto buses by armed guards; and the endless clatter of the helicopters with their harsh white beams. A Dutch woman once told me it seemed altogether "un-American."

3 But the Mexicans keep on coming—and the Guatemalans, the Salvadorans, the Panamanians, the Colombians. The seven-mile stretch of Interstate 5 nearest the Mexican border is, at times, so congested with Latin American pedestrians that it resembles a town square.

4 They stick to the center island. Running down the length of the island is a cement wall. If the "illegals" (currently, "undocumented workers"; formerly, "wetbacks") are walking north and a Border Patrol vehicle happens along, they simply hop over the wall and trot south. The officer will have to drive up to the 805 interchange, or Dairy Mart Road, swing over the overpasses, then drive south. Depending on where this pursuit begins, his detour could entail five to ten miles of driving. When the officer finally reaches the group, they hop over the wall and trot north. Furthermore, because freeway arrests would endanger traffic, the Border Patrol has effectively thrown up its hands in surrender.

5 It seems jolly on the page. But imagine poverty, violence, natural disasters, or political fear driving you away from everything you know. Imagine how bad things get to make you leave behind your family, your friends, your lovers; your home, as humble as it might be; your church, say. Let's take it further—you've said good-bye to the graveyard, the dog, the goat, the mountains where you first hunted, your

grade school, your state, your favorite spot on the river where you fished and took time to think.

6   Then you come hundreds—or thousands—of miles across territory utterly unknown to you. (Chances are, you have never traveled farther than a hundred miles in your life.) You have walked, run, hidden in the backs of trucks, spent part of your precious money on bus fare. There is no AAA or Travelers Aid Society available to you. Various features of your journey north might include police corruption; violence in the forms of beatings, rape, murder, torture, road accidents; theft; incarceration. Additionally, you might experience loneliness, fear, exhaustion, sorrow, cold, heat, diarrhea, thirst, hunger. There is no medical attention available to you. There isn't even Kotex.

7   Weeks or months later, you arrive in Tijuana. Along with other immigrants, you gravitate to the bad parts of town because there is nowhere for you to go in the glittery sections where the *gringos* flock. You stay in a rundown little hotel in the red-light district, or behind the bus terminal. Or you find your way to the garbage dumps, where you throw together a small cardboard nest and claim a few feet of dirt for yourself. The garbage-pickers working this dump might allow you to squat, or they might come and rob you or burn you out for breaking some local rule you cannot possibly know beforehand. Sometimes the dump is controlled by a syndicate, and goon squads might come to you within a day. They want money, and if you can't pay, you must leave or suffer the consequences.

8   In town, you face endless victimization if you aren't streetwise. The police come after you, street thugs come after you, petty criminals come after you; strangers try your door at night as you sleep. Many shady men offer to guide you across the border, and each one wants all your money now, and promises to meet you at a prearranged spot. Some of your fellow travelers end their journeys right here—relieved of their savings and left to wait on a dark corner until they realize they are going nowhere.

9   If you are not Mexican, and can't pass as *tijuanense,* a local, the tough guys find you out. Salvadorans and Guatemalans are routinely beaten up and robbed. Sometimes they are disfigured. Indians—Chinantecas, Mixtecas, Guasaves, Zapotecas, Mayas—are insulted and pushed around; often they are lucky—they are merely ignored. They use this to their advantage. Often they don't dream of crossing into the United States: a Mexican tribal person would never be able to blend in, and they know it. To them, the garbage dumps and street vending and begging in Tijuana are a vast improvement over their former lives. As Doña Paula, a Chinanteca friend of mine who lives at the Tijuana garbage dump, told me, "This is the garbage dump. Take all you need. There's plenty here for *everyone!*"

10   If you are a woman, the men come after you. You lock yourself in your room, and when you must leave it to use the pestilential public bathroom at the end of your floor, you hurry, and you check every corner. Sometimes the lights are out in the toilet room. Sometimes men listen at the door. They call you "good-looking" and "bitch" and "*mamacita,*" and they make kissing sounds at you when you pass.

11   You're in the worst part of town, but you can comfort yourself—at least there are no death squads here. There are no torturers here, or bandit land barons riding into

your house. This is the last barrier, you think, between you and the United States—
los Yunaites Estaites.

12   You still face police corruption, violence, jail. You now also have a wide variety of
new options available to you: drugs, prostitution, white slavery, crime. Tijuana is not
easy on newcomers. It is a city that has always thrived on taking advantage of a sucker.
And the innocent are the ultimate suckers in the Borderlands.

UNDERSTANDING CONTEXT

1. Urrea has called the border a "battlefield." How does his description illustrate this
    view?
2. What problems do the undocumented aliens face in their attempt to cross the border?
3. How are non-Mexican refugees treated in Tijuana?
4. What is the plight of refugee women on the border?
5. *Critical thinking:* Urrea quotes a Dutch woman who used the term "un-American" to
    describe the border patrols. What is un-American about fences and helicopter pa-
    trols? Does this response to immigration clash with the Statue of Liberty's promise to
    welcome the tired and poor?

EVALUATING STRATEGY

1. How effective is the use of the second person? Does it really put you in the scene?
    Does it help dramatize the plight of people many readers might choose to ignore?
2. What details does Urrea use to dramatize conditions along the border?

APPRECIATING LANGUAGE

1. Throughout the description, Urrea uses lists—"beatings, rape, murder, torture, road
    accidents . . ." How effective are they? Can listing words become tedious?
2. Select the words that create the most powerful images of the border. Why do they
    make strong impressions?

WRITING SUGGESTIONS

1. Write an essay describing a place that highlights a social problem. Select a location
    you have personal knowledge of, and try to convey the conditions residents face
    through lists of details.
2. *Collaborative writing:* Ask a group of fellow students to respond to Urrea's account.
    Consider the issues his description of the border raises. Ask members to suggest how
    conditions could be improved, and then draft a short *persuasion* essay outlining your
    ideas.

CRITICAL ISSUES

Immigration crossing sign

Immigration

Immigration reform is perhaps the most important challenge facing America. How America resolves this challenge will not only determine what kind of country America will be, but whether or not America will remain a country at all.

Tom Tancredo

I reject the idea that America has used herself up in the effort to help outsiders in, and that now she must sit back exhausted, watching people play the cards fate has dealt them . . . We have no right to be content, to close the door to others now that we are safely inside.

Mario M. Cuomo

America is a nation of immigrants. Since its founding, the United States has absorbed waves of new arrivals from around the world. Settled primarily by the English, French, and Dutch in the seventeenth century, America attracted large numbers of Germans in the early nineteenth century. During the potato famine of the 1840s and 1850s, 1,700,000 Irish emigrated to the United States. Near the end of the century, millions more arrived from Italy and Eastern Europe. By 1910, 15 percent of American residents were foreign born.

These immigrants filled American cities, adding to their commerce and diversity. European immigrants provided the labor for the country's rapid industrial expansion. Chinese workers laid the railroad tracks that unified the nation and opened the West to economic expansion.

But immigrants also met with resistance. Groups like the Know Nothings opposed the influx of Irish Catholics. As late as the 1920s, help-wanted ads in many newspapers contained the statement "No Irish Need Apply." California passed laws denying rights to the Chinese. Ivy League universities instituted quotas to limit the enrollment of Jewish students. Despite discrimination and hardships, these immigrants and their descendents entered mainstream American society and prospered. Today, some 40 percent of Americans can trace their roots to ancestors who passed through Ellis Island during the peak years of immigration a century ago.

The United States is experiencing the largest increase in immigration in its history. Between 1990 and 2000 the number of foreign-born residents increased 57 percent, reaching 31 million in 2000. Today's immigrants come primarily from Mexico, Asia, and the Middle East. This new wave of immigration is changing the nation's demographics, so that Hispanics, not African Americans, are the largest minority group. Within decades Muslims may outnumber Jews, making Islam America's second-largest religion.

This flow of immigrants, both legal and illegal, has fueled a debate about whether immigration benefits or hurts the United States. Supporters of immigration argue that immigrants offset a declining birthrate, adding new workers and consumers needed to expand the nation's economy. Critics argue that the United States has a limited capacity to absorb immigrants, especially the unskilled. Although immigrants provide employers with cheap labor, they tax the local governments that must provide them and their children with educational and health care services. Because of their numbers and historic ties to the land, Mexicans are changing the cultural fabric of the Southwest. In response, Americans concerned about national identity call for tighter border controls, restricted immigration, and the establishment of English as an official language.

Additionally, the terrorist attacks of September 11, 2001, led to new concerns about immigration, border controls, and national security. At the same time, economists are concerned that America is suffering a "brain drain" of talented foreign students who are compelled to leave the United States after graduating with advanced degrees.

Before reading the articles, consider the following questions:

1. *Where did your ancestors come from?* Were they immigrants? Did they encounter discrimination when they arrived? Did they struggle to maintain their own language and culture or seek to assimilate into American society?

2. *Should people who entered the country illegally be given legal status?* Should amnesty be given to illegal immigrants who have lived and worked in the United States for several years?

3. *Do wealthy countries like the United States have a moral obligation to accept immigrants?* The United States has historically accepted immigrants fleeing war and oppression. After Castro assumed power, 250,000 Cubans fled to the United States. Tens

of thousands of Vietnamese refugees entered the United States after the fall of South Vietnam. Does a prosperous nation also have an obligation to absorb some of the world's poor?

4. *How should the United States determine the number and type of immigrants allowed to enter the country each year?* Should talented immigrants be given priority over the unskilled? Should the number of immigrants be limited during times of recession and high unemployment?

5. *Does admitting immigrants improve the country by adding consumers and workers or weaken it by draining resources and taxing public services?*

E-READINGS ONLINE

Use InfoTrac College Edition, available through your English CourseMate at **www.cengagebrain.com,** to find the full text of each article online.

Jon Meacham. "Who We Are Now."
The 1965 Immigration and Nationality Act signed by Lyndon Johnson will have profound consequences well into the twenty-first century, when whites will constitute only 47 percent of the population, making them the nation's largest minority group.

Robert J. Bresler. "Immigration: The Sleeping Time Bomb."
Although past waves of immigrants have enriched this country, Bresler argues that unless immigration is limited our population could swell to 500 million in less than fifty years, reducing the quality of life for all citizens.

Anna Quindlen. "Undocumented, Indispensable; We Like Our Cheap Houses and Our Fresh Fruit."
Our borders remain porous because, despite concerns about illegal immigrants, Americans benefit from people willing to work hard for little pay.

Robert Samuelson. "The Hard Truth of Immigration: No Society Has a Boundless Capacity to Accept Newcomers, Especially When Many of Them Are Poor and Unskilled Workers."
Samuelson argues that immigration reform is needed to stem illegal immigration while granting legal status to illegal immigrants already living in the United States. "The stakes are simple," he argues. "Will immigration continue to foster national pride and strength or will it cause more and more weakness and anger?"

Peter Duignan. "Do Immigrants Benefit America?"
Duigan believes that most of today's immigrants "will be an integral part of a revised American community" but warns that "past success does not guarantee that history will repeat itself."

Arian Campo-Flores. "America's Divide. The Lawmakers See Legals and Illegals."
Americans tend to see immigrants as being illegal or legal, but many families are blended. Deporting an illegal immigrant may force American citizens to leave the country of their birth.

Charles Scaliger. "Double Standard on Immigration."
While Mexico calls for an open border with the United States, it maintains a tough policy on its own southern border, deporting more illegal immigrants than does the United States.

Steven Camarota. "Our New Immigration Predicament."
"Rather than changing our society to adapt to existing immigration," Camarota insists, "it would seem to make more sense to change the immigrant stream to fit our society."

Vivek Wadhwa. "A Reverse Brain Drain."
Having started 52 percent of Silicon Valley's technology companies and contributed 25 percent of America's global patents, highly skilled immigrants are vital to the nation's economy and their loss threatens our country's future.

Michael Elliott. "A Fresh Look at Immigration."
When the developed world attracts the best and brightest minds, it deprives poor nations of the talent they need to modernize.

Warren Mass. "Immigration as a Win-Win Affair."
Mass asserts that immigration has benefited the nation's culture and economy—when it has been properly regulated and controlled.

CRITICAL READING AND THINKING

1. What do authors see as the major costs and benefits of immigration?
2. What reasons do the authors give for the country's unwillingness to address illegal immigration?
3. What drives immigrants, both legal and illegal, to enter the United States?
4. How will the current wave of immigration change American society?
5. What motivates people to demand restrictions on immigration?

WRITING SUGGESTIONS

1. Write an essay about your own family history. Were you or your ancestors immigrants? When did they arrive? Did they encounter any discrimination or hardships? Did they assimilate into mainstream American society or seek to maintain ties to their native language, culture, and traditions?
2. *Collaborative writing:* Discuss immigration with other students and develop an essay presenting your group's views on one aspect of immigration—tightening border security, giving amnesty to illegal aliens, developing a guest-worker program, or prosecuting employers who hire illegal aliens. If members have differing opinions, consider developing opposing statements.
3. *Other modes:*
   - Write an essay that examines the *definitions* and terms used to discuss illegal immigrants, such as "undocumented workers," "illegal immigrants," and "illegal aliens." Note the role that connotation plays in shaping attitudes toward illegal immigrants.

- *Compare* current immigrants with those who entered Ellis Island a century ago.
- Use *process* to explain how immigrants can obtain citizenship.
- Write a *division* essay to outline the major problems that recent immigrants face in finding employment, housing, and health services in the United States.
- Use *classification* to rank suggestions for immigration reform from the most to the least restrictive, or from the most to the least acceptable to the public and politicians.

RESEARCH PAPER

You can develop a research paper about immigration by conducting further research to explore a range of issues.

- How effectively does law enforcement prosecute companies that hire illegal aliens?
- How has the concern about terrorism affected immigration policies? Do immigrants from Muslim countries face greater scrutiny? Has Homeland Security viewed the borders as potential weak spots?
- What does current research reveal about the status of Mexican Americans? Are immigrants from Mexico entering the middle class at a similar rate to immigrants from other countries?
- How will the new wave of immigrants influence American society, culture, economy, and foreign policy?
- Examine the impact immigration has had on other developed countries, such as Canada, Britain, France, Germany, and Italy. What problems, if any, have immigrant populations posed in these nations?

FOR FURTHER READING

To locate additional sources on immigration, enter *immigration policy* as a search term in InfoTrac College Edition, available through **CourseMate for *The Sundance Writer*,** or one of your college library's databases, and examine readings under the following key subdivisions:

analysis	economic aspects
cases	evaluation
comparative analysis	political aspects

ADDITIONAL SOURCES

Using a search engine such as Yahoo! or Google, enter one or more of the following terms to locate additional sources:

immigration	green cards
visa lotteries	Ellis Island
citizenship	bilingual education
Mexican Americans	English only

See the Evaluating Internet Source Checklist on page xxx. See Chapter 24 for using and documenting sources.

Paul M. Barrett has been a reporter and editor at the *Wall Street Journal* for over eighteen years and now directs the investigating reporting team at *Business Week*. His books include *The Good Black: A True Story of Race in America* (1999) and *American Islam: The Struggle for the Soul of a Religion* (2007).

American Islam

Source: Excerpt from "Muslims in America" from *American Islam* by Paul M. Barrett. Copyright © 2004 by Paul Barrett. By permission.

In this section from American Islam, *Barrett uses* example, narration, *and* comparison *to provide readers with a general description of American Muslims. Note how he presents objective details to counter commonly held misconceptions about Islam in the United States.*

1 Most American Muslims are not Arab, and most Americans of Arab descent are Christian, not Muslim. People of South Asian descent—those with roots in Pakistan, India, Bangladesh, and Afghanistan—make up 34 percent of American Muslims, according to the polling organization Zogby International. Arab-Americans constitute only 26 percent, while another 20 percent are native-born American blacks, most of whom are converts. The remaining 20 percent come from Africa, Iran, Turkey, and elsewhere.

2 Muslims have no equivalent to the Catholic pope and his cardinals. The faith is decentralized in the extreme, and some beliefs and practices vary depending on region and sect. In America, Muslims do not think and act alike any more than Christians do. That said, all observant Muslims acknowledge Islam's "five pillars": faith in one God, prayer, charity, fasting during Ramadan, and pilgrimage to Mecca. Muslims are also united in the way they pray. The basic choreography of crossing arms, bowing, kneeling, and prostrating oneself is more or less the same in mosques everywhere.

3 The two major subgroups of Muslims, Sunni and Shiite, are found in the United States in roughly their global proportions: 85 percent Sunni, 15 percent Shiite. Ancient history still animates the rivalry, which began in the struggle for Muslim leadership after the Prophet Muhammad's death in 632. Shiites believe that Muhammad intended for only his blood descendants to succeed him. Muhammad's beloved cousin and son-in-law Ali was the only male relative who qualified. Ali's followers became known as Shiites, a derivation of the Arabic phrase for "partisans of Ali." Things did not go smoothly for them. The larger body of early Muslims, known as Sunnis, a word related to Sunnah, or way of the Prophet, had a more flexible notion of who should succeed Muhammad. In 661, an extremist assassinated Ali near Najaf in what is now Iraq. Nineteen years later Sunnis killed his son, Hussein, not far away in Karbala. These deaths permanently divided the aggrieved Shiite minority from the Sunni majority.

4 Sunnis historically have afflicted the weaker Shiites, accusing them of shaping a blasphemous cult around Ali and Hussein. At the Karbala Islamic Education Center in Dearborn, Michigan, a large mural depicts mourning women who

have encountered the riderless horse of Hussein after his final battle. "You see our history and our situation in this," says Imam Husham al-Husainy, a Shiite Iraqi émigré who leads the center. In Dearborn, Shiite Iraqis initially backed the American invasion to depose Saddam Hussein, who persecuted Iraq's Shiite majority. Most Sunnis in Dearborn condemned the war as an exercise in American imperialism.

5   Sufism, another important strain of Islam, is also present in the United States. Sufis follow a spiritual, inward-looking path. Only a tiny percentage of American Muslims would identify themselves primarily as Sufis, in part because some more rigid Muslims condemn Sufism as heretical. But Sufi ideas crop up among the beliefs of many Muslims without being labeled as such. Sufism's emphasis on self-purification appeals to New Age seekers and has made it the most common avenue into Islam for white American converts such as Abdul Kabir Krambo of Yuba City, California. Krambo, an electrician who grew up in a conservative German Catholic family, helped build a mosque amidst the fruit arbors of the Sacramento Valley, only to see it burn down in a mysterious arson. Once rebuilt, the Islamic Center of Yuba City was engulfed again, this time by controversy over whether Krambo and his Sufi friends were trying to impose a "cult" on other worshipers.

6   Although there is a broad consensus that Islam is the fastest-growing religion in the country and the world, no one has provable numbers on just how many American Muslims there are. The Census Bureau doesn't count by religion, and private surveys of the Muslim population offer widely disparate conclusions. A study of four hundred mosques nationwide estimated that there are two million people in the United States "associated with" Islamic houses of worship. The authors of the survey, published in 2001 under the auspices of the Council on American-Islamic Relations (CAIR), a Muslim advocacy group, employed a common assumption that only one in three American Muslims associates with a mosque. In CAIR's view, that suggests there are at least six million Muslims in the country. (Perhaps not coincidentally the American Jewish population is estimated to be slightly below six million.) Other Muslim groups put the number higher, seeking to maximize the size and influence of their constituency.

7   Surveys conducted by non-Muslims have produced much lower estimates, some in the neighborhood of only two million or three million. These findings elicit anger from Muslim leaders, who claim that many immigrant and poor black Muslims are overlooked. On the basis of all the evidence, a very crude range of three million to six million seems reasonable. Rapid growth of the Muslim population is expected to continue, fueled mainly by immigration and high birthrates and, to a lesser extent, by conversion, overwhelmingly by African-Americans. In the next decade or two there probably will be more Muslims in the United States than Jews. Worldwide, the Muslim head count is estimated at 1.3 billion, second among religions only to the combined membership of Christian denominations.

8   American Muslims, like Americans generally, live mostly in cities and suburbs. Large concentrations are found in New York, Detroit, Chicago, and Los Angeles. But they also turn up in the Appalachian foothills and rural Idaho, among other

surprising places. Often the presence of several hundred Muslims in an out-of-the-way town can be explained by proximity to a large state university. Many of these schools have recruited foreign graduate students, including Muslims, since the 1960s. In the 1980s Washington doled out scholarships to Arab students as part of a campaign to counter the influence of the 1979 Iranian Revolution. Some of the Muslim beneficiaries have stayed and raised families.

9   In New York, Muslims are typecast as cab drivers; in Detroit, as owners of grocery stores and gas stations. The overall economic reality is very different. Surveys show that the majority of American Muslims are employed in technical, white-collar, and professional fields. These include information technology, corporate management, medicine, and education. An astounding 59 percent of Muslim adults in the United States have college degrees. That compares with only 27 percent of all American adults. Four out of five Muslim workers earn at least twenty-five thousand dollars a year; more than half earn fifty thousand or more. A 2004 survey by a University of Kentucky researcher found that median family income among Muslims is sixty thousand dollars a year; the national median is fifty thousand. Most Muslims own stock or mutual funds, either directly or through retirement plans. Four out of five are registered to vote.

10   Relative prosperity, high levels of education, and political participation are indications of a minority population successfully integrating into the larger society. By comparison, immigrant Muslims in countries such as Britain, France, Holland, and Spain have remained poorer, less well educated, and socially marginalized. Western European Muslim populations are much larger in percentage terms. Nearly 10 percent of French residents are Muslim; in the United Kingdom the figure is 3 percent. In the more populous United States the Muslim share is 1 to 2 percent, depending on which Muslim population estimate one assumes. It's unlikely that American cities will see the sort of densely packed, volatile Muslim slums that have cropped up on the outskirts of Paris, for example.

11   America's social safety net is stingy compared with those of Western Europe, but there is greater opportunity for new arrivals to get ahead in material terms. This may attract to the United States more ambitious immigrants willing to adjust to the customs of their new home and eager to acquire education that leads to better jobs. More generous welfare benefits in Europe allow Muslims and other immigrants to live indefinitely on the periphery of society, without steady jobs or social interaction with the majority. Europeans, who for decades encouraged Muslim immigration as a source of menial labor, have shown overt hostility toward the outsiders and little inclination to embrace them as full-fledged citizens. Partly as a result, violent Islamic extremism has found fertile ground in Western Europe.

UNDERSTANDING CONTEXT

1. What are some of the more striking facts Barrett presents about American Muslims? Would most Americans be surprised to learn that most Muslims in this country are not Arabs and have higher than average incomes?

2. How does Barrett explain the difference between Sunni and Shia Muslims? What percentage of American Muslims are Sunni?

3. Barrett states that Muslims have a faith that is "decentralized in the extreme." What basic beliefs do most Muslims share?

4. Why is it difficult to ascertain exactly how many Americans are Muslim?

5. *Critical thinking:* How is the Muslim American community different from those found in Western Europe? Does America's history of absorbing diverse immigrant groups create a different environment for Muslims? Why or why not?

EVALUATING STRATEGY

1. How difficult is it to objectively describe a religion? Do you think Barrett is successful? Why or why not?

2. Which facts about American Muslims do you consider the most significant? How can a writer determine which facts are important and which are trivial?

3. *Blending the modes:* How does Barrett use *comparison* to develop and organize his description?

APPRECIATING LANGUAGE

1. Do you think Barrett uses objective and neutral language in describing American Muslims? Can you detect any terms some readers might find insensitive or biased?

2. Barrett states that some Muslims condemn Sufi Muslims as "heretics" trying to impose a "cult" on other Muslims. Look up the words *heretic* and *cult* in a dictionary. What do these words mean? Are these terms objective or subjective?

WRITING SUGGESTIONS

1. Write a description essay that objectively describes a group of people. You might provide details about the residents of your apartment building, coworkers, or members of a sports team. Use neutral language and include factual details.

2. *Collaborative writing:* Working with a group of students, review Barrett's description and select three facts about American Muslims you think most significant. Which ones would surprise most Americans? Write a brief set of factual statements that might be used on billboards or blogs to educate the public.

WRITING BEYOND THE CLASSROOM

Want ads describe ideal job candidates. This want ad describes a print shop manager position in New Orleans.

◆ ◆ ◆ ◆

Bayou Printing

1500 Magazine Street
New Orleans, LA 70130
(504) 555-7100
www.bayouprinting.com

JOB ANNOUNCEMENT

Join a winning team!

Bayou Printing, New Orleans's largest independent chain of print shops, needs a creative, dynamic store manager to join our team. Bayou offers successful managers unique opportunities unavailable in national firms:

- Performance bonuses
- Profit sharing
- Full medical and dental coverage
- Education benefits

Requirements:

- Experience in hiring, training, and supervising employees in a high-volume retail operation.
- Full knowledge of state-of-the-art printing technology.
- Strong leadership and communications skills.
- Proven ability to lower employee turnover and overhead costs.

To apply for this job and join our winning team, e-mail us at info@bayouprinting.com.

UNDERSTANDING CONTEXT

1. How does the ad describe the position at Bayou Printing?
2. What are the most important requirements for the job?
3. What kind of person does Bayou Printing want to attract?
4. *Critical thinking:* What are the limits of any want ad? Can a job be fully described in a few sentences? Why can't employers address all their interests and concerns? How much of anyone's success in a job depends on personality as well as skills and experience?

EVALUATING STRATEGY

1. Why does the ad first list the job's benefits, then its requirements?

2. How effective are the use of bulleted points? Would this ad be less successful if written in standard paragraphs?

APPRECIATING LANGUAGE

1. What impact does the phrase "winning team" have? Why would it appeal to job seekers?

2. What words does the ad use to describe the ideal candidate?

WRITING SUGGESTIONS

1. Write a want ad for a job you once had. Model yours after ones you have seen in newspapers or online. Remember to keep your ad as short and easy to read as possible.

2. *Collaborative writing:* Work with a group of students and create a want ad. Imagine you are hiring a part-time secretary for your writing group who would organize your communications, schedule meetings, and conduct online research. Determine the skills needed, major duties, and the wording of the ad. You might have each member create a draft, then compare versions to select the most effective want ad.

RESPONDING TO IMAGES

Seattle Street Youths, 1983   Mary Ellen Mark

1. Describe your first reactions to this picture. Did you feel anger, disgust, fear, concern? What kind of young people are drawn to guns? Describe the problem these boys represent.

(Continued)

RESPONDING TO IMAGES

2. This photograph was taken in 1983. What do you assume happened to the boys in the picture? Where might they be today? Describe what you think may have happened to them.

3. *Visual analysis:* What do the hats, clothing, and demeanor suggest about these two boys? What do you see in the face of the boy on the left— defiance, resignation, or anger? What does the position of the weapon imply?

4. *Collaborative writing:* Discuss this picture with a group of students and describe how it might be used in a political ad about gun control, juvenile programs, tougher laws, or improved social programs. Write the text to accompany the ad. Pay attention to word choice and connotation.

5. *Other modes:*
   - Write a *narrative* to accompany this picture. Invent dialogue for the two boys.
   - Write a *cause-and-effect* essay and outline the causes or effects of youth crime.
   - Develop a *process* paper detailing the steps it would take for a youth program to intervene in these boys' lives.
   - Write a *persuasive* letter to the editor clearly stating your views on gun control. Would handgun bans keep young people from obtaining firearms?

DESCRIPTION CHECKLIST

✔ Have you limited your topic?

✔ Does your support suit your context? Should it be objective, subjective, or a blend?

✔ Is your description focused and clearly organized, or is it only a random list of facts and observations?

✔ Have you avoided including unnecessary details and awkward constructions?

✔ Does sensory detail include more than sight? Can you add impressions of taste, touch, sound, or smell?

✔ Do you avoid overly general terms and focus on specific impressions? Have you created dominant impressions?

✔ Do you *show* rather than *tell*? Can you add action to your description to keep it from being static?

✔ Do you keep a consistent point of view?

✔ Read your paper aloud. How does it sound? Do any sections need expansion? Are there irrelevant details to delete or awkward expressions to revise?

 Access the English CourseMate for this text at **www.cengagebrain.com** for additional information on writing description.

Narration

Relating Events

What Is Narration?

Narration relates an event or tells a story. Short stories and novels form narratives, as do fables, legends, biographies, annual reports, and history books. Narratives can be imaginative or factual, fiction or nonfiction. Narrative writing includes most newspaper articles, magazine stories, blogs, and biographies. All narratives seek to answer a simple question—*what happened?*

Physicians write narratives when they record a patient's history or trace the course of a treatment schedule. Attorneys use narrative writing to relate the details of a crime or justify their client's actions in a civil matter. A store manager filing an accident report will summarize an incident, relating the chain of events preceding the accident.

The Writer's Purpose and Role

Writers tell stories to inform, entertain, enlighten, or persuade. In some instances the writer's goal is to reconstruct a chain of events as accurately as possible. The purpose of a brief news story or an accident report is to supply readers with an objective statement of facts. In other cases, writers relate a story in order to provide an insight, share an experience, or teach a lesson. The writer will be selective, highlighting key events and describing them in ways to shape readers' perceptions. Some writers prefer to let a story speak for itself, assuming people will understand their point without an actual thesis statement. James Dillard (page 211), however, provides a clear thesis, stating what he learned after he treated an accident victim. Realizing that a malpractice lawsuit could have ended his medical career, he looks back on the incident, explaining the lesson the accident taught him:

> I took an oath to serve the sick and the injured. I remembered truly believing I would be able to do just that. But I have found out it isn't so simple. I understand now what a foolish thing I did that day. Despite my oath, I know what I would do on that cold roadside near Gettysburg today. I would drive on.

The writer of a narrative can be the central character, an eyewitness, or a researcher who reconstructs a chain of events from remaining evidence or interviews. Narration can be *objective* or *subjective*, depending on the writer's goal and context. **Objective narration** is generally stated in the third person to give the writer's account a sense of neutrality. In objective narration, the author is not a participant but a collector

Sam Diephuis/jupiterimages

Maria Toutoudaki/jupiterimages

and presenter of facts. In "Thirty-Eight Who Saw Murder and Didn't Call the Police" (pages 207–208), Martin Gansberg chronicles a murder victim's last movements:

> Twenty-eight-year-old Catherine Genovese, who was called Kitty by almost everyone in the neighborhood, was returning home from her job as manager of a bar in Hollis. She parked her red Fiat in a lot adjacent to the Kew Gardens Long Island Rail Road Station, facing Mowbray Place. Like many residents of the neighborhood, she had parked there day after day since her arrival from Connecticut a year ago, although the railroad frowns on the practice.
>
> She turned off the lights of her car, locked the door, and started to walk the 100 feet to the entrance of her apartment at 82-70 Austin Street, which is in a Tudor building with stores on the first floor and apartments on the second.

In contrast, **subjective narration** highlights the role of the writer, either as an eyewitness to events or as a main participant. James Dillard provides a gripping personal account of trying to resuscitate his victim (page 211), focusing not only on the objective appearance of the injured driver but also his own subjective feelings and his role as a participant:

> He was still out cold, limp as a rag doll. His throat was crushed and blood from the jugular vein was running down my arms. He still couldn't breathe. He was deep blue-magenta now, his pulse was rapid and thready. The stench of alcohol turned my stomach, but I positioned his jaw and tried to blow air down into his lungs. It wouldn't go.

Focus

Related closely to the writer's purpose and role is the narrative's *focus*. A biography of Abraham Lincoln can be a general account of his entire life or a psychological study of his battle with depression during the Civil War. A book about World War II can provide an overview of events or a detailed account of the role of women in the defense industry. An article on recycling may provide a survey of national trends or an in-depth history of tire recycling in a single city. Focus determines the details the writer includes in the narrative and the kind of evidence he or she relies on. A narrative does not have to include each event and every detail as the following one does:

> For our tenth anniversary my husband and I planned a trip to Hawaii. The seven-hour flight was exhausting, but as soon as I saw the Easter egg blue of the sky and the bright yellows and reds of the flowers I was energized. We rented a car at the airport and drove to our hotel. On the first day we went to the mountains. The scenery was incredible. The following day it rained, so we took the opportunity to visit a local art museum and dine in a Chinese restaurant. The next day we went to the beach.

Attempting to capture a ten-day vacation in a five-hundred-word essay, the student produces only a catalog, a listing of events. Like a video in fast-forward, the narrative sweeps readers through brief scenes that offer only superficial impressions. It is more effective to concentrate on a single event, as if highlighting a single scene from a movie or chapter in a book.

In "The Fender-Bender" (page 203), Ramón "Tianguis" Pérez focuses on a single incident, a minor traffic accident. As an illegal alien without papers, he fears that any contact with law enforcement could lead to an investigation of his status and deportation. Pérez does not bother explaining how he immigrated to America, why he left Mexico, or even the date or location of the incident, but immediately plunges his reader into the event:

> One night after work, I drive Rolando's old car to visit some friends, and then head towards home. At a light, I come to a stop too late, leaving the front end of the car poking into the crosswalk. I shift into reverse, but as I am backing up, I strike the van behind me. Its driver immediately gets out to inspect the damage to his vehicle. He's a tall Anglo-Saxon, dressed in a deep blue work uniform. After looking at his car, he walks up to the window of the car I'm driving.
>
> "Your driver's license," he says, a little enraged.
>
> "I didn't bring it," I tell him.
>
> He scratches his head. He is breathing heavily with fury.
>
> "Okay," he says. "You park up ahead while I call a patrolman."
>
> The idea of calling the police doesn't sound good to me, but the accident is my fault. So I drive around the corner and park at the curb. I turn off the motor and hit the steering wheel with one fist. I don't have a driver's license. I've never applied for one. Nor do I have with me the identification card that I bought in San Antonio. Without immigration papers, without a driving permit, and having hit another car, I feel as if I'm just one step from Mexico.

This single, almost incidental, event reveals more about the status of an illegal alien than a three-page summary of the author's life history. By including dialogue, Perez creates an active narrative instead of a summary of events.

WRITING ACTIVITY

Select examples of narrative writing from your textbooks, readings from this chapter, online articles, brochures, short stories, or passages from novels.

1. Can you identify the writer's purpose? Are some narratives written solely to inform, while others also seek to persuade or entertain readers?

2. What role does the author play in these narratives? Are some written in the first person? Is the writer the main participant, a minor character, or a witness of the events?

3. How do the various writers focus their narratives? What details do they leave out? How do they introduce background material?

4. Do the writers include dialogue and action to advance the narratives?

Chronology

Chronology or time is a central organizing element in narrative writing. Writers do not always relate events in a straight timeline. A biography, for instance, does not have to open with birth and childhood. Writers often alter the time sequences of their stories to dramatize events or limit their topics. A biographer of Franklin Roosevelt might choose to highlight a key event or turning point in his life. The narrative could open with his polio attack, flash back to his childhood and early political career, then flash forward to his recovery and entry into national and international politics. Other writers find it more dramatic to open a narrative with a final event and explain what led up to it. The first chapter of a biography about Czar Nicholas II could describe his execution and then flash back to the events leading to his downfall and death.

Each method of organizing a narrative has distinct advantages and disadvantages:

- **Beginning at the beginning** creates an open-ended narrative, providing readers with few hints about later events. Writers who relate complex stories with many possible causes can use a straight chronology to avoid highlighting a single event. Using a direct beginning-to-end approach is the most traditional method of telling a story. One of the difficulties can be determining exactly when the narrative should start. Often the beginning of a story consists of incidental background information that readers may find uninteresting.

- **Beginning at the middle or turning point** can arouse reader interest by opening with a dramatic scene. This method of organizing plunges the reader directly into the narrative and can give the chain of events a clear focus. This is a commonly used pattern in popular biographies. Critics, however, may argue that altering the chronology can be distorting. Not all historians, for instance, might agree that Roosevelt's polio attack was the "turning point" of his life. Some biographers may feel that this approach overemphasizes his physical disability and overshadows the political significance of Roosevelt's career.

- **Beginning at the end** dramatizes the final event. Organizing a narrative in this way can suggest that the conclusion was inevitable. When everything is presented in flashback, readers see events, actions, and thoughts in hindsight. The elements of suspense and randomness are removed, providing a stronger sense of cause and effect. Some readers will object to this method because it implies the final outcome was unavoidable, when in fact events just as easily could have led to alternative endings.

WRITING ACTIVITY

Select sample narratives from this chapter or look at one of your favorite books—fiction or nonfiction—and examine how the writers organized the chronology of events.

1. What pattern appears to be the most common?

2. Do any of the authors use flashbacks or flash forwards? If so, what impact do they have? How do the authors blend these sections into the main narrative without confusing their readers?

3. How do the writers use transitional statements and paragraph breaks to move the narrative and signal changes in time?

4. How do the writers use chronology to establish meaning? Do they use time relationships to indicate cause and effect?

5. How do the writers slow or speed up the narrative to emphasize important events or skim through minor ones?

Strategies for Writing Narration: Prewriting and Planning

Critical Thinking and Prewriting

1. **List topics suitable to your goal.** Consider the nature of the narrative assignment. What subjects would best suit your purpose?

2. **Determine your purpose.** Does your narrative have a goal beyond telling a story? What details or evidence do readers need to accept your point of view?

3. **Define your role.** As a narrator you can write in the first person, as either the major participant or the witness to events. You can write in the third person to establish greater objectivity, inserting personal opinion if desired.

4. **Consider your readers.** Define your readers' perceptual world. How much background information will you have to supply for readers to appreciate the significance of events?

5. **Review the discourse community or writing situation.** If you are writing a narrative report as an employee, study samples to determine how you should present your story.

6. **Freewrite for a few minutes on the most likely two or three topics to generate ideas.**

Planning

1. **Develop a clear thesis.** A narrative usually has a goal of doing more than simply listing a chain of events.
   - What is the purpose of your narrative—to persuade, to entertain, or to teach readers a lesson?
   - Should the thesis be clearly stated or implied?

2. **Identify the beginning and end of your narrative.** You may find it helpful to place background information in a separate foreword or introduction and limit comments on the ending to an afterword or epilogue. This can allow the body of the work to focus on a specific chain of events.

3. **Select a chronological pattern.** After reviewing the context of the narrative, determine which pattern would be most effective for your purpose—using a straight chronology, opening with a mid- or turning point, or presenting the final event first.

4. **Select key details that support your thesis.** Focus on those impressions of sight, sound, smell, taste, and touch that will bring your narrative to life.
   - Avoid minor details about times, dates, and locations unless they serve a clear purpose.

5. **Draft a timeline, listing main events of the narrative to guide your draft.** Leave space between each item on the timeline for last-minute additions.

Strategies for Writing Narration: Writing the First Draft

Writing the First Draft

1. **Use your plan as a guide, but be open to new ideas.**

2. **Use dialogue to advance the narrative.** If your narrative contains interactions between people, reconstruct conversations in direct quotations rather than summaries. Allowing people to speak for themselves gives you the opportunity to use word choice to convey a person's level of education, attitude, and lifestyle.

3. **Use transitional statements.** To prevent readers from becoming confused, make clear transitional statements to move the narrative. Such statements as "two days later" or "later that afternoon" can help readers follow the passage of time. Clear transitions are important if you alter the chronology with flashbacks and flash-forwards.
   - Paragraph breaks can be very important in narratives. They can function like chapters in a book to signal changes, isolate events, and highlight incidents.

4. **Monitor your length as you write.** If your draft begins to run too long, make notes or list points, and try to complete a full version.

Strategies for Writing Narration: Revising and Editing

Revising

1. **Review your thesis, plan, and goal.** Examine your prewriting notes and outline to determine if changes are needed.

2. **Read the first draft to get an overall view of your narrative.**
   - Does the opening generate interest and plunge readers into the story, or does it simply announce the topic or state the time and location?
   - Does the narrative have a thesis, a clear point?
   - Is the narrative easy to follow? Do transitional statements and paragraph breaks help dramatize shifts between main points?
   - Does the narrative end with a memorable impression, thought, or question?

3. **Examine the draft and isolate the narrative's key events.**
   - Can these elements be heightened or expanded?
   - Should these elements be placed in a different order?

4. **Decide whether the narrative should be expanded or narrowed.** If the draft is too short or seems to stall on a minor point or uninteresting detail, consider expanding the scope of the narrative by lengthening the chain of events.
   - If the draft is too long or reads like a summary of events, tighten the focus by eliminating minor events. *Remember, your narrative does not have to record everything that happened.*

(Continued)

5. **Determine whether the narrative can be improved by adding details, including dialogue, or altering the chronological pattern.**

Editing and Proofreading

1. **Review subsequent drafts for content, style, and tone.** Make sure that your choice of words suits the subject matter, mood, and thesis of the narrative.
   - Review your choice of words to make sure their connotations are appropriate.
2. **Make sure the narrative does not shift tense without reason.** In relating a narrative, you can write in present or past tense. In some cases, you may shift from past to present to express different actions, but you will otherwise want to remain consistent with your choice of tense.
   Acceptable: I *drive* to work every day, but that morning I *took* the bus.
   Awkward: Smith *rushes* into the end zone and the game *was* won.
3. **Avoid shifts in person or stance.** Narratives can be related in first, second, or third person. In most instances, avoid shifts in person, unless there is a clear shift in focus.
   Acceptable: I found working on a farm fascinating, though *you* might find it tedious and boring.
   Awkward: I crossed the bridge where all *you* can see is desert.

STUDENT PAPER

This paper was written in response to the following assignment:

Write a 300- to 500-word narrative essay based on a personal experience or observation. Limit your topic, select details, and use figurative language to recreate what you experienced.

FIRST DRAFT WITH INSTRUCTOR'S COMMENTS

weak intro   *Add title open with stronger image*

This paper is about a trip I made last spring to San Diego to visit my aunt and uncle. I saw a

one-day

lot during that week but the most meaningful part I remember was a one day trip to Mexico.

it's

I think it really changed the whole way I think about things. Sometimes its the minor things

you remember as important.

(Continued)

run-on
I got off the San Diego Trolley and I knew that I was going to start an adventure.

sp   *Fragment*
Tijuana. As I neared the entrance to cross the boarder there is a priest with a plastic bowl.

Avoid shift from past to present / delete "to myself"
With a picture of some kids saying "feed Tijuana's homeless children." Yeah, right, I think

to myself, just another scam, this guy probably isn't even a priest.

Tijuana. Just the name of the city brings back a special smell. A smell that you will only

know if you have been there. It only takes one time and you can relate to what I am trying to

Fragment
say to you. A smell that will permeate your olfactory senses forever. The smell was terrible.

sp   *shift*
As I cross the boarder the first thing that hits you is the smell I just mentioned. Then you

witness the terrible suffering and horrible poverty. It makes you realize how terrible many

people have it in this world.

Once I get past the few blocks of poverty and handed out all I can, I wandered upon a

Avoid shifts from past to present & "I" to "you"
busy little plaza where you could see all kinds of people having fun and partying.

Add detail
As I continued my journey, I reached a bridge. The bridge was horrible. Toward the mid-

span of the bridge, I experienced one of the most touching moments in my whole life, one of

sp
those happy ones where it's not clear weather you should laugh or cry. There was this little
Add details about children
child playing the accordion and another one playing a guitar.

It was getting to be late, and I started to get ready to leave. But this time as I passed the

Good image
priest I filled his plastic bowl with the rest of my money.

Like I stated, this one afternoon is what I remember from my whole trip. I still think

vague
about those people and the way they lived their lives. We as Americans take way too
Ending could be stronger, conclude with a strong image
much for granted and never realize how bad other people have it in this world today.

(Continued)

REVISION NOTES

This is a good topic for a narrative. There are changes you can make to create a stronger essay.

1. *Delete the first and last paragraphs; they are vague and general. Let the experience speak for itself. Focus on the event rather than telling readers how significant it was.*

2. *Add details to explain general terms such as "horrible" and "terrible."*

3. *Avoid illogical shifts in time. Describe your actions in the past tense: "I got off the trolley," "I walked," or "I saw." You can use present tense to explain general ideas or impressions not restricted to this specific event: "Tijuana is poor."*

4. *Avoid awkward shifts from "I" to "you." Write "I walked into the plaza where I could see" instead of "I walked into the plaza where you could see."*

5. *Edit for fragments and run-ons.*

REVISED DRAFT
Spare Change

As I stepped off the San Diego Trolley, I knew I was going to embark on a great adventure. Tijuana. As I neared the entrance to cross the border, I saw a priest with a plastic bowl with a picture of some kids. The caption of the picture said, "Feed Tijuana's homeless children." Yeah, right, I thought, just another scam. This man, I was convinced, probably was not even a priest.

Tijuana

© Les Stone/Sygma/Corbis

(Continued)

Tijuana. Just the name of the city brings back a distinct smell, one that will permeate my olfactory senses forever. A thousand different scents compounded into one. A smell of fast food, sweat, sewage, and tears hung over the city.

As I crossed the border the first thing that hit me was the smell. Then I witnessed countless victims of unforgettable poverty and suffering. A man without legs begged for money from a makeshift wagon. A woman with her children huddled around her stared at me, waving an old grease-stained wax cup at me, asking for help. The children, dressed in Salvation Army hand-me-downs, ripped pants and mismatched shoes, surrounded me, begging for money. Their tiny hands plucked at jacket pockets, looking for change or something to eat.

Once I got past the few blocks of human suffering and handed out all I could, I wandered upon a busy little plaza. This place was reasonably clean and clear of trash, and I heard the deafening music coming from a row of flashy clubs and saw dozens of young Americans drinking and partying. Tourists, who had spent the day in the outlet stores, trudged past distressed and exhausted from a day of hard shopping. They lugged huge plastic bags jammed with discount jeans, shoes, purses, and blouses. A score of children held out little packs of colored Chicklets, a local gum they sold to Americans at whatever price the tourists could haggle them down to. It is pathetic to think tourists feel the need to haggle over the price of gum with a child, but this is Tijuana.

Americans and tourists come from all over the world to drink, to shop, to haggle with children. This is just the way it is, the way it will always be. As I continued my journey, I reached a bridge. The bridge was horrible. Along the sides there was trash and rubbish. Towards the midspan of the bridge, I experienced one of the most touching moments of my life, one of those happy ones where I didn't know if I should shed a tear from happiness or out of despair. A small boy played an accordion and another played a guitar. He was singing a Spanish song; well actually, it sounded like he was screaming as his compadre strummed a guitar. He had a little cup in front of him, and I threw a coin into it. He just smiled and kept singing. I turned around and left, but as I passed the priest at the border, I filled his plastic bowl with the rest of my change.

QUESTIONS FOR REVIEW AND REVISION

1. This student was assigned a 300- to 500-word narrative in a composition class. How successfully does this paper meet this goal?

2. How does the student open and close the narrative? Does the opening grab attention? Does the conclusion make a powerful statement?

3. What devices does the student use to advance the chronology?

4. Most writers focus on visual details. This student includes the senses of sound and smell as well. How effective is this approach?

5. Did the student follow the instructor's suggestions? Do you see any errors the student should identify to improve future assignments?

6. Read the paper aloud. What changes would you make? Can you detect passages that would benefit from revision or rewording?

7. In the final draft the student included a photograph. Does this add value to the essay? Why or why not? Would you suggest keeping or deleting this image? Why?

WRITING SUGGESTIONS

1. Using this essay as a model, write a short narrative about a trip that exposed you to another culture. Try to recapture the sights, sounds, and smells that characterized the experience.

2. *Collaborative writing:* Ask a group of students to assign a grade to this essay and then explain their evaluations. What strengths and weaknesses does the group identify?

Suggested Topics for Writing Narration

General Assignments

Write a narrative on any of the following topics. Your narrative may contain passages making use of other modes, such as *description* or *persuasion*. Choose your narrative structure carefully and avoid including minor details that add little to the story line. Use flashbacks and flash-forwards carefully. Transitional statements, paragraphing, and line breaks can help clarify changes in chronology.

- Your first job interview
- Moving into your first apartment
- The event or series of events that led to you take some action, such as quitting a job, ending a relationship, or joining an organization
- A sporting event you played in or observed, perhaps limiting the narrative to a single play
- A first date, using dialogue as much as possible to set the tone and advance the narrative
- An event that placed you in danger
- An experience that led you to change your opinion about a friend or coworker
- The events of the best or worst day you experienced in a job
- An accident or medical emergency, focusing on creating a clear, minute-by-minute chronology
- A telephone call that changed your life, using dialogue as much as possible

Writing in Context

1. Imagine you are participating in a psychological experiment measuring stressors students face: lack of sleep, deadlines, financial problems, scheduling conflicts,

decreased contact with family and friends. Write a diary for a week, detailing instances when you experience stress.

2. Write a letter to a friend relating the events of a typical day in college. Select details your friend may find interesting or humorous.

3. Preserve on paper for your children and grandchildren a favorite story told by your grandparents or other relatives. Include needed background details and identify characters. Consider what you want your descendants to know about their ancestors.

4. You have been accused of committing a crime last Tuesday. Create a detailed log to the best of your recollection of the day's events to establish an alibi.

Strategies for Reading Narration

When reading the narratives in this chapter, keep these questions in mind:

Context

1. What is the author's narrative purpose—to inform, entertain, enlighten, share a personal experience, or provide information required by the reader? Does the writer have a goal beyond simply telling a story?

2. Does the writer include a thesis statement? If so, where does it appear in the essay?

3. What is the writer's role? Is the writer a participant or a direct witness? Is he or she writing in a personal context, focusing on internal responses, or in a professional context, concentrating on external events?

4. What audience is the narrative directed toward—general or specific? How much knowledge does the author assume readers have?

5. What is the nature of the discourse community or writing situation? Is the narration subjective or objective? Does the original source of the narrative—newsmagazine, book, or professional publication—reveal anything about its context?

Strategy

1. How does the author open and close the narrative?

2. What details does the writer select? Are some items summarized or ignored? If so, why?

3. What kind of support does the writer use—personal observation or factual documentation?

(Continued)

4. Does the author use dialogue or special effects like flashbacks or flash-forwards to advance the narrative?

5. What transitional devices does the writer use to prevent confusion? Does the author use paragraph breaks or time references such as "two hours later" or "later that day"?

Language

1. What does the level of vocabulary, tone, and style suggest about the writing context?

2. How is the author's attitude toward the subject or intended readers reflected by his or her choice of words?

READING TO LEARN

As you read the narratives in this chapter, note techniques you can use in your own writing:

- **"Take This Fish and Look at It" by Samuel Scudder** uses repetition to drive home an experience that taught him a valuable lesson.

- **"The Fender-Bender" by Ramon "Tianguis" Perez** uses a single incident to demonstrate how precarious life can be for undocumented workers. Perez includes extensive dialogue to advance his narrative.

- **"Thirty-Eight Who Saw Murder and Didn't Call the Police" by Martin Gansberg** is a fact-driven objective newspaper account of a murder. The first sentence, which many critics view as misleading, helped transform this incident into a national controversy.

- **"A Doctor's Dilemma" by James Dillard** uses the story of an accident to demonstrate why many doctors, fearing lawsuits, refuse to administer first aid to victims.

- **"Shooting an Elephant" by George Orwell** relates an event where a police-man feels pressured by a crowd to act against his better judgment.

- **"Incident Report" by Roisin Reardon** objectively records a hotel employee's observations and actions during a disturbance.

Samuel Scudder (1837–1911) attended Williams College. In 1857 he entered Harvard, where he studied under the noted scientist Louis Agassiz. Scudder held various positions and helped found the Cambridge Entomological Club. He published hundreds of papers and developed a comprehensive catalog of three hundred years of scientific publications. While working for the United States Geological Survey, he named more than a thousand species of fossil insects. Much of Scudder's work is still admired for its attention to detail.

Take This Fish and Look at It

Today educators stress critical thinking, which begins with close observation. As you read this essay, consider how effective the professor's teaching method is. Does it rest on the age-old notion that "people learn by doing"?

1   It was more than fifteen years ago that I entered the laboratory of Professor Agassiz, and told him I had enrolled my name in the Scientific School as a student of natural history. He asked me a few questions about my object in coming, my antecedents generally, the mode in which I afterwards proposed to use the knowledge I might acquire, and, finally, whether I wished to study any special branch. To the latter I replied that, while I wished to be well grounded in all departments of zoology, I purposed to devote myself specially to insects.

2   "When do you wish to begin?" he asked.

3   "Now," I replied.

4   This seemed to please him, and with an energetic "Very well!" he reached from a shelf a huge jar of specimens in yellow alcohol. "Take this fish," he said, "and look at it; we call it a haemulon; by and by I will ask what you have seen."

5   With that he left me, but in a moment returned with explicit instructions as to the care of the object entrusted to me.

6   "No man is fit to be a naturalist," said he, "who does not know how to take care of specimens."

7   I was to keep the fish before me in a tin tray, and occasionally moisten the surface with alcohol from the jar, always taking care to replace the stopper tightly. Those were not the days of ground-glass stoppers and elegantly shaped exhibition jars; all the old students will recall the huge neckless glass bottles with their leaky, wax-besmeared corks, half eaten by insects, and begrimed with cellar dust. Entomology was a cleaner science than ichthyology, but the example of the Professor, who had unhesitatingly plunged to the bottom of the jar to produce the fish, was infectious; and though this alcohol had a "very ancient and fishlike smell," I really dared not show any aversion within these sacred precincts, and treated the alcohol as though it were pure water. Still I was conscious of a passing feeling of disappointment, for gazing at a fish did not commend itself to an ardent entomologist. My friends at home, too, were annoyed when they discovered that no amount of eau-de-Cologne would drown the perfume which haunted me like a shadow.

Intro sets time

brief summary

uses dialogue

gives direction

Sam Diephuis/jupiterimages

8   In ten minutes I had seen all that could be seen in that fish, and started in search of the Professor—who had, however, left the Museum; and when I returned, after lingering over some of the odd animals stored in the upper apartment, my specimen was dry all over. I dashed the fluid over the fish as if to resuscitate the beast from a fainting fit, and looked with anxiety for a return of the normal sloppy appearance. This little excitement over, nothing was to be done but to return to a steadfast gaze at

my mute companion. Half an hour passed—an hour—another hour; the fish began to look loathsome. I turned it over and around; looked it in the face—ghastly; from behind, beneath, above, sideways, at three-quarters' view—just as ghastly. I was in despair; at an early hour I concluded that lunch was necessary; so, with infinite relief, the fish was carefully replaced in the jar, and for an hour I was free.

9   On my return, I learned that Professor Agassiz had been at the Museum, but had gone, and would not return for several hours. My fellow-students were too busy to be disturbed by continued conversation. Slowly I drew forth that hideous fish, and with a feeling of desperation again looked at it. I might not use a magnifying-glass; instruments of all kinds were interdicted. My two hands, my two eyes, and the fish: it seemed a most limited field. I pushed my finger down its throat to feel how sharp the teeth were. I began to count the scales in the different rows, until I was convinced

that was nonsense. At last a happy thought struck me—I would draw the fish; and now with surprise I began to discover new features in the creature. Just then the Professor returned.

10   "That is right," said he; "a pencil is one of the best of eyes. I am glad to notice, too, that you keep your specimen wet, and your bottle corked."

11   With these encouraging words, he added: "Well, what is it like?"

12   He listened attentively to my brief rehearsal of the structure of parts whose names were still unknown to me: the fringed gill-arches and movable operculum; the pores of the head, fleshy lips and lidless eyes; the lateral line, the spinous fins and forked tail; the compressed and arched body. When I finished, he waited as if expecting more, and then, with an air of disappointment:

13   "You have not looked very carefully; why," he continued more earnestly, "you haven't even seen one of the most conspicuous features of the animal, which is plainly before your eyes as the fish itself; look again, look again!" and he left me to my misery.

14   I was piqued; I was mortified. Still more of that wretched fish! But now I set myself to my task with a will, and discovered one new thing after another, until I saw how just the Professor's criticism had been. The afternoon passed quickly; and when, towards its close, the Professor inquired:

15   "Do you see it yet?"

16   "No," I replied, "I am certain I do not, but I see how little I saw before."

17   "That is next best," said he, earnestly, "but I won't hear you now; put away your fish and go home; perhaps you will be ready with a better answer in the morning. I will examine you before you look at the fish."

18   This was disconcerting. Not only must I think of my fish all night, studying, without the object before me, what this unknown but most visible feature might be; but

also, without reviewing my discoveries, I must give an exact account of them the next day. I had a bad memory; so I walked home by Charles River in a distracted state, with my two perplexities.

19   The cordial greeting from the Professor the next morning was reassuring; here was a man who seemed to be quite as anxious as I that I should see for myself what he saw.

20   "Do you perhaps mean," I asked, "that the fish has symmetrical sides with paired organs?"

21   His thoroughly pleased "Of course! of course!" repaid the wakeful hours of the previous night. After he had discoursed most happily and enthusiastically—as he always did—upon the importance of this point, I ventured to ask what I should do next.   *asks for help*

22   "Oh, look at your fish!" he said, and left me again to my own devices. In a little more than an hour he returned, and heard my new catalogue. "That is good, that is good!" he repeated; "but that is not all; go on"; and so for three long days he placed that fish before my eyes, forbidding me to look at anything else, or to use any artificial aid. "Look, look, look," was his repeated injunction.   *repeated command*

23   This was the best entomological lesson I ever had—a lesson whose influence has extended to the details of every subsequent study; a legacy the Professor has left to me, as he has left it to so many others, of inestimable value, which we could not buy, with which we cannot part.   *thesis/value of lesson*

24   A year afterward, some of us were amusing ourselves with chalking outlandish beasts on the Museum blackboard. We drew prancing starfishes; frogs in mortal combat; hydra-headed worms; stately crawfishes, standing on their tails, bearing aloft umbrellas; and grotesque fishes with gaping mouths and staring eyes. The Professor came in shortly after, and was as amused as any at our experiments. He looked at the fishes.   *flash-forward to humorous incident*

25   "Haemulons, every one of them," he said; "Mr. —— drew them."

26   True; and to this day, if I attempt a fish, I can draw nothing but haemulons.

27   The fourth day, a second fish of the same group was placed beside the first, and I was bidden to point out the resemblances and differences between the two; another and another followed, until the entire family lay before me, and a whole legion of jars covered the table and surrounding shelves; the odor had become a pleasant perfume; and even now, the sight of an old, six-inch, worm-eaten cork brings fragrant memories.

28   The whole group of haemulons was thus brought in review; and, whether engaged upon the dissection of the internal organs, the preparation and examination of the bony framework, or the description of the various parts, Agassiz's training in the method of observing facts and their orderly arrangement was ever accompanied by the urgent exhortation not to be content with them.

29   "Facts are stupid things," he would say, "until brought into connection with some general law."   *conclusion*

30   At the end of eight months, it was almost with reluctance that I left these friends and turned to insects; but what I had gained by this outside experience has been of greater value than years of later investigation in my favorite groups.

UNDERSTANDING CONTEXT

1. What is Scudder's purpose in this narrative? Why is this essay more than a typical "first day at school" story?

2. What did Professor Agassiz mean when he stated that "a pencil is one of the best of eyes"?

3. *Critical thinking:* How effective was Professor Agassiz's teaching method? By directing a new student to simply "look, look again," did he accomplish more than if he had required Scudder to attend a two-hour lecture on the importance of observation? Does this method assume that students have already acquired basic skills? Would this method work for all students? Why or why not?

4. What has this essay taught you about your future career? How can keen observation and attention to detail help you achieve your goals?

EVALUATING STRATEGY

1. How does Scudder give the narrative focus? What details does he leave out?

2. Scudder does not bother describing Professor Agassiz. Would that add or detract from the narrative?

3. *Other modes:* How does Scudder use *description* of the fish, specimen bottles, and smells to provide readers with a clear impression of the laboratory?

APPRECIATING LANGUAGE

1. How much scientific terminology does Scudder use in the narrative? What does this suggest about his intended audience?

2. This essay contains little action. Essentially it is a story about a man interacting with a dead fish. What words add drama and humor to the narrative?

WRITING SUGGESTIONS

1. Apply Professor Agassiz's technique to a common object you might use every day. Take your clock radio or a can of your favorite soft drink and study it for five minutes. Write a description of what you have observed. List the features you never noticed before.

2. Professor Agassiz gave his student little direction other than a simple command. Write a brief account about a time when a parent, teacher, coach, or boss left you to act on your own. What problems or challenges did you encounter? Did you feel frustrated, afraid, angry, or confident? What did you learn?

3. *Collaborative writing:* Working with three or four other students, select an object unfamiliar to the group. Allow each member to study the object and make notes. Compare your findings, and work to create a single description incorporating the findings of the group.

Ramón "Tianguis" Pérez is an undocumented immigrant and does not release biographical information.

The Fender-Bender

Source: "The Fender Bender" from *Diary of an Undocumented Immigrant* by Ramon "Tianguis" Perez. Copyright © 1991 by Arte Publico Press–University of Houston. By permission.

As you read the essay, notice how Pérez uses dialogue to advance the narrative. Pay attention to the role common documents such as a driver's license or a letter play in the drama.

1 One night after work, I drive Rolando's old car to visit some friends, and then head towards home. At a light, I come to a stop too late, leaving the front end of the car poking into the crosswalk. I shift into reverse, but as I am backing up, I strike the van behind me. Its driver immediately gets out to inspect the damage to his vehicle. He's a tall Anglo-Saxon, dressed in a deep blue work uni form. After looking at his car, he walks up to the window of the car I'm driving.

2 "Your driver's license," he says, a little enraged.

3 "I didn't bring it," I tell him.

4 He scratches his head. He is breathing heavily with fury.

5 "Okay," he says. "You park up ahead while I call a patrolman."

6 The idea of calling the police doesn't sound good to me, but the accident is my fault. So I drive around the corner and park at the curb. I turn off the motor and hit the steering wheel with one fist. I don't have a driver's license. I've never applied for one. Nor do I have with me the identification card that I bought in San Antonio. Without immigration papers, without a driving permit, and having hit another car, I feel as if I'm just one step away from Mexico.

7 I get out of the car. The white man comes over and stands right in front of me. He's almost two feet taller.

8 "If you're going to drive, why don't you carry your license?" he asks in an accusatory tone.

9 "I didn't bring it," I say, for lack of any other defense.

10 I look at the damage to his car. It's minor, only a scratch on the paint and a pimple-sized dent.

11 "I'm sorry," I say. "Tell me how much it will cost to fix, and I'll pay for it; that's no problem." I'm talking to him in English, and he seems to understand.

12 "This car isn't mine," he says. "It belongs to the company I work for. I'm sorry, but I've got to report this to the police, so that I don't have to pay for the damage."

13 "That's no problem," I tell him again. "I can pay for it."

14 After we've exchanged these words, he seems less irritated. But he says he'd prefer for the police to come, so that they can report that the dent wasn't his fault.

15 While we wait, he walks from one side to the other, looking down the avenue this way and that, hoping that the police will appear.

16 Then he goes over to the van to look at the dent.

17 "It's not much," he says. "If it was my car, there wouldn't be any problems, and you could go on."

18   After a few minutes, the long-awaited police car arrives. Only one officer is inside. He's a Chicano, short and of medium complexion, with short, curly hair. On getting out of the car, he walks straight towards the Anglo.

19   The two exchange a few words.

20   "Is that him?" he asks, pointing at me.

21   The Anglo nods his head.

22   Speaking in English, the policeman orders me to stand in front of the car and to put my hands on the hood. He searches me and finds only the car keys and my billfold with a few dollars in it. He asks for my driver's license.

23   "I don't have it," I answered in Spanish.

24   He wrinkles his face into a frown, and casting a glance at the Anglo, shakes his head in disapproval of me.

25   "That's the way these Mexicans are," he says.

26   He turns back towards me, asking for identification. I tell him I don't have that, either.

27   "You're an illegal, eh?" he says.

28   I won't answer.

29   "An illegal," he says to himself.

30   "Where do you live?" he continues. He's still speaking in English.

31   I tell him my address.

32   "Do you have anything with you to prove that you live at that address?" he asks.

33   I think for a minute, then realize that in the glove compartment is a letter that my parents sent to me several weeks earlier.

34   I show him the envelope and he immediately begins to write something in a little book that he carries in his back pocket. He walks to the back of my car and copies the license plate number. Then he goes over to his car and talks into his radio. After he talks, someone answers. Then he asks me for the name of the car's owner.

35   He goes over to where the Anglo is standing. I can't quite hear what they're saying. But when the two of them go over to look at the dent in the van, I hear the cop tell the Anglo that if he wants, he can file charges against me. The Anglo shakes his head and explains what he had earlier explained to me, about only needing for the police to certify that he wasn't responsible for the accident. The Anglo says that he doesn't want to accuse me of anything because the damage is light.

36   "If you want, I can take him to jail," the cop insists. The Anglo turns him down again.

37   "If you'd rather, we can report him to Immigration," the cop continues.

38   Just as at the first, I am now almost sure that I'll be making a forced trip to Tijuana. I find myself searching my memory for my uncle's telephone number, and to my relief, I remember it. I am waiting for the Anglo to say yes, confirming my expectations of the trip. But instead, he says no, and though I remain silent, I feel appreciation for him. I ask myself why the Chicano is determined to harm me. I didn't really expect him to favor me, just because we're of the same ancestry, but on the other hand, once I had admitted my guilt, I expected him to treat me at least fairly. But even against the white man's wishes, he's trying to make matters worse for me.

I've known several Chicanos with whom, joking around, I've reminded them that their roots are in Mexico. But very few of them see it that way. Several have told me how when they were children, their parents would take them to vacation in different states of Mexico, but their own feeling, they've said, is, "I am an American citizen!" Finally, the Anglo, with the justifying paper in his hands, says good-bye to the cop, thanks him for his services, gets into his van and drives away.

39   The cop stands in the street in a pensive mood. I imagine that he's trying to think of a way to punish me.

40   "Put the key in the ignition," he orders me.

41   I do as he says.

42   Then he orders me to roll up the windows and lock the doors.

43   "Now, go on, walking," he says.

44   I go off taking slow steps. The cop gets in his patrol car and stays there, waiting. I turn the corner after two blocks and look out for my car, but the cop is still parked beside it. I begin looking for a coat hanger, and after a good while, find one by a curb of the street. I keep walking, keeping about two blocks away from the car. While I walk, I bend the coat hanger into the form I'll need. As if I'd called for it, a speeding car goes past. When it comes to the avenue where my car is parked, it makes a turn. It is going so fast that its wheels screech as it rounds the corner. The cop turns on the blinking lights of his patrol car and leaving black marks on the pavement beneath it, shoots out to chase the speeder. I go up to my car and with my palms force a window open a crack. Then I insert the clothes hanger in the crack and raise the lock lever. It's a simple task, one that I'd already performed. This wasn't the first time that I'd been locked out of a car, though always before, it was because I'd forgotten to remove my keys.

UNDERSTANDING CONTEXT

1. What is the author's purpose in telling the story? What do we learn from this experience?

2. Pérez answers the Chicano patrolman in Spanish. Was this a mistake? What does their exchange reveal about cultural conflicts within the Hispanic community?

3. *Critical thinking:* Pérez implies that Chicanos have been offended when he has reminded them of their Mexican heritage; they insist on being seen as American citizens. What does this say about assimilation and identity? Does the Chicano officer's comment about Mexicans reveal contempt for immigrants? Have other ethnic groups—Jews, Italians, the Irish—resented the presence of unassimilated and poorer arrivals from their homelands?

EVALUATING STRATEGY

1. Why is a minor incident like a fender-bender a better device to explain the plight of the undocumented immigrant than a dramatic one?

2. How does Pérez use dialogue to advance the narrative? Is it better to let people speak for themselves?

APPRECIATING LANGUAGE

1. What words does Pérez use to trivialize the damage caused by the accident?

2. What word choices and images highlight the importance of documents in the lives of illegal immigrants?

WRITING SUGGESTIONS

1. Write a short narrative detailing a minor event that taught you something. A brief encounter with a homeless person may have led you to change your opinions of the poor. Perhaps you discovered your dependence on energy one afternoon when your apartment building lost power and you were unable to use your computer to finish an assignment, watch the evening news, prepare dinner, or even open the garage door to get your car.

2. *Collaborative writing:* Working with a group of students, discuss your views on immigration. Take notes and write a brief statement outlining your group's opinion. If major differences emerge during your discussion, split into subgroups and draft pro and con statements.

Martin Gansberg (1920–1995) grew up in Brooklyn and worked as a reporter, editor, and book reviewer for the *New York Times* for over forty years. His 1964 article about a woman who was fatally stabbed while her neighbors watched but failed to call the police stunned readers and caused a national outrage. Psychologists blamed the impact of television for causing what they called "the bystander effect." Editorials cited the incident as sign of urban alienation and social apathy. Critics later claimed that Gansberg's article exaggerated events and that his dramatic opening line created the false impression that the neighbors passively watched the entire incident from beginning to end. In fact, most witnesses only heard what they thought was a late-night argument, and the most vicious part of the attack occurred out of sight of many neighbors. The man convicted of the 1964 murder of Kitty Genovese, Winston Moseley, remains in prison. He was denied parole for the thirteenth time in 2008.

Thirty-Eight Who Saw Murder and Didn't Call the Police

This article appeared four months after the assassination of President Kennedy, when many commentators and most of the public were troubled by social unrest, crime, violence, and a growing sense that America was, as some put it, a "sick society." Consider how today's cable news commentators and bloggers would react to a similar event.

1   For more than half an hour 38 respectable, law-abiding citizens in Queens watched a killer stalk and stab a woman in three separate attacks in Kew Gardens.

2   Twice their chatter and the sudden glow of their bedroom lights interrupted him and frightened him off. Each time he returned, sought her out, and stabbed her again. Not one person telephoned the police during the assault; one witness called after the woman was dead.

3   That was two weeks ago today.

4   Still shocked is Assistant Chief Inspector Frederick M. Lussen, in charge of the borough's detectives and a veteran of 25 years of homicide investigations. He can give a matter-of-fact recitation on many murders: But the Kew Gardens slaying baffles him— not because it is a murder, but because the "good people" failed to call the police.

5   "As we have reconstructed the crime," he said, "the assailant had three chances to kill this woman during a 35-minute period. He returned twice to complete the job. If we had been called when he first attacked, the woman might not be dead now."

6   This is what the police say happened beginning at 3:20 A.M. in the staid, middle-class, tree-lined Austin Street area:

7   Twenty-eight-year-old Catherine Genovese, who was called Kitty by almost everyone in the neighborhood, was returning home from her job as manager of a bar in Hollis. She parked her red Fiat in a lot adjacent to the Kew Gardens Long Island Rail Road Station, facing Mowbray Place. Like many residents of the neighborhood,

Sam Diephuis/jupiterimages

she had parked there day after day since her arrival from Connecticut a year ago, although the railroad frowns on the practice.

8   She turned off the lights of her car, locked the door, and started to walk the 100 feet to the entrance of her apartment at 82-70 Austin Street, which is in a Tudor building with stores in the first floor and apartments on the second.

9   The entrance to the apartment is in the rear of the building because the front is rented to retail stores. At night the quiet neighborhood is shrouded in the slumbering darkness that marks most residential areas.

10   Miss Genovese noticed a man at the far end of the lot, near a seven-story apartment house at 82-40 Austin Street. She halted. Then, nervously, she headed up Austin Street toward Lefferts Boulevard, where there is a call box to the 102nd Police Precinct in nearby Richmond Hill.

11   She got as far as a streetlight in front of a bookstore before the man grabbed her. She screamed. Lights went on in the 10-story apartment house at 82-67 Austin Street, which faces the bookstore. Windows slid open and voices punctuated the early-morning stillness.

12   Miss Genovese screamed: "Oh, my God, he stabbed me! Please help me! Please help me!"

13   From one of the upper windows in the apartment house, a man called down: "Let that girl alone!"

14   The assailant looked up at him, shrugged, and walked down Austin Street toward a white sedan parked a short distance away. Miss Genovese struggled to her feet.

15   Lights went out. The killer returned to Miss Genovese, now trying to make her way around the side of the building by the parking lot to get to her apartment. The assailant stabbed her again.

16   "I'm dying!" she shrieked. "I'm dying!"

17   Windows were opened again, and lights went on in many apartments. The assailant got into his car and drove away. Miss Genovese staggered to her feet. A city bus, 0–10, the Lefferts Boulevard line to Kennedy International Airport, passed. It was 3:35 A.M.

18   The assailant returned. By then, Miss Genovese had crawled to the back of the building, where the freshly painted brown doors to the apartment house held out hope for safety. The killer tried the first door; she wasn't there. At the second door, 82-62 Austin Street, he saw her slumped on the floor at the foot of the stairs. He stabbed her a third time—fatally.

19   It was 3:50 by the time the police received their first call, from a man who was a neighbor of Miss Genovese. In two minutes they were at the scene. The neighbor, a 70-year-old woman, and another woman were the only persons on the street. Nobody else came forward.

20   The man explained that he had called the police after much deliberation. He had phoned a friend in Nassau County for advice, and then he had crossed the roof of the building to the apartment of the elderly woman to get her to make the call.

21   "I didn't want to get involved," he sheepishly told police.

22   Six days later, the police arrested Winston Moseley, a 29-year-old business machine operator, and charged him with homicide. Moseley had no previous record. He is married, has two children and owns a home at 133-19 Sutter Avenue, South Ozone Park, Queens. On Wednesday, a court committed him to Kings County Hospital for psychiatric observation.

23   When questioned by the police, Moseley also said that he had slain Mrs. Annie May Johnson, 24, of 146-12 133d Avenue, Jamaica, on Feb. 29 and Barbara Kralik, 15, of 174-17 140th Avenue, Springfield Gardens, last July. In the Kralik case, the police are holding Alvin L. Mitchell, who is said to have confessed to that slaying.

24   The police stressed how simple it would have been to have gotten in touch with them. "A phone call," said one of the detectives, "would have done it." The police may be reached by dialing "0" for operator or SPring 7-3100.

25   Today witnesses from the neighborhood, which is made up of one-family homes in the $35,000 to $60,000 range with the exception of the two apartment houses near the railroad station, find it difficult to explain why they didn't call the police.

26   A housewife, knowingly if quite casually, said, "We thought it was a lovers' quarrel." A husband and wife both said, "Frankly, we were afraid." They seemed aware of the fact that events might have been different. A distraught woman, wiping her hands in her apron, said, "I didn't want my husband to get involved."

27   One couple, now willing to talk about that night, said they heard the first screams. The husband looked thoughtfully at the bookstore where the killer first grabbed Miss Genovese.

28   "We went to the window to see what was happening," he said, "but the light from our bedroom made it difficult to see the street." The wife, still apprehensive, added: "I put out the light and we were able to see better."

29   Asked why they hadn't called the police, she shrugged and replied: "I don't know."

30   A man peeked out from a slight opening in the doorway to his apartment and rattled off an account of the killer's second attack. Why hadn't he called the police at the time? "I was tired," he said without emotion. "I went back to bed."

31   It was 4:25 A.M. when the ambulance arrived to take the body of Miss Genovese. It drove off. "Then," a solemn police detective said, "the people came out."

UNDERSTANDING CONTEXT

1. What details of this murder transformed it from a local crime story into an event that captured national attention?

2. How did the duration of the attack add to the significance of the neighbors' failure to call the police?

3. What reasons did the residents of Kew Gardens give for not taking action?

4. Gansberg mentions that William Moseley is a married homeowner with two children. Would these details surprise readers? Do most people have stereotyped notions about violent criminals?

5. Gansberg describes the neighborhood as being middle class. Is this significant? Why or why not?

6. *Critical thinking:* Do you think this article describes an isolated event or captures common-place attitudes and behaviors? Would most people call 911 today? Have you or anyone you know reported a crime in progress? Do you believe that urban life and television violence have desensitized people to crime and led them to passively watch rather than help? Do you think the same situation could occur in a small town? Is it a fact of modern life or human nature that leads people to avoid getting involved?

EVALUATING STRATEGY

1. What impact does the first line have? Although it states facts and not a point of view, can you consider it a thesis statement? Why or why not?

2. Gansberg includes details such as times and addresses. Why is this expected in a newspaper article? Does the author's inclusion of objective facts give the article greater authority?

3. Gansberg includes several direct quotations by neighbors explaining their actions that night. Are direct quotes more effective than paraphrases? Why?

4. *Critical thinking:* Does the opening line imply to you that all the witnesses passively watched the attack from beginning to end? Do writers, especially reporters, have an ethical responsibility to be accurate? Do you believe some journalists distort or exaggerate events to make their stories more dramatic?

APPRECIATING LANGUAGE

1. Gansberg uses passive voice to describe the actions of neighbors that night, stating "lights went out" and "windows opened." What impact does this have?

2. What verbs does Gansberg use to describe the victim's calls for help? What effect do they have?

3. What words does Gansberg use to describe the witnesses after the attack?

4. Gansberg uses the word "shrugged" to describe both the killer and a witness. Do you think this was deliberate? Why or why not?

WRITING SUGGESTIONS

1. Write a brief narrative about a recent incident and try objectively to reconstruct an accurate timeline of events. Include details about times, dates, locations, and participants, as for a newspaper report.

2. *Collaborative writing:* Discuss Gansberg's article with a group of students. Are they aware of similar incidents? Have they observed people's reaction to the plight of a person in distress? Do they believe most people are apathetic to victims of violence? Why or why not? Use division to organize your group's responses. If the group comes up with opposing viewpoints, consider using comparison to prepare contrasting statements.

James Dillard is a physician who specializes in rehabilitation medicine. In this narrative, first published in the "My Turn" column in *Newsweek,* he relates an incident that nearly ended his medical career.

A Doctor's Dilemma

Source: From *Newsweek,* June 12, 1995. Copyright © 1995 The NewsweekDaily Beast Company LLC. All rights reserved. Used by permission.

As you read this narrative, keep in mind how most people expect physicians to respond in an emergency.

1   It was a bright, clear February afternoon in Gettysburg. A strong sun and layers of down did little to ease the biting cold. Our climb to the crest of Little Roundtop wound past somber monuments, barren trees and polished cannon. From the top, we peered down on the wheat field where men had fallen so close together that one could not see the ground. Rifle balls had whined as thick as bee swarms through the trees, and cannon shots had torn limbs from the young men fighting there. A frozen wind whipped tears from our eyes. My friend Amy huddled close, using me as a wind breaker. Despite the cold, it was hard to leave this place.

2   Driving east out of Gettysburg on a country blacktop, the gray Bronco ahead of us passed through a rural crossroad just as a small pickup truck tried to take a left turn. The Bronco swerved, but slammed into the pickup on the passenger side. We immediately slowed to a crawl as we passed the scene. The Bronco's driver looked fine, but we couldn't see the driver of the pickup. I pulled over on the shoulder and got out to investigate.

3   The right side of the truck was smashed in, and the side window was shattered. The driver was partly out of the truck. His head hung forward over the edge of the passenger-side window, the front of his neck crushed on the shattered windowsill. He was unconscious and starting to turn a dusky blue. His chest slowly heaved against a blocked windpipe.

4   A young man ran out of a house at the crossroad. "Get an ambulance out here," I shouted against the wind. "Tell them a man is dying."

5   I looked down again at the driver hanging from the windowsill. There were six empty beer bottles on the floor of the truck. I could smell the beer through the window. I knew I had to move him, to open his airway. I had no idea what neck injuries he had sustained. He could easily end up a quadriplegic. But I thought: he'll be dead by the time the ambulance gets here if I don't move him and try to do something to help him.

6   An image flashed before my mind. I could see the courtroom and the driver of the truck sitting in a wheelchair. I could see his attorney pointing at me and thundering at the jury: "This young doctor, with still a year left in his residency training, took it upon himself to play God. He took it upon himself to move this gravely injured man, condemning him forever to this wheelchair . . ." I imagined the millions of dollars in award money. And all the years of hard work lost. I'd be paying him off for the rest of my life. Amy touched my shoulder. "What are you going to do?"

7   The automatic response from long hours in the emergency room kicked in. I pulled off my overcoat and rolled up my sleeves. The trick would be to keep enough

traction straight up on his head while I moved his torso, so that his probable broken neck and spinal-cord injury wouldn't be made worse. Amy came around the driver's side, climbed half in and grabbed his belt and shirt collar. Together we lifted him off the windowsill.

8   He was still out cold, limp as a rag doll. His throat was crushed and blood from the jugular vein was running down my arms. He still couldn't breathe. He was deep blue-magenta now, his pulse was rapid and thready. The stench of alcohol turned my stomach, but I positioned his jaw and tried to blow air down into his lungs. It wouldn't go.

9   Amy had brought some supplies from my car. I opened an oversize intravenous needle and groped on the man's neck. My hands were numb, covered with freezing blood and bits of broken glass. Hyoid bone—God, I can't even feel the thyroid cartilage, it's gone . . . OK, the thyroid gland is about there, cricoid rings are here . . . we'll go in right here . . .

10   It was a lucky first shot. Pink air sprayed through the IV needle. I placed a second needle next to the first. The air began whistling through it. Almost immediately, the driver's face turned bright red. After a minute, his pulse slowed down and his eyes moved slightly. I stood up, took a step back and looked down. He was going to make it. He was going to live. A siren wailed in the distance. I turned and saw Amy holding my overcoat. I was shivering and my arms were turning white with cold.

11   The ambulance captain looked around and bellowed, "What the hell . . . who did this?" as his team scurried over to the man lying in the truck.

12   "I did," I replied. He took down my name and address for his reports. I had just destroyed my career. I would never be able to finish my residency with a massive lawsuit pending. My life was over.

13   The truck driver was strapped onto a backboard, his neck in a stiff collar. The ambulance crew had controlled the bleeding and started intravenous fluid. He was slowly waking up. As they loaded him into the ambulance, I saw him move his feet. Maybe my future wasn't lost.

14   A police sergeant called me from Pennsylvania three weeks later. Six days after successful throat-reconstruction surgery, the driver had signed out, against medical advice, from the hospital because he couldn't get a drink on the ward. He was being arraigned on drunk-driving charges.

15   A few days later, I went into the office of one of my senior professors, to tell the story. He peered over his half glasses and his eyes narrowed. "Well, you did the right thing medically of course. But, James, do you know what you put at risk by doing that?" he said sternly. "What was I supposed to do?" I asked.

16   "Drive on," he replied. "There is an army of lawyers out there who would stand in line to get a case like that. If that driver had turned out to be a quadriplegic, you might never have practiced medicine again. You were a very lucky young man."

17   The day I graduated from medical school, I took an oath to serve the sick and the injured. I remember truly believing I would be able to do just that. But I have found out it isn't so simple. I understand now what a foolish thing I did that day. Despite my oath, I know what I would do on that cold roadside near Gettysburg today. I would drive on.

UNDERSTANDING CONTEXT

1. What was Dillard's goal in publishing this narrative in a national newsmagazine?

2. Does this narrative serve to contrast idealism and reality? How does Dillard's oath conflict with his final decision?

3. Does the fact that the victim was drinking have an impact on your reactions to the doctor's actions? Does Dillard seem to show contempt for his patient?

4. *Critical thinking:* Does this essay suggest that there is an undeclared war between doctors and lawyers? Do medical malpractice suits improve or diminish the quality of medicine? Are lawyers to blame for the writer's decision to "drive on"?

EVALUATING STRATEGY

1. *Other modes:* Does this narrative also serve as a persuasive argument? Is the story a better vehicle than a standard argumentative essay that states a thesis and presents factual support?

2. Does this first-person story help place the reader in the doctor's position? Is this a more effective strategy than writing an objective third-person essay about the impact of malpractice suits?

3. Why does Dillard mention that the patient later disobeyed his doctors' orders and left the hospital so he could get a drink?

4. How do you think Dillard wanted his readers to respond to the essay's last line?

APPRECIATING LANGUAGE

1. What words does Dillard use to dramatize his attempts to save the driver's life? How do they reflect the tension he was feeling?

2. What language does Dillard use to demonstrate what he was risking by trying to save a life?

3. What kind of people read *Newsweek?* Do you find this essay's language suitable?

WRITING SUGGESTIONS

1. Relate an emergency situation you experienced or encountered. Using Dillard's essay as a model, write an account capturing what you thought and felt as you acted.

2. Write a letter to the editor of *Newsweek* in response to Dillard's essay. Do you find his position tenable? Are you angry at a doctor who vows not to help accident victims? Or do you blame the legal community for putting a physician in this position?

3. *Collaborative writing:* Discuss Dillard's essay with a small group of students and compose a short letter to the editor as a response. If members of your group have conflicting points of view, consider developing opposing letters.

- Will corporations pressure employees to accept fewer health care benefits to compete in the global economy?
- Can advances in medical technology lower health care costs by diagnosing diseases at an earlier stage or identifying conditions that can be prevented with drugs or changes in lifestyle?

FOR FURTHER READING

To locate additional sources on health care, enter *health care industry* as a search term in InfoTrac College Edition (available through your English CourseMate at **www.cengagebrain.com**) or one of your college library's databases, and examine readings under the following key subdivisions:

analysis	economic aspects
beliefs, opinions, attitudes	ethical aspects
case studies	political aspects

ADDITIONAL SOURCES

Using a search engine, enter one or more of the following terms to locate additional sources:

health care costs	medical malpractice
Medicare	medical malpractice insurance
health care crisis	national health insurance
right to die	euthanasia
living wills	HMOs

See the Evaluating Internet Source Checklist on pages 553–554. See Chapter 24 for documenting sources.